MW01688745

Instructor's Resource Manual

Edited by and Discography compiled by

WILLIAM E. ANDERSON

fifth edition

JAZZ STYLES

history & analysis

MARK C. GRIDLEY

Heidelberg College

Tiffin, Ohio 44883

prentice hall englewood cliffs, new jersey 07632

© 1994 by PRENTICE-HALL, INC.
A Paramount Communications Company
Englewood Cliffs, N.J. 07632

All rights reserved.

10 9 8 7 6 5 4 3 2 1

ISBN 0-13-176900-6

Printed in the United States of America

CONTENTS

Page

Preface

This manual should ease your job and help your students get the most out of their brief semester with you. The contents reflect experiences of numerous other professors and their students who shared observations with me. Much of the material represents teaching techniques and materials that I devised while teaching jazz history to nonmusicians during 23 semesters at Case Western Reserve University.

This manual is keyed to the **fifth** edition of JAZZ STYLES: HISTORY AND ANALYSIS, the JAZZ STYLES DEMONSTRATION CASSETTE/CD, and the JAZZ CLASSICS CASSETTE/CD. If you are missing any of those items, contact your Prentice-Hall sales representative, phone 1-800-526-0485, or write College Humanities Marketing, Prentice-Hall, Inc., Englewood Cliffs, NJ 07632.

A **TEST BANK FOR JAZZ STYLES**, FIFTH EDITION is available to teachers who contact Prentice-Hall sales representatives. It contains approximately one thousand test items. The test bank is also available on computer disc in Macintosh and IBM formats, with test editing and test generating capacities and instructions.

This teachers' manual has a 122-page companion volume called **HOW TO TEACH JAZZ HISTORY** (available from the International Association of Jazz Educators, Box 724, Manhattan, Kansas 66502; phone 913-776-8744). It offers numerous lecture-demonstration ideas, motivational strategies, listening exercises, exam items and testing strategies that are not found in the Prentice-Hall teachers manuals or test banks. Topics include ideas for cultivating an appreciation for textural improvisation, illustrating the emancipation of the modern jazz rhythm section, introducing premodern jazz, developing appreciation for bop, demonstrating connections between jazz and African music, how to apportion treatment of the different styles, how to make recordings come alive, graphing solo lines, making musician identifications fun, getting students to learn about jazz outside the classroom, revising your course to fulfill critical thinking requirements, what is realistic to expect students to know before they take your course, etc.

The chapter titled "If You Are Teaching This Course For The First Time" originally appeared in altered form as "Teaching Jazz History for the First Time." This article is reprinted from the JAZZ EDUCATORS JOURNAL, Volume XIX, #4, the official publication of the International Association of Jazz Educators, Box 724, Manhattan, Kansas 66502, by permission of the editors. Portions of the material in this manual were presented to the National Association of Jazz Educators Convention held in Columbus, Ohio on January 15, 1984 and the International Association of Jazz Educators convention held in Boston, Massachusetts on January 14, 1994.

In the preparation of this manual, I am especially grateful for detailed suggestions from William E. Anderson formerly of Cleveland State University, Ola Jones of San Diego State University, Lewis Porter of Rutgers University, Lawrence Gushee of University of Illinois, Wallace Rave of Arizona State University, Rosemary Snow of John Carroll University, Terry Steele of Slippery Rock State College, Richard Davis of the University of Wisconsin, Chas Baker of Kent State University, Anita Clark of the University of Nebraska at Omaha, Bill Kirk of Saddleback Community College, and John Specht of Queensborough Community College. Thanks also go to Chuck Braman, Victor Schonfield, John Richmond, and Karl Koenig who commented on many drafts of these materials.

ABOUT THE AUTHOR

Mark C. Gridley is an active professional jazz musician with a life-long involvement in educating the public about jazz. He created and produced "Jazz, That Lively Art" for WOAK-FM radio in Detroit from 1962 to 1965. From 1971 to 1981, he taught "History and Styles of Jazz" for nonmusicians at Case Western Reserve University in Cleveland, where he earned M.S. and Ph.D. degrees. During 1976 he led the jazz demonstration unit for the Cleveland chapter of Young Audiences.

By the time he earned a B.S. degree at Michigan State University, Gridley had won honors playing flute, oboe and saxophone, and he had led numerous bands in Michigan. (The Mark Gridley Quartet was finalist at the 1968 Notre Dame Collegiate Jazz Festival in which Gridley won the "Best Flutist" award.) Gridley has performed and toured with several name bands (Harry "Sweets" Edison, Ralph Marterie, Les Elgart, Ray McKinley) and accompanied numerous popular singers (Lou Rawls, Sammy Davis, Tony Bennett, Yolande Bavan, Vic Damone, Marlena Shaw, Steve Lawrence, The Fifth Dimension, The Jacksons, The Temptations, etc.). He has performed with the Chautauqua Symphony Orchestra in New York, and he continues to maintain the steady schedule of performances with his own jazz groups that he began in the Cleveland area in 1969.

Gridley's critically acclaimed text, JAZZ STYLES: HISTORY AND ANALYSIS, has been translated into Bulgarian, Japanese, Danish and Polish, and it has earned its author a listing in WHO'S WHO IN THE MIDWEST, as well as commissions that led to extensive contributions in the ENCYCLOPAEDIA BRITANNICA, THE NEW GROVE DICTIONARY OF AMERICAN MUSIC and THE NEW GROVE DICTIONARY OF JAZZ. Gridley has done field research in all the jazz centers of the U.S. as well as Africa, South America and the Caribbean. He frequently addresses scholarly conferences as well as lecturing at colleges and universities throughout the U.S.

Beginning with its 1985 edition, JAZZ STYLES became America's most widely-used introduction to jazz. During the 1980's, Gridley's articles about jazz appeared in THE MUSICAL QUARTERLY, THE INSTRUMENTALIST, THE BLACK PERSPECTIVE IN MUSIC, POPULAR MUSIC AND SOCIETY, JAZZ EDUCATOR'S JOURNAL, and BLACK MUSIC RESEARCH JOURNAL. In 1987, The Educational Press Association of America gave Gridley its Distinguished Achievement Award.

IF YOU ARE TEACHING THIS COURSE FOR THE FIRST TIME

You might be apprehensive when you are first assigned to teach an entire semester of an academic course, especially if your training is in bandleading or choirleading, not in musicology. The job looms even larger if the course is in jazz history and you do not already have a long standing interest in the area and a large personal collection of jazz records. But it is not difficult to get past your apprehensions as soon as you begin realizing that such an undertaking is going to be fun. You will enjoy it because of the immense freedom you have in choosing material and the great opportunity you will have to hear so much new jazz with your students in the classroom. So, the first idea to keep in mind is that, more than anything else, music appreciation classes are taught because listening to music is fun, and people like yourself already understand so much about music that you are in a position to help others derive more enjoyment from music. It is always a kick to watch others enjoy jazz for their first time.

The course becomes all the more rewarding when you realize that, first, you will be coaching listening skills that your students will carry with them the rest of their lives and, second, that you will be introducing students to styles that many will like enough to go and share with their friends. I have never met anyone who teaches this course who said he/she did not enjoy it. In fact, one prof remarked to me that he had resisted taking the position of teaching it because he thought he would not like teaching nonmusicians, yet now he finds he likes it more than conducting (and this is a conductor with a good reputation and a string of successful bands and albums under his directorship). In other words, if you keep reminding yourself that the basic purpose is musical pleasure for you and your students, not only will you succeed in making the course fun for yourself and your students but also you will have created a good course and enhanced your reputation as a stimulating teacher.

You probably dread the prospect of trying to create a new course and still get through an entire semester without sacrificing your other responsibilities, health and sanity. But you really **CAN** teach a respectable course in jazz appreciation, as long as you keep in mind that **YOU DO NOT HAVE TO COVER EVERYTHING.** Basically you are your own boss, free to allocate whatever you are best able to handle. (At almost no colleges is this course a prerequisite for any other course.) If you ignore that consideration, you will be testing the limits of your health and sanity, and, most importantly, you will run the real risk of alienating the same students you were hired to stimulate.

Here is a telling example of the flexibility that is available to you. These are strategies I suggested to a first-time instructor who was hired at the last minute to teach a one-semester course in jazz and rock. I advised him to first introduce some "how to listen" ideas via demonstration of instruments and analysis of song forms (as explained on pages 372-391 and Chapter 3 and illustrated on the JAZZ STYLES DEMONSTRATION CASSETTE/CD), then to present an African retentions sequence (as explained in pages 40-51 and illustrated on tracks 1-6 of the JAZZ CLASSICS CASSETTE/CD). After that, he moved smoothly to jazz-rock, because jazz-rock has more Africanisms than any other jazz style has, and because his course title implied current popular music. Both he and his students were familiar with Spyro Gyra. So that music became a good point of departure. Joe Zawinul's "Birdland" was another handy point of departure because his students had heard the Manhattan Transfer or Quincy Jones versions and could recognize the resemblance to the riff band style of Count Basie's "One O'Clock Jump." Then he presented whatever pop music he could scrape together on short notice (Motown, the Jacksons, James Brown, Ray Charles) and showed its African connections via discussions in pages 40-51, 324-331, and in the Demonstrating African Connections chapter of my teachers' manual HOW TO TEACH JAZZ HISTORY (NAJE Press, 1984; IAJE Press, 1994). He keyed it all to the chart of parallel streams that appears in pages 326-327. Then, for the remainder of the course, he chose a few key jazz styles such as swing and bop and discussed only a few, absolutely essential figures (Louis Armstrong, Duke Ellington, Count Basie, Charlie Parker, Dizzy Gillespie, Miles Davis, and John Coltrane).

Two other basic considerations are worth pondering. One is that probably you will be hired to teach the course again somewhere, someday. Therefore, all those things that dawn on you during the semester, that you wish you'd have realized sooner, are not wasted ideas after all. You can use them the **NEXT** time. (All good teachers are continuously refining, as they see what they **SHOULD HAVE** done differently.) In other words, try to not get caught despairing what you cannot do or what you **DIDN'T** do. Try to savor what you **CAN** do and **ARE** doing.

Preventing Confrontations About Grades

The other consideration is the single greatest damper on your having fun in this course: issues surrounding tests and grading. Students take such things so seriously that they often forget the purpose of the course, then they accidentally lead you to dwell on such matters, to the exclusion of your main purposes. Therefore it is advisable to announce in your syllabus and to frequently reiterate in your first lectures that the purpose of the course is two-fold: 1. "to turn you on to jazz" and 2. "to improve your hearing, without surgery." If you acknowledge all this ahead of time, you can forestall the agonies and hostilities that **ALWAYS** arise otherwise.

The only strategy that ever worked for me in avoiding testing and grading hostilities was to present a very detailed syllabus (some of mine ran to 14 pages of single-spaced typing that spelled out every assignment's textbook page numbers, listening selections, specific hints for focusing particular aspects in the listening experience, etc.) and all the course requirements:

a. exam dates,

b. exam content,

c. exam format,

d. where and how exam results will be available,

e. whether exam grades are contestable (if so, what is the appeals procedure),

f. due dates for term papers and reviews (Due dates for outlines and rough drafts are also helpful.),

g. grading criteria,

h. absence policy (what are the consequences of missing class?),

i. missed exam policy (scheduling make-up's),

j. what constitutes an acceptable record review or concert review (Provide models and lists of the critical features.).

(See sample learning goals and grading criteria at the end of this chapter. But note that it is **NOT** a syllabus. It is only the **GRADING SCHEME** for one. A true syllabus includes all lecture topics, assignments listed by textbook page numbers, tape and record selections, all of which are detailed for every date of the semester.)

Sample tests and quizzes were provided, along with scoring criteria and final grade computation formulae. Then I said, in class, that I was willing to spend any time necessary during the first week of the semester to discuss any aspect of course grading that anyone wished for as long as anyone cared to spend. In addition, I tape recorded all the first week's class discussions, made spare copies of all the tapes and announced that they were available to anyone who missed hearing the discussions. But I also told them that, after the first week, I would never again spend **ANY** time discussing tests or grading, in class or outside of class. The only topic to which I would devote any time was **JAZZ**. After laying out something that comprehensive, you should be free to relax and have fun with the music, and so should your students. Where there is little uncertainty about what is expected and when it is due, there is little anxiety. And where there is little anxiety, there is even less hostility and confrontation about tests and grading.

Here is a model for a grading scheme to include in your syllabus. This is not a syllabus itself. This is just a set of goals **THAT MIGHT BE INCLUDED IN A SYLLABUS** to help your students focus their studying. A syllabus also includes the lecture topics and textbook pages and record and tape selections that are assigned for each class meeting. A syllabus also includes the due dates for any assignments that must be handed in, and it has the criteria by which each assignment will be graded.

GRADING SCHEME

This course is a perceptual learning experience. There is no way to measure more than a fraction of the new auditory skills you will acquire, and most of the following recognition skills would ordinarily be acquired, almost as incidental learning, by anyone who seriously pursues the task of widening their appreciation for jazz by doing the required listening, reading and by attending all the lecture-demonstrations in a course such as this or by self-study with the aid of musician friends. However, grades must be assigned because this is a credit course in college. Therefore, the following guidelines are offered to help you gear some of your learning to quiz formats that will be used in the class. Dates are attached to the listening skills goals so that you need not be caught short when quizzes are administered. A few information goals are also included with some of the listening skills goals. Quizzes will occasionally draw upon the information outlined in those goals.

NOTE: Try not to think **ONLY** in terms of the material needed for quiz passing. This course is supposed to help you **ENJOY** jazz more. Quizzes and grading are only a tiny part of the experience.

Goals for Learning

By January 10, be able to

1. offer several different definitions of jazz
2. identify jazz when you hear it and say how its sound qualifies it for the jazz label

By January 15, be able to

1. distinguish an improvisation based on the 12-bar blues format from one based on a 32-bar A-A-B-A format
2. identify when the bridge occurs while you are listening to an improvisation based on a 32-bar A-A-B-A form
3. identify a passage containing soloists trading fours or eights with the drummer
4. identify a stop-time solo break when it occurs in a performance
5. identify double-time feeling when it occurs in a ballad performance

By January 21, be able to

1. identify the type of saxophone playing on a record, and be confident in differentiating the sounds and appearances of soprano, alto, tenor sax and clarinet
2. notice when a chord changes within an accompaniment for an improvisation

By January 24, be able to

1. differentiate the sound of a trumpet from a trombone from a saxophone
2. differentiate the sound of a muted trumpet from an unmuted trumpet

By January 31, be able to

1. distinguish the sound and the appearance of a ride cymbal from that of the high-hat
2. distinguish time-keeping drumming from coloristic drumming
3. distinguish the sound of the snare drum from that of the tom-tom
4. distinguish the sounds made by drum sticks from those made by brushes
5. explain comping and ride rhythms, and know when you are hearing them
6. explain the special musical skills possessed by the improviser
7. list the unwritten rules that help organize jam sessions
8. match each of the drummer's four limbs with its traditional function in the jazz drum set

By February 14, be able to

1. tell what instrument is played by
    a. Miles Davis
    b. Louis Armstrong
    c. Charlie Parker
    d. Dizzy Gillespie
    e. Duke Ellington
2. distinguish music with counterpoint from music without counterpoint
3. distinguish tone with vibrato from tone without vibrato
4. distinguish pitch bending ornaments from unornamented tones
5. list at least 5 reasons why Louis Armstrong is historically significant
6. list arranging concepts that Duke Ellington pioneered
7. identify growl-style trumpet playing within a recorded passage
8. identify growl style trombone playing within a recorded passage

By February 19, be able to

1. distinguish the sound of Johnny Hodges from that of Charlie Parker
2. distinguish pre-bop jazz piano sound from bop piano sound
3. distinguish the sound of Louis Armstrong from that of Dizzy Gillespie
4. list at least 3 reasons for Charlie Parker's significance

By February 26, be able to

1. differentiate the four roles of bass playing when you hear any single example or combination of them in a recording
2. differentiate the sound of swing, bop, and free drumming
3. list the historical contributions of Jimmy Blanton, Scott LaFaro and Jaco Pastorius
4. distinguish among the sounds of Lester Young, Charlie Parker, Johnny Hodges and John Coltrane
5. indicate when John Coltrane is playing tenor and when he is playing soprano sax (soprano examples are on "The Promise" in JAZZ CLASSICS CASSETTE/CD)
6. differentiate the sound of John Coltrane from that of Cannonball Adderley on selections from the KIND OF BLUE album, such as "Flamenco Sketches" in JAZZ CLASSICS CASSETTE/CD
7. argue the various definitions of free jazz and its associated elements
8. tell who Bill Evans is and why he is historically significant

By the end of the semester, be able to

1. do all of the above, plus
2. tell why John Coltrane was important as a composer
3. list at least 5 players who currently show the influence of Coltrane
4. tell who Elvin Jones is and why he is important
5. tell what Weather Report is and why it is historically significant
6. explain how misleading the jazz-rock term is
7. distinguish the sound of funk bass from nonrepetitive-interactive style
8. list the ways that jazz-rock/jazz-funk differs from
    a. hard bop
    b. swing
    c. rock
9. identify jazz swing feeling when you hear it on a record and distinguish it from jazz-funk feeling
10. list at least four ways that jazz differs from rock
11. explain similarities between African music and jazz-rock
12. distinguish improvised parts from prewritten parts

SAMPLE COURSE REQUIREMENTS

A. Attend at least 2 live jazz concerts and/or jazz night club engagements. (One can be by a local group, but at least one must be by a national group.) Each attendance must be accompanied by a 2 page, typewritten, **THOROUGHLY PROOFREAD**, review which must be completed and handed in at least two weeks before the final class meeting. (Two points of extra credit, equivalent to quiz points, will be granted for every review that is handed in at the first class meeting that occurs after the event.) Ticket stub and/or program must be stapled to the review. In addition to **WHATEVER YOU FEEL IS SIGNIFICANT TO SAY ABOUT YOUR EXPERIENCE**, you must also list

1. the instruments that were played,
2. the form of at least one piece you heard,
3. the performers,
4. the time,
5. date,
6. place,
7. price of the event,
8. a detailed account of your personal impressions of the music (what you liked and disliked about it **AND WHY**).

B. Complete the graphing of recorded solo lines that occasionally will be assigned in class. In order to receive credit, the work must be handed in within one week of its being announced in class.

C. Complete a two-page, thoroughly proofread, typewritten review of one jazz album, your own or a borrowed one. If you want advice about what to buy, consult the textbook's SMALL BASIC CD COLLECTION (page 1), and consider albums mentioned in footnotes and in chapter endnotes. Within your review, be certain to describe the music in terms of the categories and musical techniques outlined in lectures (bass roles, drum roles, era, instruments, etc.) and the form of at least one piece on it (12-bar blues, 32-bar A-A-B-A, etc.). An alternative to buying or borrowing an album is taping a hour-long jazz program from the radio and treating it as an album. (Note that you still need to list correct personnel, tune titles and instruments for all selections just as you would in a standard record review.) In order to receive credit for it, this must be handed in at least one week before the last class meeting.

D. Take at least 8 out of the 9 quizzes that will be administered during the semester on the dates that are listed in the above course goals. Each quiz counts 3 points. No make-up quizzes will be given to anyone without a written excuse from the Dean. All make-ups must be completed before the last class meeting. Your course grade will otherwise be computed by point total from remaining quizzes. Assuming on-time completion of all the activities outlined in A-C above, your course grade will be determined by the semester total from the quiz grades (and extra credit outlined in A):

23-27 points = 4.0
21-22 points = 3.5
20 points = 3.0
19 points = 2.5
18 points = 2.0
17 points = 1.5
16 points = 1.0
fewer than 16 points total quiz scores and/or missing any work or deadlines from A-C above = 0.0

Keep track of all your assignment completions and quiz grades. Make a log for yourself, and enter each item as soon as it is completed. Then you will never need to ask the professor about your standing or your course grade.

GETTING ORGANIZED IS HALF THE BATTLE

Using The Text As Smorgasbord Because You Cannot Cover Everything

The biggest problem teaching jazz history is that you cannot do justice to every major style. You cannot do it in a 13 to 15 week semester, and you cannot even come close to doing it in a 10 week quarter. So, when devising your syllabus, it might be best to take a deep breath, grit your teeth, and cut a few of your favorite styles. Note that you can lessen the pain by alternating what you cut. Leave out some styles some semesters, other styles other semesters. Incidentally, even after my own book JAZZ STYLES (Prentice-Hall, 1978) came out, I never used more than half of it in a single semester course. In fact, the only styles I covered in depth every single time were Armstrong, Ellington, Parker, Gillespie, Davis, and Coltrane. And the extensive time that most instructors devote to the origins of jazz (Africa, ragtime, blues, gospel) I devoted to jazz styles instead. Then I always devoted the last week or two to putting current styles in historical perspective and giving students insight about the musical techniques being employed by their contemporaries. (If a jazz giant came to town, a representative albums were put in the listening lab. Then at least a half a week was devoted to his music. I then organized car pools and went to see the band with my students.) All other styles were on again off again, though I nearly always spent at least a week a piece on early jazz, swing, bop, hard bop, and jazz-rock. The alternations were done partly for expediency and partly to keep me from getting stale. (Twenty-three semesters is a lot of repetition if you cover exactly the same styles and examples every time!)

A strategy for managing the heartbreak you experience upon realizing you won't be able to share all your favorites with every semester of students is to pick a different set of stars to represent each period on alternate semesters. For example, when covering jazz-rock, one semester you might focus solely on post-1968 Miles Davis and John McLaughlin's Mahavishnu Orchestra. Another semester you might focus on just Weather Report and Herbie Hancock. When covering swing, I sometimes just spent a week on Ellington and a week on Basie. Other semesters, I decreased my time on Basie and introduced Hawkins, Tatum, Goodman, Eldridge, and Lunceford, and, when there were any guitarists in class, I would allot more time to Django Reinhardt and Charlie Christian. During some semesters, you could devote an entire week to the Miles Davis-Claude Thornhill-Lennie Tristano origins of the cool school, whereas the same slot could be filled during other semesters exclusively by such giants of West Coast style as Dave Brubeck, Gerry Mulligan, and Art Pepper. In treating bop, I often presented only Parker, Gillespie, Monk, and Powell. Though sometimes I also presented Dexter Gordon and Stan Getz, it always seemed to cut into the time allowed for depth in my Parker and Gillespie coverage. It is also distressing to realize that if you do Monk and Powell justice, there is rarely any time left for Shearing and Peterson. The solution to that dilemma is to remember that you need not cover everything **IN CLASS**. You need only assign textbook coverage, and put representative tapes in the listening lab for any players you neglect in class, then require your students to fill in the gaps themselves by matching textbook coverage with listening assignments.

Most instructors and textbook authors overlook the facts that a) the past 20 year period constitutes almost a third of recorded jazz history, and b) that students often feel cheated when their instructor fails to treat this period. Therefore, you might consider devoting a few weeks to historical perspective on your students' favorites and on explaining the improvisational methods and materials of our time. (Many of my own students said they enrolled in the course for precisely that knowledge.) This is apparently difficult to do. Most jazz history instructors fail to distribute their lectures across the semester in manners that allow sufficient time for treating music of the past twenty years. Many sheepishly concede that they rarely manage to get as far as Ornette Coleman or John Coltrane, much less doing justice to such recent styles as Weather Report and Keith Jarrett. Some instructors even skip the entire Bill Evans school (Evans, Herbie Hancock, Chick Corea, Keith Jarrett). That is almost equivalent to forgetting Art Tatum, Bud Powell, and Lennie Tristano! The result of such loose scheduling is usually to be an apologetic professor asking forgiveness from his students. And, though he wishes in vain to be hired to teach a year-long jazz history sequence and redeem himself, accidentally he continues to cheat his students out of precisely what they had entrusted him to teach them.

Students also complain about the professors who throw a kaleidoscopic range of styles at them during every lecture, dropping names at a furious pace and never stopping to rehear a solo or praise a particularly inspired turn of phrase. These professors rarely assemble listening labs for their students. And, though they **COVER** all of jazz history, they convey little more than what might be gleaned from radio programs run by historically minded disc jockeys. Many instructors inadvertently end up running their classes in this frantic way because they feel compelled to live up to the course title of Jazz **HISTORY**. They accidentally sacrifice depth for the sake of completeness.

Another type of professor who elicits bemused comments from students is one who gets so mired in analyses of Afro-American traditions when he begins the course that he barely reaches modern jazz, much less the jazz styles that show the most obvious African traits: jazz-rock (chapter 16) and the music of the AACM (chapter 14). Such instructors often spend a week on Africa, a week on the blues, a week on ragtime. They fail to provide an adequate sequence on how jazz is made and how to listen to it (what improvisation is, how improvising musicians follow unwritten rules, what the different instruments and song forms sound like, etc.). Then they fly through the New Orleans, Chicago, and swing eras, only to confront the end of the semester, falling 20 to 30 years short.

The only solution to these problems that ever worked for me was to rigidly adhere to a detailed syllabus that allowed no more than one week per ten year period. That is all that could be allotted if the first three or four weeks were already devoted to helping students learn to differentiate the basic instrument sounds (trumpet from fluegelhorn, alto sax from tenor, muted brass from unmuted, clarinet from soprano sax, bass viol from Fender bass, etc.; as illustrated on the JAZZ STYLES DEMONSTRATION CASSETTE/CD) and understand the basics of making jazz (as explained in the Elements of Music appendix, pages 358-391 and in Chapter 3: Appreciating Jazz Improvisation). I found that, when these basics were not learned, the week by week chronology reached students only superficially when they did their listening assignments. In other words, teaching jazz **HISTORY** can actually cheat students out of gaining jazz **APPRECIATION**. But if you first spend sufficient time on jazz appreciation, then you **CAN STILL** teach a lot of jazz history. However, this is true only if you are well organized and you stick to your syllabus.

The JAZZ STYLES text was designed as a smorgasbord of selections so readers would have a flexible reference source. Many sections of chapters and several entire chapters can be skipped without doing serious damage to an introductory course in jazz appreciation or a single-semester course in jazz history. Numerous deletions and rearrangements of the book's contents have supplied workable sequences for hundreds of jazz courses since the first edition appeared in 1978.

No technical knowledge of music is required to understand the contents of JAZZ STYLES, and the text's vocabulary has proven to be comprehensible for high school students as well as college students. Past editions have been used effectively in high schools and community colleges as well as in universities. Many instructors have successfully taught their courses from this book without devoting any attention to technical terms. Other instructors have used the "Elements of Music" appendix (pages 358-391) at the beginning of their course to introduce basic technical concepts before discussing selected jazz styles.

With the **JAZZ STYLES DEMONSTRATION CASSETTE/CD** and the **JAZZ CLASSICS CASSETTE/CD**, this text can serve as the core of a self-paced course of study in which the reader/listener becomes familiar with the sights and sounds of jazz, separate from the presentations made by the instructor. Technical concepts that otherwise require lecture/demonstrations by professional musicians can be learned by pairing the cassette with the accompanying text pages. The contents of the JAZZ STYLES DEMONSTRATION CASSETTE/CD also can be used as reinforcement of lecture/demonstrations performed by the instructor because they provide a handy source of review materials for study outside of class. Exceptionally efficient professors have required that their students learn the contents of the JAZZ STYLES DEMONSTRATION CASSETTE/CD outside of class. Then, with the resulting savings in class time, they presented additional historic styles. Some professors have used Steve Gryb's videocassette adaptation of the JAZZ STYLES DEMONSTRATION CASSETTE/CD for the same effect (available as LISTENING TO JAZZ, distributed by Prentice-Hall Publishers as ISBN 0-135328624; phone 515-284-6751; FAX 515-284-2607). No matter what approach is taken to using the book and its cassettes, every individual and class is encouraged to listen to as much jazz, both recorded and live, as possible. The book will be an effective guide only if reading is accompanied by extensive listening.

JAZZ STYLES was originally conceived in an omnibus format whose organization was intended to provide a flexible reference for learning about jazz. The next five paragraphs outline approaches that have proven successful in colleges and universities where previous editions of this book have been required.

The text provides the essentials for a course in **UNDERSTANDING JAZZ** if it is accompanied by a well-chosen collection of records (the albums cited in endnotes provide a good start) and several carefully conceived, in-class demonstrations by musicians. For those demonstrations, many instructors follow the guidelines described in "Getting the Most From a Drumming Demonstration and Live Rhythm Section" in HOW TO TEACH JAZZ HISTORY (Mark C. Gridley, NAJE Press, 1984/1994; available from the International Association of Jazz Educators, Box 724, Manhattan, Kansas 66502; phone 913-776-8744). They also use the strategies that are demonstrated in "Teaching Jazz History to Nonmusicians" and "Where's the Melody" (1984 NAJE Convention Cassettes #37 and 38, available from Mark Records, 10815 Bodine Road, Clarence, NY 14031; phone 716-759-2600). Previous editions of the text have been used in this way at several colleges, with these chapters providing the keys: Elements of Music Appendix (pages 358-391), chapter 2 (What is Jazz?), chapter 3 (Appreciating Jazz Improvisation), and chapter 4 (Origins of Jazz). Much emphasis was placed on the listening guides that appear throughout the text. Instructors usually supplemented that material with selected portions of styles chapters. The portions that give readers the greatest insight into how jazz is made are the nonbiographical units that appear at the beginnings of chapters 5, 6, 9, 14, and 16.

The text provides the essentials for a historically organized **INTRODUCTION TO JAZZ STYLES**. Again, a basic collection of records is essential. The skeleton of the course is contained in the "styles" chapters: chapter 5 (Early Jazz), chapter 6 (Swing), chapter 9 (Bop), chapter 10 (Cool), chapter 11 (Hard Bop), chapter 14 (Avant-Garde/Free Jazz), and chapter 16 (Jazz/Rock). Instructors frequently preface their styles sequence with appendix materials and the introductory chapters, and they frequently select more specialized chapters to use as supplements (the chapters devoted to Duke Ellington and Miles Davis, for instance).

The text provides the essentials for a course concerned primarily with **MAJOR FIGURES IN JAZZ**: Louis Armstrong (covered in chapter 5), Duke Ellington (chapter 7), Charlie Parker/Dizzy Gillespie (chapter 9), Miles Davis (chapters 12 and 16), and John Coltrane (chapter 13). For those who wish to explore more than just the top five or six figures, the text also includes substantial coverage of such other giants as Jelly Roll Morton (chapter 5), Earl Hines (chapter 5), Count Basie (chapter 8), Lester Young (chapter 8), Lennie Tristano (chapter 10), Ornette Coleman (chapter 14), Charles Mingus (chapter 14), Bill Evans (chapter 15), Sun Ra (chapter 14), and Stan Kenton (chapter 10), to name just a few.

For a course in **THE HISTORY OF JAZZ**, the text can be used intact, though minor juggling of contents can make the final five chapters more chronological. The main treatment of Miles Davis (chapter 12) runs from the 1950's to 1970; so the instructor may wish to postpone coverage of its second half until John Coltrane (chapter 13) and Bill Evans (chapter 15) have been covered. Similarly, the instructor may wish to postpone the final two thirds of chapter 15 until the 1970's have been covered, because the bulk of its material overlaps the same span, and then spills into the 1980's with its updates on Herbie Hancock and Chick Corea. The coverage of Charles Mingus in chapter 14 runs from the 1940's to the 1970's, as does that of Sun Ra. The end of chapter 14 (Art Ensemble of Chicago, Anthony Braxton, World Saxophone Quartet) overlaps the same time period as jazz-rock (chapter 16).

JAZZ STYLES has also been used in courses called "American Music," "Contemporary Music," "Twentieth Century Music," "Popular Music in America," "Afro-American Music," and "Black Music." The last third of the text is used in many courses called "Rock", "The History of Rock and Roll," and "Jazz/Rock Foundations." The "Elements of Music" appendix is used in numerous music appreciation courses. The "For Musicians" appendix is used in many courses in "jazz theory" and "Introduction to Jazz Styles," "Jazz Survey," and "Jazz Perspectives." At least one professor requires the text to be read by students in courses called "jazz trumpet," "jazz trombone," "jazz saxophone," "jazz piano," "jazz bass," and "jazz drums."

A number of professors have said that this book has too much information in it, and, in particular, that it is impossible for them to cover some chapters, such as those on Ellington and Coltrane, in a single-semester college course. These professors are correct. However, if they are unduly frustrated by this, they are overlooking two considerations. First is that this book, like most good textbooks, is intended to be merely a resource, not a rigid syllabus for a particular course. It was never intended to be studied line by line, cover to cover by novice listeners in a single-semester jazz appreciation course. The second consideration is that part of a teacher's job is to make judicious choices from the assortment of information offered in a textbook and then guide students to a comprehensible sampling that is suitable for them.

Students are often confused and frustrated in the courses where professors do not routinely follow a detailed syllabus that tells what pages, terms, and musicians the students must know. Textbooks tend to be overwhelming when students assume that they must learn everything in them. Helpful teachers tell their students what not to be overly concerned with. A few examples will clarify this. Whereas some teachers consider sideman names to be superfluous, others believe that familiarity with every musician in the Ellington chapter is essential for a minimum understanding of the music. Whereas some teachers feel that to know Coltrane was an important post-Parker saxophonist is sufficient, other teachers consider an appreciation of Coltrane's McCoy Tyner-Jimmy Garrison-Elvin Jones rhythm section also to be essential. And some teachers want students to remember not only that Coltrane had roots in the style of Lester Young, but also that Coltrane influenced such current giants as David Liebman and Michael Brecker. Some teachers believe that a basic introduction to jazz involves learning to discriminate soprano from tenor saxophone timbre. Other teachers feel that such a skill exceeds reasonable expectations for nonmusician students. Whereas some teachers feel that students should be able to recognize the sound of a 12-bar blues before receiving a passing grade in an introductory course, other teachers are more concerned that their students remember the birthplaces of famous musicians. Some teachers believe that an immersion in the sounds of jazz is sufficient and students need not acquire knowledge about how jazz is made. Regardless of a teacher's philosophy of education, students benefit from being told what that philosophy is, what pages to read, what examples on the cassettes to study, and what they will be expected to remember from those materials.

CAN YOU TEACH JAZZ HISTORY WITHOUT ACCOUNTING FOR YOUR STUDENTS' PERCEPTUAL SKILLS?

The instructor who has listened to jazz for many years finds no difficulty in distinguishing many different styles. For some instructors, it is incomprehensible that other people cannot immediately recognize the distinctive features of tone quality and melodic conception that set Clifford Brown apart from Miles Davis or that separate Bix Beiderbecke from Louis Armstrong. However, most first-time listeners rarely notice such aspects. Even upon repeated listening, many bright, highly motivated students are unable to match a musician's name with his sound.

If you acknowledge the low level listening skills that many students bring with them, you can help them and prevent losing their interest. First, build a respectable listening lab by making up tapes of all the essential sounds (the different instruments, the different song forms, back-to-back contrasts of the major players performing the same tunes, etc.). Second, provide students with adequate playback facilities. (Buy a few Walkmans or Discmans if your school has no music library or language lab, then make them available for check-out at the reserve reading desk of your main library.) Third, require recognition of players on only a few instruments in each era. Fourth, hold students responsible for identifying the styles of only two major figures per instrument per era. (Names of major figures are bold-faced in the text.)

If you do not spend a week or two discussing the Elements of Music appendix (pages 358-391) before launching your chronology of styles, consider first requiring familiarization with the contents of the **JAZZ STYLES DEMONSTRATION CASSETTE/CD** and/or the Steve Gryb videocassette **LISTENING TO JAZZ** and devoting a week to Chapter 3 (Appreciating Jazz Improvisation).

When you cover Chord Progressions and Tune Construction (Chapter 3) and the JAZZ STYLES DEMONSTRATION CASSETTE/CD, you might assign pages 274-276 for discussing how free is free jazz. It describes how chord changes guide solo improvisations. This is a splendid time to bring musicians into class, run a question and answer session, and make the musicians and your students pick apart the musical roles of improvisers. This may reveal how musicians know what to do at a jam session.

Chapter 3 (Appreciating Jazz Improvisation) requires much classroom illustration before it affects the listening skills of your students. Therefore, if you are a jazz musician, your students will be grateful when you bring in your own combo and demonstrate each principle (12-bar blues, 32-bar A-A-B-A format, stop-times, double-times, bridges, comping, trading fours, ride rhythms, walking bass patterns, etc.). If your own combo is not available, throw together a combo of student musicians. During demonstrations, it is handy to have students turn to page 378 and follow along. Pages 377-381 provide a useful guide for your lecture/demonstration as well as a review that your students can study later. They can use it to accompany their own listening assignments, too. If you do not have the cooperation of a group of musicians, use Music Minus One records or the Play-Along format available in Jamey Aebersold's series of recordings: A NEW APPROACH TO JAZZ IMPROVISATION. (I like VOL. 6, CHARLIE PARKER - "ALL BIRD" because it has a twelve-bar blues, a couple of 32 bar A-A-B-A pieces, and stop-time solo breaks. And it has stereo separation that allows you to play the walking bass sound in isolation if you want to demonstrate that style, and/or improvise over it yourself.) You can get the Aebersold recordings (available on LP, audio cassette, or compact disc) quickly via a toll-free number: 1-800-456-1388; by fax: 1-812-949-2006; or by writing Jamey Aebersold, P.O. Box 1244C, New Albany, IN 47151-1244. Current prices appear in recent issues of DOWN BEAT and INTERNATIONAL MUSICIAN.

If you don't play jazz yourself, it is especially handy for your students to have a guest player visit class and explain and demonstrate it. You might be able to get by with only a pianist and bassist, but a trio or quartet would be more comprehensive. The earlier in the semester this happens, the more your students will get out of their remaining listening assignments because they will know what happened in the recording studios to make the music, and they will have a better appreciation for the extent of spontaneity in jazz. (For a more detailed illustration of demonstration activities, order cassette taped presentations originally made by Howie Smith and me at the 1984 National Association of Jazz Educators conference when we were asked to explain techniques of teaching jazz appreciation to nonmusicians. Order from Mark Records, 10815 Bodine Road, Clarence, New York 14031. Phone 1-716-759-2600. Ask for the 1984 NAJE tape 37: Teaching Jazz History to Nonmusic Majors, and tape 38: Where's the Melody?)

It is important to help students learn to distinguish instrument sounds that are common to different eras in jazz history. So in addition to requiring familiarity with the JAZZ STYLES DEMONSTRATION CASSETTE/CD and the Steve Gryb LISTENING TO JAZZ videocassette, consider comparing these pairs of sounds in live demonstrations:

drummer using sticks vs. drummer using brushes (on drum and on cymbal)
electric piano vs. acoustic piano
muted trumpet vs. unmuted trumpet (bring in Harmon and cup mutes)
trumpet vs. trombone
alto sax vs. tenor sax

To further help students distinguish saxophone timbres, play recordings by musicians who play similar styles but blow different sized horns. For example, play:

Johnny Hodges vs. Ben Webster (1940's) (contrast "Prelude to a Kiss" with "Cottontail" in the JAZZ CLASSICS CASSETTE/CD)

Charlie Parker vs. Sonny Rollins (1950's)

Lee Konitz vs. Stan Getz (Cool) (both play on "No Figs" in the JAZZ CLASSICS CASSETTE/CD)

Cannonball Adderley vs. John Coltrane (early 1960's) (both play on "Flamenco Sketches" on the JAZZ CLASSICS CASSETTE/CD)

David Sanborn vs. Michael Brecker (1970's)

CONVEYING THE EXTENT OF SPONTANEITY IN JAZZ

Students in jazz appreciation classes need to understand that most of what they're hearing on recordings was being made up by the musicians **AS THEY WERE PERFORMING IT**. Instructors tell me that their students often come back from attending live performances and report that the musicians were playing memorized solos and/or reading all the music from sheets! If such students were attending jazz combo performances, they were obviously confusing nonjazz formats with jazz format. As speaker at a booking agents conference, I discovered that most agents are also unaware. Classical soloists frequently perform without sheet music. However they do this because they have memorized, note-for-note, their entire part. Jazz musicians, on the other hand, usually perform without sheet music, not because they are playing memorized parts, but because what they are playing **IS NOT WRITTEN DOWN**. It is being created at the very moment the audience hears it. If they have memorized anything, it is the chord progressions providing the harmonic basis for their improvisations. It is therefore essential to stress to your students that jazz musicians do not perform without sheets because they have memorized, note-for-note, their entire part. The **ONLY** part the jazz musician has memorized is the set of underlying harmonies to the piece. All the rest of the solo is being made up as he goes along. Explain that when jazz musicians do perform from sheet music, it is usually for the purpose of following the chord changes. In fact, jazz musicians rarely refer to the music as a score or as sheet music. They call it a chart, probably because that is exactly what it looks like. (Let your students examine a chart so that they can see long stretches of nothing but the chords and slashes that indicate the organizing harmonies and their respective durations.)

Another confusing experience for the novice jazz fan is to witness a performance by a large jazz ensemble. This presents complications because little of the music in such big bands really IS improvised. It is just a swinging concert band, with most of the musicians reading, note-for-note, all their parts. (You can get around the problem by endorsing primarily combo performances as concerts that will fulfill course requirements.) But if the students do attend a big band gig, you must explain to them beforehand that when a musician stands up alone and plays a solo, that solo is improvised. And if the musician looks like he is **READING** his part, it is the sequence of chords that he is reading, not a note-for-note copy of his solo. In the case of combo performances, the musicians might have memorized preset introductions, endings and transitions, as well as theme statements at the beginning and end of a piece. However, such organizational aspects should not be allowed to confuse the listeners into thinking that the bulk of the performance, namely the solos themselves, is also memorized. **THE BULK OF THE PERFORMANCE IS SPONTANEOUS**. The solos are spontaneous, and the accompaniments for the solo improvisations are spontaneous.

Jazz is improvised music. However, for most people, the idea that a musician can simultaneously compose and perform coherent music that has not been rehearsed is quite difficult to comprehend, impossible to believe. Therefore, the instructor must spend considerable class time explaining and demonstrating this. Many courses are taught in a strictly historical manner, and unfortunately the graduates of those courses attend jazz performances without really knowing that they are hearing spontaneously conceived music resulting from little prearrangement, far less prearrangement than is used in most other music familiar to them.

Demonstrating the act of improvisation is easy for the instructor who himself is a jazz musician. All he needs to do is tell the class that he is about to make up something new for them, and then proceed to play it. He must assure them that what he is doing is genuinely off the top of his head, and sometimes it helps when he uses themes and melodic fragments that his students supply. Those instructors who are not players might be a bit nervous about demonstrating improvisation. But they should not be. They can discuss the analogy to speech. When asked the question, "Is everything you say something that you have said in exactly the same way before?," students will say, "Of course not." Just explain that, "We choose from words we already know, and we improvise sentences with them, just as jazz musicians choose notes and rhythms to improvise **MUSICAL** sentences." Another way is to draw upon recordings that show how jazz musicians rarely play the same tune the same way twice. Find a couple versions of the same song by the same player. Two versions of Embraceable You are in SCCJ. Two versions of several John Coltrane tunes can be found by getting the compact disc of John Coltrane, GIANT STEPS (Atlantic: 1311-2). (In the LP format, John Coltrane, ALTERNATE TAKES (Atlantic: SD 1668) contains the alternate takes.) Another strategy is to simply teach your students a song such as I Got Rhythm (use the version by Don Byas in SCCJ). Then indicate the chorus lengths within improvised solos. Once your students can determine when one chorus starts and another leaves off, tell them to compare solo choruses. Short of playing the first few measures of two versions of the same ballad by the same improviser in the same key at the same tempo, this should help convey the principle of improvisation to your students. Note: If everything is totally new to the listener, he is unlikely to be capable of recognizing what is different from one version to another or from one chorus to the next. For example, if a student does not know the melody to Body and Soul, Coleman Hawkins' **ENTIRE** solo will sound improvised! For this reason, first employ only the simplest melodies and the simplest improvisations. I had much success with Freddie the Freeloader from the Miles Davis album, KIND OF BLUE, Columbia: CK 40579. The piece is a 12-bar blues, a form you would already have taught. The melody line is very clear and uncomplicated, and the Miles Davis trumpet solo is easy to sing along with. Just get the students to learn it, sing along with it, then compare each successive chorus. By the third chorus of the Davis solo, students will have grasped the idea of improvisation.

IT IS EASY TO HELP STUDENTS HEAR THE CHORD CHANGES

If you are not a musician, you might be intimidated by the prospect of helping your students hear chord changes. However, if you take a moment to run through the exercises in the Elements of Music appendix (pages 372-376), you will be adequately equipped to provide your students with all the help they need. Just find a piano, and then follow the step-by-step instructions that have the piano keyboard illustrations (follow the dots). Then require students to study those same examples as they are heard on the DEMONSTRATION CASSETTE. Several nonmusician instructors have told me that they use the appendix routinely at the beginning of the course. Some even require their nonmusician students to compose an original 12-bar blues! A number of students told me that, independent of their course requirements, they performed the Elements of Music exercises with no trouble. (Some became so interested that they decided to go on and get formal music lessons after that brief introduction.)

Most students are not sufficiently motivated to complete all the exercises independently. Therefore, it is a good idea to perform several of the counting/listening exercises in lecture and require students to review them on the DEMONSTRATION CASSETTE. Don't feel shy about pulling the 12-bar blues illustration directly from the book. Your students will thank you for coaching them on something they can then try again by themselves. The same goes for the listening guides found in the Duke Ellington, Count Basie and Miles Davis chapters.

It is essential that you teach your students how to determine the tempo of a piece and how to find where the first beat of a measure is. Only when you have assured yourself that they can do this can you expect them to do it for a grade. For instance, something as complex as Harlem Airshaft (on side 1 of JAZZ CLASSICS CASSETTE) requires your loudly counting every beat as it goes by and announcing each section as it arrives. Some instructors make stereo tape recordings in which one channel has music while the other has counting. Students can use both channels until they get the hang of it, then switch off the counting channel when they are ready to listen without such cues. All the listening guides in JAZZ STYLES tell how many seconds pass for each event. In that way, the students can verify their perceptions of musical events against a stop watch while the music is playing. Some profs require students to construct event diagrams for at least one brief passage of one selection each week. The ups and downs of the solo line indicate pitch, and line lengths indicate durations. Expression of accompanying sounds can be made graphically, organized in terms of beats in the song form. You might choose to have students juxtapose beats, song form, and seconds. Some instructors base their listening exams on such formats. One of the easiest places to begin training for such a task is the very slow Flamenco Sketches, available on side 2 of the JAZZ CLASSICS CASSETTE/CD. The selection is based on five modes and analyzed, measure-by-measure, in the listening guide on pages 228-230.

Students catch on to these principles and acquire these skills quickly if you first count each beat out loud with the music: 1234 2234 3234 4234 5234, etc., all the time using a pointer to indicate on an overhead projection or a chalkboard chart of the piece's construction. (Remember that it is too much to expect students to identify the **ACTUAL CHORD**. You need only expect them to identify the **MOVEMENT** when the chord **CHANGES**. Illustrations are in the JAZZ STYLES CASSETTE/CD.) The goal is to provide them with a glimpse into the mental activities of the improvisor by providing information about one thing the improvisor must always keep track of while he creates his lines. All of this is explained in detail in Chapter 3 (Appreciating Jazz Improvisation). However, that material usually doesn't mean much unless it is preceded by the basics that are found in the Elements of Music appendix (pages 367-387), accompanied by about a week's worth of demonstrations, question and answer sessions, and close study of examples on the DEMONSTRATION CASSETTE.

PITFALLS TO AVOID

Now let's turn to a few pitfalls that almost everyone encounters one time or another. Having talked with dozens of instructors during their first semesters of teaching this course, I have identified these **ASSUMPTIONS THAT CAN TRIP YOU**:

1. The book has 16 chapters, and I **MUST** cover them **ALL**.

No, don't even try. Just take five to ten that you feel comfortable with, and then do justice to each, and forget the rest. However, do try to spend at least a week on contemporary sounds. Your students will be very disappointed if you don't give some respectful attention to their favorites, or at least to musicians who are still living and performing.

2. People already know how to listen, they've been listening all their lives.

Not true. Observations by professors combined with my own studies of listener cognitions, show that most nonmusicians do not actively listen, they do not focus on individual parts. Note that this statement requires important qualification. It does **NOT** say that nonmusicians are **INCAPABLE** of focusing. It says only that frequently they are **NOT IN THE HABIT** of focusing. In fact, several reputable studies have shown that nonmusician listeners are just as capable as musician listeners. Once they are told how to follow a sound or a group of sounds, they can attend as well as musicians can.

3. Students already know who Benny Goodman is, who Miles Davis is, Louis Armstrong, John Coltrane, etc.

No, they don't. Even those few students who might recognize the names, rarely know what instruments were played by these musicians, much less their respective era or sound. For the most part, your students are going to be learning a foreign language from you, a language in which almost all the names and sounds are fresh. So when you are lecturing, keep in mind that you and your students do **NOT** share a common frame of reference. You must provide **ALL** their prerequisite knowledge before proceeding in your course.

4. In one week, I can explain the fundamental principles behind chord change-based improvisation, mode-based improvisation and free-form improvisation via demonstrations and many examples of the 12-bar blues and 32-bar A-A-B-A forms.

No, you can't. You might be able to **MENTION** all these principles, or review them aloud for yourself in a week. But you cannot get your students to the point of **COMPREHENDING** what it means for an improviser to select his notes from the framework of the 12-bar I-IV-I-V-I progression or alter his phrasing when he comes to the bridge of a 32-bar A-A-B-A song form and what rules keep strangers at a jam session playing well enough together to create a respectable performance without knowing each other or having any prior discussion among themselves. However, you **COULD** do it **IF YOU ALLOWED YOURSELF MORE TIME**, perhaps 2 or 3 weeks. And you could do it **IF YOU**:

a. frequently brought musicians to class and

b. played "Misty" or the "(Meet the) Flintstones" theme (the only 32-bar A-A-B-A songs they are all likely to know) while

c. counting measures aloud and

d. used charts on the chalk board to guide the listening of your students **WHILE THE MUSICIANS ARE PLAYING** (for graphic illustrations, see JAZZ STYLES appendix pages 378-388)

e. first played several slow, simple, blues pieces (by B.B. King or T-Bone Walker, perhaps), then

f. gradually moved to more complex pieces (from blues by Bessie Smith to blues by Count Basie to Charlie Parker to John Coltrane),

g. all the while, requiring your students, **OUTSIDE OF CLASS**, to practice counting the beats to blues pieces that were on reserve in their library listening booths and/or available in albums you brought to class for sale.

5. Students already know the instruments in jazz bands.

No, they don't. You must show them and demonstrate them. Remember that saxophones are not common, especially in symphony orchestras and even in rock bands. Furthermore, even if a nonmusician **DOES** see one, if no one tells him what it is that he is seeing, he will **STILL NOT KNOW** what a saxophone is, and he will know nothing about the differences among soprano, alto, tenor, and baritone saxophones. (The first time they saw one, most of my students thought the soprano sax was a **METAL CLARINET**.)

Perhaps a few anecdotes will give us more perspective. A dean at my college, who knew that I played flute, was reading the newspaper and saw a photo of me holding my flute, and exclaimed, "Mark, I didn't know you played **CLARINET, TOO**." (And this was a man who previously had reported to me that he was "a jazz fan"!) I also remember a particular night club gig in which I was playing flute with my guitarist and acoustic bassist, and one enthusiastic patron ran up to us to compliment my bassist on his "cello" solo and me on my great "clarinet" playing. (This was the same patron who had previously told me how much he liked jazz and how large his record collection was!) It may also be instructive to note that several of my students confused the saxophone with the trumpet in listening to their copies of the Miles Davis album KIND OF BLUE.

A few more anecdotes should help complete our perspective on the normal extent of ignorance in the population at large. Once I was being interviewed on radio by a well known jazz disc jockey. And, after listening to a Stan Getz record and hearing me say that "This featured Stan Getz on tenor sax," the disc jockey said to the audience that she'd assumed that Getz was playing alto sax. That makes me recall the time I was driving my young bassist to a gig, while the car stereo was playing an Eric Dolphy bass clarinet improvisation, and my bassist commented, "What an unusual tone that alto saxophonist has!" Then there was my gig for a private party at a millionaire's house. When we took a break, I set my flute on the piano and sat on the couch, away from the guests, but still within earshot. Soon a guest sat down at the piano and started playing old Irish songs, and several other guests gathered around him. One looked at my flute, and said to the other, "That's an oboe, isn't it?" The other replied, "No, it's a clarinet." And the guest kept on playing piano. No one offered any further corrections. Not even the piano-playing guest seemed to know.

These anecdotes are cited, not for their comedy value, but because they reflect the limits of instrument familiarity you are likely to encounter among your students. Humility in this concern might be afforded when you ask yourself how many jazz friends of yours can differentiate a viola from a violin, by sound OR appearance. Yet classical players find this to be a major distinction, though it is no better known a distinction among outsiders than are the distinctions between the alto and tenor sax or between the clarinet and soprano sax. And how many people do you know who can open the hood of their car and name all the engine parts underneath? The point is that we all possess specialized knowledge that we accidentally assume is possessed by the population at large. So, at least in the case of instrument identifications, one solution is to frequently direct your students to the instrument photos in their textbook **WHILE** they are listening to recordings of the sounds made by those instruments. Another solution is to require students to familiarize themselves with all the instrument sounds on the JAZZ STYLES DEMONSTRATION CASSETTE/CD. Incidentally, many probably will not do that unless you promise to require such identifications on exams.

TROMBONES ARE PICTURED ON PAGES 62, 108, 113 & 291

SOPRANO SAXOPHONES ARE PICTURED ON PAGES 76, 264, 333 & 339

CLARINETS ARE PICTURED ON PAGES 62, 76, 85, 94, 271

FLUTE AND PICCOLO ARE PICTURED ON PAGE 290 & 291

BASS CLARINET IS PICTURED ON PAGE 290 & 349

FLUEGELHORN IS PICTURED ON PAGE 113 & 349

TUBA IS PICTURED ON PAGE 78

BASS SAXOPHONE IS PICTURED ON PAGES 78 & 294

BARITONE SAXOPHONE IS PICTURED ON PAGES 78, 88, 174 & 300

VIBRAHARP IS PICTURED ON PAGE 150 & 168

TENOR SAXOPHONES ARE PICTURED ON PAGES 2, 11, 88, 96, 108, 128, 138, 161, 215, 219, 235, 251, 252, 257, 294, 296, 300

ALTO SAXOPHONES ARE PICTURED ON 88, 125, 139, 140, 174, 189, 195, 219, 272, 275, 300

TRUMPETS ARE PICTURED ON PAGES 4, 62, 71, 72, 94, 145, 215 & 251

CORNETS ARE PICTURED ON PAGES 52, 52, 72 & 195

BASS VIOLS ARE PICTURED ON PAGES 11, 22, 128, 139, 177, 189, 257, 275, 284, 296 & 323

BANJO IS PICTURED ON 43 & 62

DRUM SET IS PICTURED ON PAGES 23, 24, 94, 108, 168, 189, 218, 232, 251, 257, 259, 289

DRUM STICKS AND BRUSHES ARE PICTURED ON PAGE 25

BASS DRUM PEDAL IS PICTURED ON PAGE 26

HIGH-HAT CYMBAL APPARATUS IS PICTURED ON PAGE 25, 138

BASS GUITAR IS PICTURED ON PAGE 22, 343 & 349

MUTES ARE PICTURED ON PAGES 388-390, **CUP MUTE** IN TRUMPET ON PAGES 2 & 128

An excellent supplement to the instrument photos in the text and their sounds on the JAZZ STYLES DEMONSTRATION CASSETTE/CD is the one-hour videocassette adaptation prepared by Steve Gryb, **LISTENING TO JAZZ** (Prentice-Hall ISBN 0-135328624; available by mail order from the publisher; phone: 515-284-6751; FAX: 515-284-2607). And, most importantly, bring musicians to class to demonstrate all the instruments and to run "blindfold tests" with your students to help the students practice identifying what sounds are associated with what instruments. Doing this more than once during the semester is a must. Of course, initially this must be done in the first few weeks of class or else the semester's listening assignments will be missing a entire dimension for your students. And it is very useful to assign the JAZZ STYLES DEMONSTRATION CASSETTE/CD for the first two weeks of classes, as well as letting students know they will be tested from it on their first quizzes and exams.

There is another method for helping students learn to match the appearance with the sound of jazz instruments, and it increases student attention and enthusiasm, too. Simply gather jazz movies and video tapes for class presentation. If your department has a budget for such materials, just watch the reviews and advertisements in DOWN BEAT and JAZZ TIMES. Then order whatever videos look intriguing. A few distributors include Original Music, 418 Lasher Road, Tivoli, NY 12583 (phone: 914-756-2767); Rhapsody Films, P.O. Box 179, New York, NY 10014 (phone: 212-243-0152); Jazzland, Box 366, Dayton, Ohio 45401 (phone: 513-222-2413); and Jamey Abersold (P.O. Box 1244C, New Albany, IN 47151-1244; phone: 1-800-456-1388). And there are other sources. Every city has at least one person who collects jazz films, and usually he videotapes jazz-related shows from television. So make friends with that person and begin borrowing materials. Libraries, especially some of the larger ones, also lend jazz-related films. Other connections often unfold when you attend the annual conventions of the International Association of Jazz Educators (every January) and JAZZ TIMES (every September). Both routinely feature presentations of videos and meetings with collectors. To keep up with much of the material in jazz pedagogy, join IAJE and subscribe to JAZZ TIMES. They review new books, albums, and videos in their publications. IAJE is reached via Box 724, Manhattan, Kansas 66502; phone: 913-776-8744. JAZZ TIMES subscriptions can be obtained via 7961 Eastern Avenue, Silver Spring, Maryland 20910-4898; phone: 1-800-866-7664 or 301-588-4114.

WHAT MATERIALS CAN I FIND IMMEDIATELY?

Many of the textbook's discussions refer to recorded performances that have been reissued in the boxed anthology called the **SMITHSONIAN COLLECTION OF CLASSIC JAZZ (SCCJ)**. Most libraries have the complete set, and some have several copies in several formats. It is a collection of recordings by historically significant jazz musicians. The contents are listed on pages 129-130 of the discography in this teachers' manual. The SCCJ is currently available on audio cassette and compact disc format via 1-800-669-1559 and by mail from Smithsonian Recordings, P.O. Box 2071, Colchester, VT 05449-2071. If your library does not have SCCJ, and you have no one to borrow it from, yet you still have to begin teaching the jazz course, you can order it. However, professors have reported that delays of 6 weeks to 6 months frequently occur before they receive their orders. Therefore you might best plan around it at first and follow some of the alternate strategies suggested below.

Finding good examples to illustrate the major jazz styles used to be rather difficult. However, with the **JAZZ CLASSICS CASSETTE/CD** that comes with the 2-cassette version of the JAZZ STYLES textbook, you already have a good start for a single-semester jazz history course. The JAZZ CLASSICS CASSETTE/CD was compiled to be suitable equally well as a substitute or a supplement to the SCCJ. Note that due to a combination of limits on running time and problems in obtaining clearances from companies owning the rights to certain historic recordings, the JAZZ CLASSICS CASSETTE/CD, like the SCCJ, is not complete in its representation of all eras and all major styles. However, you can piece together a fair representation of jazz history if you pair it with the SMITHSONIAN COLLECTION OF CLASSIC JAZZ, and supplement with a few examples footnoted in the textbook for Art Blakey, Cannonball Adderley, Sonny Stitt, Horace Silver, Joe Henderson, Freddie Hubbard, Albert Ayler, Sun Ra, Gerry Mulligan, Stan Kenton, and Keith Jarrett. An assortment of fusion artists would also be useful, especially 1970's recordings footnoted in the textbook for Miles Davis, Chick Corea, and John McLaughlin. If you are teaching a course concerned with popular music and the jazz that became popular music, you will also need to supplement with popular jazz recordings from each era. The recordings included in the SMITHSONIAN COLLECTION OF CLASSIC JAZZ and the JAZZ CLASSICS CASSETTE/CD tend to be the artistic successes, not the popular successes.

Another easy-to-obtain supplement is the 77-minute compact disc of jazz classics (**CONCISE GUIDE CD**) that was issued in conjunction with the CONCISE GUIDE TO JAZZ textbook, the abridged version of JAZZ STYLES: HISTORY AND ANALYSIS. The CD is available from Prentice-Hall as **ISBN 0-13-174475-5**. (The ISBN is essential to distinguish it from the JAZZ CLASSICS COMPACT DISC FOR JAZZ STYLES; ISBN 0-13-111429-8.) Instructors who have required their students to buy the CONCISE GUIDE TO JAZZ textbook are entitled to free copies of the CD (phone: 1-800-526-0485). Bookstores can obtain it for student purchase if instructors request that a quantity be kept on hand. Individuals can obtain the CD from Prentice-Hall Publishers by phoning 515-284-6751 (FAX: 515-284-2607). Its selections for Original Dixieland Jazz Band, Louis Armstrong, Duke Ellington, Count Basie, Bill Evans, and Chick Corea duplicate items for those artists on the JAZZ CLASSICS COMPACT DISC FOR JAZZ STYLES. The remaining selections are Sobbin' Hearted Blues by Bessie Smith & Louis Armstrong, Back in Your Own Back Yard by Billie Holiday & Lester Young, Tiger Rag by Art Tatum, Body and Soul by Coleman Hawkins, I've Got It Bad by Johnny Hodges, Ko-Ko by Charlie Parker, Things to Come by Dizzy Gillespie big band, Dexter Digs In by Dexter Gordon, Bud Powell & Max Roach, Sax of a Kind by Lee Konitz & Lennie Tristano, Two Bass Hit by John Coltrane & Cannonball Adderley, Blue in Green by Miles Davis, Bill Evans & John Coltrane, Get Happy by J. J. Johnson, Clifford Brown & Jimmy Heath, Cloning by Ornette Coleman & Don Cherry, Your Lady by John Coltrane, McCoy Tyner, Jimmy Garrison & Elvin Jones, and Birdland by Weather Report.

Another manual in addition to the one you are now reading is 120 pages long, with hundreds of listening goals, information goals, essay exams, and many chapters explaining how to organize demonstrations such as the African connections, how to develop an appreciation for textural improvisation in free jazz, how to demonstrate the emancipation of the modern jazz rhythm section, how to relate chord notes to melody notes, how to make the most of a live band in your class by using the rhythm section as demonstration unit, how to ease students into appreciating bop, how to help them appreciate early jazz sounds, etc. It is **HOW TO TEACH JAZZ HISTORY**, available from the International Association of Jazz Educators, Box 724, Manhattan, Kansas 66502, phone: 913-776-8744.

A one-hour cassette tape of demonstrations and advice that I presented to the 1984 convention of the National Association of Jazz Educators is also available. In addition to general advice and anecdotes, the cassette contains excerpts from important albums and it is organized to show

a. how you can demonstrate the continuity from African music to jazz-rock,

b. how you can demonstrate the influence of Bill Evans on Herbie Hancock, Chick Corea and Keith Jarrett,

c. how you can demonstrate the differences between bop, cool and hard bop,

d. how you can demonstrate the influence of Art Tatum on Bud Powell,

e. how you can help students understand the relationship between chords and the notes that are improvised to be compatible with the chords.

It is available as tape #37: **TEACHING JAZZ HISTORY TO NONMUSICIANS**/1984 NAJE CONVENTION, distributed by Mark Records, 10815 Bodine Road, Clarence, New York 14031, phone: 716-759-2600.

HOW TO USE THE JAZZ STYLES DEMONSTRATION CASSETTE/CD

Introducing Sounds in Isolation Before Listening in Context

The most effective way to help listeners detect something in context is to expose them to it first in isolation. For instance, if you want someone to notice walking bass within a bop combo improvisation, first bring a bassist to class, and have him demonstrate the walking technique. If you want listeners to notice the sound of drummer Jo Jones keeping time with a Count Basie combo, let your students first see and hear a drummer play a ride rhythm on high-hat cymbals in class. Only after that experience, will neophyte listeners feel confident in pinning a label on that aspect of the rhythm section sound within a jazz recording. And having labelled it perceptually, they might begin to appreciate the contribution that element makes to the overall Basie band sound. For that reason, the JAZZ STYLES textbook comes in several different formats: book with cassette of 171 instrument demonstrations (ISBN 0-13-175977-9); book with 2 cassettes: the demonstrations cassette plus a cassette of 26 historic recordings (ISBN 0-13-175969-8); book alone (ISBN 0-13-102245-8) with option to purchase compact disc versions of the cassettes separately: **JAZZ STYLES DEMONSTRATION COMPACT DISC** (ISBN 0-13-176918-9) and **JAZZ CLASSICS COMPACT DISC FOR JAZZ STYLES** (ISBN 0-13-111429-8). Each of these is available free to instructors who require their students to buy any version of the textbook. For your complimentary copy, contact your local Prentice-Hall field representative, phone: 1-800-526-0485, or write College Humanities Marketing, Prentice-Hall, Inc., Englewood Cliffs, NJ 07632.

Perhaps some personal recollections will illustrate my sympathy for your situation. When I began teaching jazz appreciation courses, I assumed that, like me and all the kids on the street where I'd grown up, everyone knew what a trumpet, saxophone, flute, snare drum, and bass drum was. So when my department chairman suggested that we make General Music ("The Listening Experience") a prerequisite for History and Styles of Jazz, I rejected his idea. But he compromised with me and put a note in the course roster, saying that the prerequisite for my course was General Music "or consent of instructor." So I began looking for advantages that might accrue from listening skills that students acquired in that prerequisite course. I reasoned that perhaps the course really could do some good by familiarizing students with basic tone colors so that I did not have to spend class time on them and would therefore have more time to introduce different jazz styles. To verify this assumption, I began interviewing the people who taught that course. But I found that they did not, as a rule, teach students to distinguish the sounds of the instruments common to jazz. I also began asking my students whether they really had taken General Music. Then I began noticing that, within recordings, some could not distinguish a sax from a trumpet sound, and that some of those who failed such a basic identification had taken the prerequisite. In other words, it didn't seem to make any difference whether they had already taken General Music. In conclusion, what I discovered was that, unlike me and the kids on the street where I'd grown up, a substantial portion of college students could not tell the difference between jazz instruments, in appearance or sound, and general music appreciation courses failed to remedy this.

Even though it took me a few semesters to recognize the situation, I eventually reorganized my syllabus and cut the number of jazz styles in my course to make way for presentations of such basics as instrument sounds and song forms. I ultimately settled on a program in which the entire first month was filled teaching basic listening skills: the names, appearances and sounds of the instruments; the construction of basic song forms (32-bar A-A-B-A, 12-bar blues, etc.); meter and syncopation; the fundamentals of listening (graphing solo lines, focusing on different instruments in the band one-at-a-time, recognizing the difference between staccato and legato, etc.). Members of my own professional bands and other free-lance musicians in the community helped me do this. By the time I'd worked the bugs out of the course and accounted for the musical ignorance of nonmusician students, I was routinely scheduling at least three weeks of demonstrations scattered throughout every semester. These were class meetings during which musicians appeared, demonstrated their instruments, and discussed how they improvised.

Luckily, I was blessed with a department chairman who suggested that the college could afford a modest honorarium for each guest musician. (It was $20 in 1971.) But, I also found out that many local professional musicians and almost all student musicians were quite willing to visit my class and demonstrate their craft for free. So, **IF YOU HAVE NO BUDGET FOR GUEST PLAYERS**, don't despair. There are at least three alternatives available:

1. Recruit volunteers

2. Do favors for the musicians. (Treat them to a free dinner or drink. Involve them in faculty recitals that will help them attain recognition in the community. Help find them private students to teach. Tell your students where the musicians are performing, thereby increasing attendance at their gigs.)

3. Dip into your own pocket for car fare. (No matter what burden this places on you, it always proves worthwhile over the long run because the demonstrations will enhance your effectiveness and reputation as a teacher.). Provide transportation for the musicians yourself, in your own car on your own time, and or in student-driven vehicles, and **ALWAYS** give the drummer a hand with his equipment, getting it up and down stairs, through security, in and out of doors, etc.

Unfortunately, we never had the opportunity to put the entire production on video, though Steve Gryb adapted my script from the JAZZ STYLES DEMONSTRATION CASSETTE and prepared a one-hour videocassette introduction for many of the basics. It is available as **LISTENING TO JAZZ** (published by Prentice-Hall as ISBN 0-13507971-3). It can be obtained by special order through any bookstore or to individuals by phone (515-284-6751) or FAX (515-284-2607). The next best thing is to provide you with an approximation of those events that occurred during the very first week of classes in my course. But before we get to that, let's briefly consider how to get students to come to class, take demonstrations seriously and earn acceptable grades.

Constructing Quizzes From The JAZZ STYLES DEMONSTRATION CASSETTE/CD

If you are afraid that your students will view musician demonstrations as entertainment instead of a method for expanding their listening skills, then organize a third of the semester's tests and quizzes around the appearances and sounds of the instruments that are demonstrated. For a quiz, just cue up the JAZZ STYLES DEMONSTRATION CASSETTE/CD to the sound of an instrument, play that brief segment for the students, making certain to give no hints about what portion of the cassette/cd held that particular sound.

When making exams, you need merely note the track number of a passage on the JAZZ CLASSICS COMPACT DISC FOR JAZZ STYLES (ISBN 0-13-50-8524-1 or 0-13-111429-8) and then play it for your students. This saves you the trouble and illegality of taping brief excerpts from historic recordings that students have studied in their out-of-class assignments. This may motivate students to learn both the sounds in isolation (from their copies of the demonstration cassette/CD) and the sounds in context (from their jazz classics cassette/CD).

To integrate this effectively, clearly state in your syllabus that

1. Some of the quiz and exam sounds will always be selected directly from the cassette/cd, and that

2. students can reinforce their learning by regularly studying the cassette/CD.

Here are some concrete examples of how to integrate the cassette/cd contents into study assignments, long-term learning, and test design.

To help students learn the parts of the drum set, frequently direct their attention to the illustrations in chapter 3. After having a drummer play in class and dissect his equipment for your students, tell the class that a quiz will require them to identify all the parts of the basic drum set. Then, when constructing your quiz, just photocopy the sketch of the drum set that appears in the book, and use Liquid Paper or White-Out to blank the labels. Use the altered photocopy as a master, and include it in your quiz.

Make all instrument names blank, but numbered as "fill-ins" (easy for you to score). For measuring the generality of your students' learning, photocopy a drum set illustration from a different chapter or from an instrument ad in a music magazine such as DOWN BEAT or JAZZ TIMES.

Here's a listening skills variation upon the above idea. Prepare an altered picture of the drum set, and put blank spaces next to all the unlabelled parts. Distribute copies to your students. Then cue up the JAZZ STYLES DEMONSTRATION CASSETTE/CD to a brief sequence or sounds produced by those parts of the drum set (high-hat, snare drum, etc.). Play the sequence, and require your students to number the sounds on the parts of the picture according to the order in which you played them.

You need not limit your selections to drum sounds, either. Copy illustrations of other instruments (trumpet, soprano sax, clarinet, etc.), and make a collage of them. Then put blanks next to each, and play the instrument sounds from the cassette/cd (minus the narrative), asking students to number the blanks in the sequence they heard the sounds. Later in the semester, do the same thing, but use recorded moments that you have excerpted from other albums that the students have studied, or from the JAZZ CLASSICS CASSETTE/CD.

A listening quiz administered during the first third of the semester could consist of the jam session that occupies the final portion of the JAZZ STYLES DEMONSTRATION CASSETTE/CD. It is track 98 (instrument quiz) on the compact disc version. (See complete contents listing elsewhere in this manual.) Each instrument is featured for at least one chorus, and none are identified in the narration. Though it is intended as a self-quizzing strategy, you could also use it repeatedly as the basis for listening exams, choosing different instruments for each test. (The JAZZ CLASSICS CASSETTE/CD also provides convenient examples of real life instrument comparisons on the same piece: clarinet, baritone sax, alto sax and tenor sax on No Figs and muted trumpet, tenor sax, and alto sax on Flamenco Sketches. The JAZZ CLASSICS COMPACT DISC FOR CONCISE GUIDE TO JAZZ features a sequence of solos by trumpet, tenor sax, and trombone on Get Happy. Each solo on these CDs has its own track number.)

It is also instructive first to tell students that some demonstration items from the cassette might be used again, and then repeat a few items each time you give a listening exam, to ensure that those students who fail an earlier test are motivated to study the cassette again because they know that they will get another chance. **NOTE:** When selecting the excerpts for a test, avoid playing the items in the order that they occur on the original. Otherwise some students will begin getting the correct answers merely because they have learned the order associated with the correct names of the sounds. And be certain to change your quizzes from semester to semester. Veteran students will coach your new students, thereby preventing new students from learning the sounds. If you do not change exam items from semester to semester, many students will learn only the test-taking strategies, not the course material.

Uses for the JAZZ STYLES DEMONSTRATION CASSETTE/CD

The JAZZ STYLES CASSETTE has at least four uses:

1. a source for reinforcing the learning that stems from in-class demonstrations

2. a means for your students to perform independent, self-directed learning

3. a source of quiz and exam items concerned with identifying instrument sounds and song forms

4. a substitute for demonstrations by live musicians, if you are completely unable to gather instruments and musicians to bring to class. If you do not have access to musicians and a sufficient variety of instruments, you might bring the JAZZ STYLES DEMONSTRATION CASSETTE/CD to class every time you begin discussing a song form that is illustrated by the cassette, and again every time you begin discussing a given musician whose instrument is illustrated by the cassette (trumpet, trombone, alto sax, tenor sax, soprano sax, clarinet, drums, bass, etc.). In other words, identify a particular instrument sound in isolation from the DEMONSTRATION CD before playing an historic recording in which that sound is important in context, such as the clarinet before playing a recording by Benny Goodman, the ride cymbal before playing a Miles Davis record with drummer Tony Williams, or the pizzicato bass before playing a Duke Ellington recording that contains a Jimmy Blanton solo.

The JAZZ STYLES DEMONSTRATION CASSETTE/CD is helpful for ensuring that your students have materials of their own to study, long after the last sounds in the classroom have faded from their ears. If you routinely list cassette contents in your syllabus, students will know what passages to study prior to a given lecture. Key the cassette listings to the textbook page assignments in your syllabus. Before you deliver your John Coltrane lecture, require your students to listen to the saxophone examples so they can learn to distinguish soprano from tenor sax. Before discussing Earl Hines, require students to listen to piano techniques so they can identify tremolo, stride and octaves. If such details are already in your syllabus, you no longer need to devote precious class time to putting it on the board or talking about it. And you won't have to worry about whether you will have time to present it all fresh during lecture. If they know they are going to be quizzed on it, students will show up for class, having already studied the appropriate sounds.

The cassette/CD should help provide what your situation does not provide, but **THE JAZZ STYLES DEMONSTRATION CASSETTE/CD IS NOT INTENDED TO SUBSTITUTE FOR DEMONSTRATIONS BY LOCAL MUSICIANS**. Live demonstrations are usually the high points of the semester for your students. And if you are a performer yourself, **PLAY FOR YOUR STUDENTS**, often. It increases your credibility with them, and it makes your teaching more specific because you can create sounds instantaneously to illustrate points in your lectures.

QUIZ MATERIALS IN THE JAZZ STYLES DEMONSTRATION CASSETTE/CD

In addition to providing a self-paced instructional program for novice listeners, the JAZZ STYLES DEMONSTRATION CASSETTE/CD provides instructors with audio materials to use for quizzes and listening exams. Your students will learn a lot on their own if you key reading assignments in the JAZZ STYLES textbook to listening assignments in the JAZZ STYLES DEMONSTRATION CASSETTE/CD. If this is all posted in your course syllabus along with the announcement that quizzes will be drawn from these materials, students can review material that you don't have time to review in class. To facilitate this, print textbook page numbers in the assignments listings of your syllabus, and be certain that they appear along with the names and locations of selections on the JAZZ STYLES DEMONSTRATION CASSETTE/CD that illustrate the points made in those text passages.

Allow students a few weeks to listen to the JAZZ STYLES DEMONSTRATION CASSETTE/CD and to study chapter 3 (Appreciating Jazz Improvisation, pages 12-30) and the Elements of Music appendix (pages 358-391). Then quiz your students by cuing up the JAZZ STYLES DEMONSTRATION CASSETTE/CD to selected examples, and playing the sounds without the identifying narration. This strategy should prove useful for evaluating students' recognition of such sounds as walking bass, comping, ride rhythms, tenor sax, Harmon-muted trumpet, etc. To be certain that students are generalizing their learning, you will also want to use other examples of the same concepts. For instance, you should have Scott LaFaro's work on Solar from the Bill Evans album AT THE VILLAGE VANGUARD SESSIONS (Riverside 60-017) to illustrate non-repetitive/interactive style of bass playing. (This selection excerpted in the JAZZ CLASSICS CASSETTE/CD that accompanies the 2-cassette version of the JAZZ STYLES textbook.) The Miles Davis KIND OF BLUE album (Columbia: CK 40579) would be handy for its back-to-back examples of alto sax (Cannonball Adderley), tenor sax (John Coltrane), and Harmon-muted trumpet. The Flamenco Sketches track from this album is in the JAZZ CLASSICS CASSETTE/CD FOR JAZZ STYLES. The Blue in Green track is in the JAZZ CLASSICS CASSETTE/CD FOR CONCISE GUIDE TO JAZZ.

To quiz your students in their ability to recognize variations in tone quality produced by the tenor saxophone, it would be useful first to urge students to become familiar with all the saxophone examples on the JAZZ STYLES DEMONSTRATION CASSETTE/CD. Expanding this exercise can be made convenient if students buy the JAZZ CLASSICS COMPACT DISC FOR JAZZ STYLES because many of the saxophone solos can be quickly accessed because they have their own track numbers on it (Ben Webster on Cottontail, Lester Young on Taxi War Dance, John Coltrane on Flamenco Sketches, Wayne Shorter on Masqualero, Stan Getz on No Figs). Then it would be convenient for you to make recordings available by Stan Getz (THE REVISED SMITHSONIAN COLLECTION OF CLASSIC JAZZ has eight measures of Getz playing Body and Soul) and Sonny Rollins (SCCJ has his Pent-Up House and Blue Seven). In fact, you can even compare different tenor saxophone tone qualities within the same piece in SCCJ because on Basie's Doggin' Around, Herschel Evans takes the first tenor solo, and Lester Young takes the second. After sufficient exposure to a wide variety of sax styles, a quiz on instrument sounds would help you assess student progress.

Numerous examples of basic jazz sounds are provided in SCCJ. To quiz your students on the clarinet sound, after having it introduced by the JAZZ STYLES DEMONSTRATION CASSETTE/CD, you could use SCCJ's Body and Soul by Benny Goodman. Or use the JAZZ CLASSICS CASSETTE/CD for Buddy DeFranco's solo on No Figs, Jimmy Strong's on West End Blues, or Barney Bigard's solo on Harlem Airshaft. After playing the plunger-muted growl examples on the JAZZ STYLES DEMONSTRATION CASSETTE/CD, you could use Duke Ellington's East St. Louis Toodle-Oo for Bubber Miley and Ellington's Koko for Tricky Sam Nanton. After introducing it on the JAZZ STYLES DEMONSTRATION CASSETTE/CD, tell your students that another example of walking bass is provided by the tenor sax-bass duo of Don Byas and Slam Stewart on I Got Rhythm. (That selection also illustrates tenor saxophone tone and 32-bar A-A-B-A song form.) Double-timing is illustrated by Coleman Hawkins on his Body and Soul (also available on the JAZZ CLASSICS CASSETTE/CD FOR CONCISE GUIDE TO JAZZ.) Double-timing and quadruple-timing is illustrated by Charlie Parker on Embraceable You. Stride-style piano playing can be heard in James P. Johnson's Carolina Shout (and in You've Got To Be Modernistic on the JAZZ CLASSICS CASSETTE/CD FOR JAZZ STYLES and Art Tatum's Tiger Rag on the JAZZ CLASSICS CASSETTE/CD FOR CONCISE GUIDE TO JAZZ). Sonny Rollins' Blue Seven has prominent piano comping. Ornette Coleman's Lonely Woman has alto saxophone. (Other alto saxophone tones are available in the JAZZ CLASSICS CASSETTE/CD by Johnny Hodges on Prelude to a Kiss and by Lee Konitz on No Figs.) Keep in mind that the value of the JAZZ STYLES DEMONSTRATION CASSETTE/CD is to alert listeners to the sounds that they will find in other jazz performances. So you might introduce the concepts in class and in listening assignments homework with SCCJ and the JAZZ STYLES cassettes or CDs, then require students to unearth examples on other recordings you are likely to use for quiz material.

For extending the JAZZ STYLES DEMONSTRATION CASSETTE/CD's presentation of the 32-bar A-A-B-A song form, a list of 32-bar A-A-B-A pieces contained in SCCJ is provided in Note 1 on page 31 of the JAZZ STYLES textbook. For examples of comping and walking bass, in addition to those provided on the JAZZ STYLES DEMONSTRATION/CASSETTE/CD and SCCJ, try Jamey Aebersold's albums of pre-recorded accompaniments. With these, you can illustrate accompaniment sounds without the solo part. Stereo separation on the Aebersold recordings allows you to isolate walking bass because it is on a channel by itself. These recordings are also excellent for illustrating 32-bar A-A-B-A and 12-bar blues forms (A NEW APPROACH TO JAZZ IMPROVISING, Vol. 6: CHARLIE PARKER - "ALL BIRD" has good examples of each). If neither you nor the jazz band director at your school has any of the Aebersold recordings (available on LP, audio cassette, or compact disc), write Jamey Aebersold, P.O. Box 1244C, New Albany, IN 47151-1244 for a catalog, phone 1-800-456-1388, or fax 1-812-949-2006.

INTRODUCTION TO SAMPLE SYLLABI
ORGANIZATION OF LECTURE TOPICS AND STUDY ASSIGNMENTS

Many professors do not provide detailed course syllabi. They announce assignments and exam times only during classes. However, such notifications are often missed because even the most conscientious students must occasionally be away from class, and many students are frequently absent. Students appreciate knowing assignments far in advance rather than having to pester the professor for updates whenever they miss class.

Other benefits come with comprehensive syllabi. Students appreciate being able to plan their assignments and apportion their time appropriately. If it is necessary to send a substitute teacher to class, a detailed syllabus will ease the transition. If a professor is ill or on tour and wants students to proceed without him, a comprehensive syllabus can help. Some school administrations require detailed accounts of course organization to monitor teaching, fulfill requirements of accrediting agencies, and use for proposing curricular changes. Administrators also need syllabi to help them handle disputes that arise between students and teachers.

Sample lecture schedules with accompanying study assignments are offered next. These outlines can be modified and incorporated with adapted versions of the sample course requirements, grading schemes, and learning goals offered above. **BUT THEY ARE NOT MEANT TO BE USED IN EXACTLY THE FORM THEY APPEAR HERE.** Even if you plan to incorporate the bulk of a given sample syllabus, your own schedule and instructional goals will necessitate adjustments. For instance, some professors do not give quizzes. Some give quizzes, but not for grades. Some professors give only quizzes, no exams. Some professors show many videos and have live bands during class time without listening homework.

The chapter assignments in each of these outlines is organized around JAZZ STYLES: HISTORY AND ANALYSIS, 5th Edition (Prentice-Hall, 1994), the JAZZ STYLES DEMONSTRATION CASSETTE/CD (**JSDC**), the JAZZ CLASSICS CASSETTE/CD (**JCC**), and THE SMITHSONIAN COLLECTION OF CLASSIC JAZZ (**SCCJ**). The revised edition of the Smithsonian collection (**SCCJ-R**) is available on cassette and compact disc from Smithsonian Recordings, P.O. Box 2071, Colchester, VT 05449-2071; phone: 1-800-669-1559. Both editions of it are available in most libraries. An abridged listing of its contents appears on pages 129-130 of the discography section in this manual. The JAZZ STYLES DEMONSTRATION CASSETTE comes with the one-cassette version of the JAZZ STYLES textbook (ISBN 0-13-175977-9). **Complete contents for the JSDC and JCC are listed on pages 59-64** after the following sample syllabi. Both the JAZZ STYLES DEMONSTRATION CASSETTE and the JAZZ CLASSICS CASSETTE come with the two-cassette version of the JAZZ STYLES textbook (ISBN 0-13-175969-8). The compact disc versions of these cassettes are available free from Prentice-Hall to instructors who require their students to buy the JAZZ STYLES textbook. (Requests for complimentary copies can be made through local Prentice-Hall field representatives, the toll-free request line (1-800-526-0485), or by writing College Humanities Marketing, Prentice-Hall, Inc., Englewood Cliffs, NJ 07632). Bookstores can order copies of the CDs for student purchase by order of instructors for JAZZ CLASSICS COMPACT DISC FOR JAZZ STYLES (ISBN 0-13-111-4298) and the JAZZ STYLES DEMONSTRATION COMPACT DISC (0-13-176918-9).

In the following syllabi, the main listening assignments for student homework and instructor demonstrations derive from the JAZZ STYLES DEMONSTRATION CASSETTE/CD and the JAZZ CLASSICS CASSETTE/CD. That music comprises the bare minimum for an introduction to jazz. The main supplements derive from the SMITHSONIAN COLLECTION OF CLASSIC JAZZ and the JAZZ CLASSICS CASSETTE/CD that accompanies the CONCISE GUIDE TO JAZZ textbook (Prentice-Hall, 1991). In the following syllabi, this is designated "**CGC**." The Concise Guide CD is available free to instructors who require their students to buy the CONCISE GUIDE TO JAZZ textbook, the abridged version of JAZZ STYLES: HISTORY AND ANALYSIS. Bookstores can order copies for student purchase upon instructors requesting CONCISE GUIDE TO JAZZ, JAZZ CLASSICS COMPACT DISC (Prentice-Hall ISBN 0-13-174475-5).

NOTE: For the sake of brevity and flexibility in presenting sample syllabi in this manual, the reading assignments are listed only in terms of chapters. **IT IS NOT ADVISABLE, HOWEVER, TO ASSIGN ENTIRE CHAPTERS OF THE JAZZ STYLES TEXTBOOK TO NOVICE LISTENERS IN A SINGLE-SEMESTER JAZZ APPRECIATION OR JAZZ HISTORY COURSE.** There is not enough time to do all the contents justice. Students will be less inclined to see the forest for the trees if entire chapters are assigned. And most students will not have the majority of recordings that are necessary to make the text passages meaningful, anyway. It is better to specify only the pages that cover the musicians whom you will discuss in class. Forget the rest. For example, instead of posting "Read Chapter 5 for Monday," veteran teachers tend to post something like "Learn pages 68-73 (Louis Armstrong) for Monday. Come to class prepared to list at least five reasons Louis Armstrong is historically significant. Listen to his "West End Blues" recording, and note what you like and dislike about it." When introducing early jazz within a single-semester, lower-level survey course, for instance, many instructors omit coverage of Johnny Dodds, Jimmie Noone, Jack Teagarden, Eddie Lang, Lonnie Johnson, Baby Dodds, etc. All these men are historically significant and represented by at least a paragraph of coverage in the JAZZ STYLES textbook. But veteran instructors know that coverage of them will be learned by students who are sufficiently curious to pursue the music further, and the semester is too short to do all figures justice for all levels of student. So instructors cover only a few of the biggest names mentioned in the JAZZ STYLES textbook, or they assign the abridged version of JAZZ STYLES: THE CONCISE GUIDE TO JAZZ (Prentice-Hall, 1992). It has about half the number of pages, 10 chapters instead of 16, a fifth the number of musician profiles, and about a fortieth the number of musician names and tune titles.

The following outlines are organized according to what surveys have shown to be the most common approaches for allocating topics across 10-week quarters and 15-week semesters, with classes meeting either three times per week, presented here as Monday-Wednesday-Friday, or meeting only two times per week, presented here as Tuesday-Thursday. Incidentally, professors tend to cover more topics when the same amount of class time is divided into three class meetings per week than two times a week. This might stem from their tendency to go into more depth (or off on more tangents) when they have a long class period. Some of these differences have been taken into account in the number of musicians and styles allocated across semesters in the sample syllabi. Also keep in mind that professors differ widely in how much attention they devote to different topics, no matter what their class meeting schedule. For example, many professors spend several weeks on the elements of music and the roles of instruments in the jazz band. Other professors dispense with elements and "how to listen"; they jump directly into a historical survey of the jazz styles. Some profs don't cover the origins of jazz. Some cover ragtime and blues but do not delve into the African retentions issues that occupy the second half of chapter 4. Others spend several weeks on it. Some don't cover jazz-rock fusion. Many devote only brief time to free jazz and the avant garde of the 1960's and 1970's. Some skip hard bop or cool jazz. Others consider cool jazz to be pivotal. Some professors allocate most of their time to a single figure in each era. Others survey numerous musicians in each era.

The following syllabi list SCCJ contents among supplemental materials for most assignments and suggested classroom listening. A brief course could be taught with just JSDC and JCC if all students bought the two-cassette version of the JAZZ STYLES textbook. However, without his own personal collection of historic recordings or a good basic collection in the music library, a professor would be missing some breadth of coverage. Possession of the albums listed on page 1 of JAZZ STYLES ("A Small Basic Collection") or a healthy sampling of the albums cited in the textbook's footnotes would be ideal. But without that advantage, it is convenient to have the SCCJ available for lectures, though at most schools it is apparently a luxury for students to have personal access to it. As valuable as SCCJ is to professors lacking large personal collections, critical opinion remains divergent about its historical value and stylistic balance. Some professors consider the SCCJ contents to be "the meat and potatoes" of historic examples. Other professors consider SCCJ highly skewed in its allocations of selections. (For instance, because it omits the Original Dixieland Jazz Band, Chick Corea, and Weather Report, both the JAZZ CLASSICS CASSETTE/CD for JAZZ STYLES and the JAZZ

CLASSICS CASSETTE/CD for CONCISE GUIDE TO JAZZ contain representative selections by those pivotal figures.) Many historians and critics question the taste of its compiler and don't necessarily consider all the choices "classic." Others treat it as a canon of jazz history. A number of professors do not use the SCCJ at all. Others require each of their students to own the complete set. One requires all his students to attain intimate familiarity with its every selection.

College schedules also vary. The routine is often interrupted with exam days, "reading" days, "free" days, field trips, religious holidays, legal holidays, etc. Semesters don't always include 15 full weeks, and quarters don't always include 10 full weeks. A Monday-Wednesday-Friday course does not always have every Monday, Wednesday, and Friday available to it, and a Tuesday-Thursday class does not always have every Tuesday and Thursday. Many semesters don't begin on a Monday or end on a Friday. Some colleges allow exams to be given during class periods, whereas others require that exams occur only on exam days. Some professors use a considerable number of class meetings for administering exams and going over the results, and this eats into the total number of topics they cover. Other professors give only a midterm and a final, and some require only a final and/or a term paper. Some professors use class time for review sessions, others use it solely for presentation of new material. Incidentally, students are more likely to skip class on Fridays than on Mondays or Wednesdays. Therefore if quizzes and exams are scheduled on Fridays, more students will attend more classes than if quizzes and exams occur on Mondays or Wednesdays.

Professors who stress development of listening skills tend to include listening items on their exams. They play an excerpt of a recording that students have studied, then ask students to identify its form, instrumentation, era, or soloists. For sample listening exams, see HOW TO TEACH JAZZ HISTORY, available from the International Association of Jazz Educators, Box 724, Manhattan, Kansas 66502; phone: 913-776-8744.

Some professors give a brief quiz every time class meets. No matter how much or how little they count, quizzes tend to motivate students to do the required reading and listening assignments. Otherwise most students do not keep up with assignments. They usually study only near exam time. Profs who want students to be prepared for classes tend to give frequent quizzes or exams.

Incidentally, if you tell your students that the textbook is "optional" ("not required"), even though you may also say that it is "highly recommended," they will tend to neither buy it nor read it. "Highly recommended" translates to "optional" which, in turn, translates to "don't bother." If you tell your students that the book is required, they might buy it. But unless they know they will be tested on its contents, many of your students will not read it. Additionally, it is significant to note that "reading" is different from "studying." Students might read the assigned pages, but not learn them unless your syllabus clearly states that students should come to class prepared to explain, orally or in writing, the contents of a particular page. In other words, it is best to assign only what you realistically expect students to learn.

Students tend to get more out of live performances than they get from recordings, even if the quality or historical significance of the live performance is far below that of your recordings. If concert reviews or album reviews are going to be required for a course grade, students will find it helpful if your syllabus lists the semester's events and the local stores that stock jazz albums. It is convenient to include names, addresses, phone numbers, maps, and prices for night clubs that feature jazz in your area. Large cities tend to have "jazz lines," 24-hour phone numbers that announce the week's activities for anyone who calls. Many professors prominently display that number in their syllabi. Whenever a nationally known musician is going to perform in your vicinity, students appreciate an album by that musician being placed on reserve at the library to hear. They also appreciate hearing the music in class, even if you have to cut some of your standard course material to make time for it. (You can put on reserve whatever course notes and recordings you cut. Then students won't miss getting them.) Some of the most enterprising instructors arrange for the musicians themselves to visit class during the week of the concert. (Big names might surprise you with their willingness to facilitate jazz appreciation!) If the campus itself is sponsoring the concert, a door is already open for soliciting a class visit by the performers. This serves a double function: it increases attendance at the concert (making it more likely that your students will actually go and hear the music), and it gives students insight into the people behind the music.

The following outlines are suggested ways of organizing a one-semester or one-quarter course in jazz history or introduction to jazz appreciation. Your schedule might not perfectly match any of them, but a usable format might be gleaned from one of them. After a little cutting and pasting, one of these schedules could save you some time organizing your course. The longer you teach, the more variations you will invent.

15-WEEK "STRAIGHT HISTORY" OF JAZZ

(no introductory emphasis on elements of music or how to listen)

Monday-Wednesday-Friday Schedule; Three Exams

<u>Week 1</u>

Monday: What is Jazz?
Read Chapters 1 and 2

Wednesday: Origins of Jazz
Read Chapter 4.
Listen to JSDC side 2 for blue notes (CD tracks 50-58).
Listen to the first 7 selections on JCC.

Friday: Origins of Jazz
same as Wednesday
Supplement: "Maple Leaf Rag" in SCCJ

The 1920's

<u>Week 2</u>

Monday: ODJB and Jelly Roll Morton
Read Chapter 5.
Listen to "Dixie Jazz Band One-Step" in JCC.
Supplement: "Black Bottom Stomp" in SCCJ

Wednesday: James P. Johnson, Joe Oliver, and Sidney Bechet
Read Chapter 5.
Listen to "You've Got To Be Modernistic" in JCC.
Supplement: "Carolina Shout," "Dippermouth Blues," "Blue Horizon," "Cake Walkin' Babies From Home" in SCCJ

Friday: Louis Armstrong and Bix Beiderbecke
Read Chapter 5.
Listen to "West End Blues" in JCC.
Supplement: "Sobbin' Hearted Blues" in CGC, "Weather Bird," "Hotter Than That," "Potato Head Blues," "Singin' the Blues," and "Struttin' With Some Barbecue" in SCCJ

The 1930's

<u>Week 3</u>

Monday: Duke Ellington
Read Chapter 7.
Listen to "Harlem Airshaft" and "Cottontail" in JCC.
Supplement: "Concerto for Cootie" and "In A Mellotone" in SCCJ
Note: These pieces were recorded in 1940, but they represent the culmination of Ellington's work in the 1930's.

Wednesday: Duke Ellington
Read Chapter 7.
Listen to "Transblucency" and "Prelude to a Kiss" in JCC.
Note: These pieces were written in the 1930's, but the JCC renditions were recorded later.
Supplement: "I've Got It Bad" in CGC

Friday: Count Basie and Lester Young
Read Chapter 8.
Listen to "Lester Leaps In" and "Taxi War Dance" in JCC.
Supplement: "Back in Your Own Back Yard" in CGC

Week 4

Monday: Coleman Hawkins, Roy Eldridge, and Art Tatum
Read Chapter 6.
Listen to "Body and Soul," "Rockin' Chair," "Willow Weep For Me," "Too Marvelous For Words," and "I Can't Believe That You're In Love With Me"in SCCJ.
Supplement: "Tiger Rag" in CGC

Wednesday: Benny Goodman and Jimmie Lunceford
Read Chapter 6.
Listen to Goodman and Lunceford selections in SCCJ.

The 1940's

Friday: Charlie Parker and Dizzy Gillespie
Read Chapter 9.
Listen to JSDC side 1 (CD 1-8) for bop drumming.
Listen to "Things to Come" and "Koko" in CGC and "Shaw Nuff" in JCC.
Supplement: Parker and Gillespie selections on SCCJ

Week 5

Monday: Thelonious Monk and Bud Powell
Read Chapter 9.
Listen to Monk and Powell selections in SCCJ.

Wednesday: Dexter Gordon and Miles Davis
Read Chapter 9.
Listen to "Dexter Digs In" in CGC.
Listen to "Bikini," "Boplicity," "Klactoveedsestene," and "Crazeology" ("Little Benny") in SCCJ.

Friday: FIRST EXAM

Week 6

The 1950's

Monday: Lennie Tristano and Lee Konitz
Read Chapter 10.
Listen to "No Figs" in JCC.
Supplement: "Boplicity" and Tristano selections in SCCJ; "Sax of a Kind" in CGC

Wednesday: Stan Getz and Miles Davis
Read Chapter 9 and 10.
Listen to "Four Brothers" and "No Figs" in JCC.

Friday: Gerry Mulligan and Dave Brubeck
Read Chapter 10.
Listen to "Boplicity" in SCCJ and assorted albums cited in endnotes of Chapter 10.

Week 7

Monday: Clifford Brown and Sonny Rollins
Read Chapter 11.
Listen to "Pent-Up House" and "Blue Seven" in SCCJ.
Supplement: "Get Happy" in CGC

Wednesday: Horace Silver and Cannonball Adderley
Read Chapter 11.
Listen to Adderley's solos on "Flamenco Sketches" in JCC and "So What" in SCCJ, plus assorted Silver and Adderley albums cited in endnotes of Chapter 11.

Friday: Miles Davis in the 1950s
Read Chapter 12.
Listen to "Flamenco Sketches" and "Fisherman, Strawberry, Devil Crab" in JCC.
Supplement: "Summertime" and "So What" in SCCJ; "Blue in Green" in CGC

The 1960's

Week 8

Monday: John Coltrane
Read Chapter 13.
Listen to "Flamenco Sketches" and "The Promise" in JCC.
Supplement: "So What" and "Alabama" in SCCJ; "Your Lady" and "Blue in Green" in CGC

Wednesday: Ornette Coleman
Read Chapter 14.
Listen to "Congeniality" and "Free Jazz" in SCCJ.
Supplement: "Cloning" in CGC

Friday: Cecil Taylor
Read Chapter 14.
Listen to "Jitney No. 2" in JCC.
Supplement: "Enter Evening" in SCCJ

Week 9

Monday: Wayne Shorter and Freddie Hubbard
Read Chapter 11 and 12.
Listen to "Masqualero" in JCC.
Supplement: assorted Shorter and Hubbard albums on Blue Note that are cited in endnotes of Chapters 11 and 12

Wednesday: Miles Davis in the 1960's
Read Chapter 12.
Listen to "Masqualero" in JCC.

Friday: SECOND EXAM

Week 10

Monday: Bill Evans
Read Chapter 15.
Listen to "Flamenco Sketches" and "Solar" in JCC.
Supplement: "So What" in SCCJ and "Blue in Green" in CGC

Wednesday: Bossa Nova
Supplement: assorted 1960's recordings by Stan Getz with Joao Gilberto and Antonio Carlos Jobim

Friday: Charles Mingus
Read Chapter 14.
Listen to Mingus selections in SCCJ and SCCJ-R.

Week 11

Monday: Sun Ra
Read Chapter 14.

The 1970's

Wednesday: ECM
Supplement: assorted ECM records of the 1970's by Gary Burton, Pat Metheny, Jan Garbarek, Keith Jarrett, and Chick Corea

Friday: Herbie Hancock
Read Chapter 12 and 15.
Listen to "Masqualero" on JCC.
Supplement: assorted Davis and Hancock albums cited in endnotes of Chapters 12 and 15

Week 12

Monday: Chick Corea
Read Chapter 15.
Listen to "Steps" in JCC.
Supplement: various ECM albums by Corea cited in endnotes of Chapter 15

Wednesday: Art Ensemble of Chicago and the World Saxophone Quartet
Read Chapter 14.
Listen to WSQ's "Steppin'" on SCCJ-R.

Friday: Keith Jarrett
Read Chapter 15.
Supplement: assorted Atlantic, Impulse and ECM recordings cited in endnotes of Chapter 15

Week 13

Monday: Miles Davis Fusion
Read Chapter 16.
Supplement: assorted post-1968 recordings cited in chapter

Wednesday: Weather Report
Read Chapter 16.
Listen to "Surucucu" in JCC.
Supplement: "Birdland" in CGC

Friday: John McLaughlin
Read Chapter 16.
Supplement: assorted recordings cited in chapter

The 1980s

Week 14

Monday: Hard Bop Revival
Supplement: assorted recordings of 1980's by the Marsalis brothers, Out of the Blue, Terrence Blanchard, and others

Wednesday: New Age
Read pages 346-348.
Supplement: assorted Windham Hill and Narada recordings

Friday: Popular Fusion
Read pages 310-313, 324-331.
Supplement: assorted popular recordings by Spyro Gyra, Kenny G, George Benson, Grover Washington, Earl Klugh, and other contemporary artists

Week 15 FINAL EXAM

15-WEEK "STRAIGHT HISTORY" OF JAZZ

(no introductory emphasis on elements of music or how to listen)

Tuesday-Thursday Schedule; Three Exams

<u>Week 1</u>

Tuesday: What is Jazz
Read Chapters 1 and 2.

Thursday: Origins of Jazz
Read Chapter 4.
Listen to JSDC side 2 for blue notes (CD tracks 50-58).
Listen to first 7 selections on JCC.

<u>Week 2</u>

Tuesday: Origins of Jazz
Read Chapter 4.
Listen to "Maple Leaf Rag" on SCCJ.

The 1920's

Thursday: ODJB and Joe Oliver
Read Chapter 5.
Listen to "Dixie Jazz Band One-Step" on JCC.
Supplement: "Dippermouth Blues" on SCCJ

<u>Week 3</u>

Tuesday: James P. Johnson and Jelly Roll Morton
Read Chapter 5.
Listen to "You've Got To Be Modernistic" in JCC.
Supplement: "Black Bottom Stomp" and "Carolina Shout" in SCCJ

Thursday: Louis Armstrong and Sidney Bechet
Read Chapter 5.
Listen to "West End Blues" in JCC.
Supplement: "Weather Bird," "Hotter Than That," "Potato Head Blues," "Blue Horizon," and "Cake Walkin' Babies From Home" in SCCJ; "Sobbin' Hearted Blues" in CGC

<u>Week 4</u>

Tuesday: Bix Beiderbecke and Fats Waller
Read Chapter 5.
Listen to "Singin' the Blues" and "I Ain't Got Noboby" in SCCJ.

The 1930's

Thursday: Duke Ellington
Read Chapter 7.
Listen to "Harlem Airshaft" and "Cottontail" in JCC.
Supplement: "Concerto for Cootie" and "In A Mellotone" in SCCJ
Note: Though these recordings were made in 1940, they represent the culmination of Ellington's work of the 1930's.

<u>Week 5</u>

Tuesday: Duke Ellington
Read Chapter 7.
Listen to "Transblucency" and "Prelude To A Kiss" in JCC.
Note: These pieces were written in the 1930's, though the JCC renditions were recorded later.
Supplement: "I've Got It Bad" in CGC

Thursday: FIRST EXAM

Week 6

Tuesday: Benny Goodman, Coleman Hawkins, and Roy Eldridge
Read Chapter 6.
Listen to "I Found a New Baby," "Body and Soul," "Rockin' Chair," and "I Can't Believe That You're In Love With Me" in SCCJ.

Thursday: Art Tatum, Count Basie, and Lester Young
Read Chapters 6 and 8.
Listen to "Taxi War Dance" and "Lester Leaps In" on JCC.
Supplement: "Willow Weep for Me" and "Too Marvelous For Words" in SCCJ; "Back In Your Own Back Yard" and "Tiger Rag" in CGC

The 1940's

Week 7

Tuesday: Charlie Parker and Dizzy Gillespie
Read Chapter 9.
Listen to JSDC side 1 for bop drumming (CD tracks 1-8).
Listen to "Shaw Nuff" on JCC.
Supplement: Parker and Gillespie selections on SCCJ; "Things to Come" and "Koko" on CGC

Thursday: Thelonious Monk and Bud Powell
Read Chapter 9.
Listen to Monk and Powell selections on SCCJ.

Week 8

Tuesday: Dexter Gordon and the Woody Herman bop bands
Read Chapter 9.
Listen to "Four Brothers" on JCC.
Supplement: "Bikini" on SCCJ; "Dexter Digs In" on CGC

The 1950's

Thursday: Lennie Tristano, Lee Konitz, and Stan Getz
Read Chapter 10.
Listen to "No Figs" on JCC.
Supplement: Tristano selections on SCCJ; "Sax of a Kind" on CGC

Week 9

Tuesday: Dave Brubeck and Gerry Mulligan
Read Chapter 10.
Supplement: assorted recordings cited in endnotes of Chapter 10

Thursday: Clifford Brown and Sonny Rollins
Read Chapter 11.
Listen to "Pent-Up House" and "Blue Seven" in SCCJ.
Supplement: "Get Happy" on CGC

Week 10

Tuesday: Horace Silver, Cannonball Adderley, and Miles Davis
Read Chapters 11 and 12.
Listen to "Flamenco Sketches" on JCC; "So What" and "Summertime" on SCCJ
Supplement: assorted albums by Silver and Adderley cited in endnotes of Chapters 11 and 12; "Blue in Green" on CGC

Thursday: SECOND EXAM

The 1960's

Week 11

Tuesday: Bill Evans and Miles Davis in the 1960's
Read Chapters 12 and 15.
Listen to "Flamenco Sketches," "Solar," and "Masqualero" in JCC.
Supplement: "So What" in SCCJ; "Blue in Green" on CGC
Note: "Flamenco Sketches" and "So What" from the album KIND OF BLUE were recorded in 1959, but the impact of the Evans and Coltrane work in them is associated more with the 1960's than the 1950's.

Thursday: Ornette Coleman and Cecil Taylor
Read Chapter 14.
Listen to "Jitney No. 2" in JCC.
Supplement: "Enter Evening," "Congeniality," and "Free Jazz" in SCCJ; "Cloning" in CGC

Week 12

Tuesday: John Coltrane
Read Chapter 13.
Listen to "Flamenco Sketches" and "The Promise" in JCC.
Supplement: "So What" and "Alabama" in SCCJ; "Your Lady" and "Blue in Green" in CGC

Thursday: Herbie Hancock, Wayne Shorter, and Freddie Hubbard
Read Chapters 11, 12 and 15.
Listen to "Masqualero" in JCC.
Supplement: assorted Blue Note albums cited in endnotes of Chapters 11, 12 and 15

The 1970's

Week 13

Tuesday: Keith Jarrett and Chick Corea
Read Chapter 15.
Listen to "Steps" on JCC.
Supplement: assorted ECM albums cited in endnotes of Chapter 15

Thursday: Sun Ra and the AACM
Read Chapter 14.

Week 14

Tuesday: Weather Report and John McLaughlin
Read Chapter 16.
Listen to "Surucucu" on JCC; "Birdland" on CGC.
Supplement: assorted McLaughlin CBS albums cited in endnotes of Chapter 16

The 1980's

Thursday: Fuzak and New Age
Read pages 346-348.
Supplement: assorted albums on Windham Hill and Narada, plus music by Kenny G, Earl Klugh, Grover Washington, George Benson, and other popular contemporary artists

Week 15

FINAL EXAM

15-WEEK INTRODUCTION TO JAZZ
(emphasizing introductory units on elements of music and how to listen)

Monday-Wednesday-Friday Schedule; Three Exams

Note: All selections accompanied by the JCC designation (for JAZZ CLASSICS CASSETTE) are represented by listening guides in the appropriate chapters.

Week 1

Monday: What is Jazz?
Read Chapters 1 and 2.

Wednesday: Elements of Music (rhythm)
Read pages 358-65.

Friday: Elements of Music (chords)
Read pages 365-73.
Listen to JSDC, side 1.

Week 2

Monday: Elements of Music (instruments)
Read pages 388-391.
Listen to JSDC, side 2 (CD tracks 59-98).
Listen to "No Figs" and "Flamenco Sketches" in JCC for instrument identifications.

Wednesday: How to Listen (song forms and performance routines--blues)
Read pages 372-381.
Listen to JSDC, side 1 (CD tracks 16-20).
Listen to "West End Blues," "Frame for the Blues," and "Steps" in JCC.

Friday: How to Listen (song forms and performance routines--A-A-B-A form)
Read pages 381-387.
Listen to JSDC side 2 (CD track 33).
Listen to "Lester Leaps In," "Taxi War Dance," "Cottontail," "Four Brothers," and "Shaw Nuff" in JCC and follow their listening guides.

Week 3

Monday: How To Listen (instrument roles; layered listening)
Read Chapter 3.
Listen to "Masqualero" and "Flamenco Sketches" in JCC.
Use layered listening approach first, then follow listening guides in Chapter 12.

Wednesday: How to Listen (graphing solo lines; detecting blues and A-A-B-A)
Read Chapter 3.
Listen to "West End Blues," "Shaw Nuff," and "Lester Leaps In" in JCC and "Two Bass Hit," "Dexter Digs In," and "Sobbin' Hearted Blues" in CGC.

Friday: Origins of Jazz
Read Chapter 4.
Listen to the first 7 selections in JCC (CD tracks 1-7).

Week 4

Monday: Origins of Jazz
Read Chapter 4.
Listen to "Maple Leaf Rag" in SCCJ.

Wednesday: Origins of Jazz
Read Chapter 4.
Listen to "Dippermouth Blues" and "Cake Walkin' Babies From Home" in SCCJ.

Friday: FIRST EXAM

The 1920's

Week 5

Monday: ODJB and Jelly Roll Morton
Read Chapter 5.
Listen to "Dixie Jazz Band One-Step" in JCC.
Supplement: "Black Bottom Stomp" and "Dippermouth Blues" in SCCJ

Wednesday: Sidney Bechet and James P. Johnson
Read Chapter 5.
Listen to "You've Got To Be Modernistic" in JCC.
Listen to "Carolina Shout," "Blue Horizon," and "Cake Walkin' Babies From Home" in SCCJ.

Friday: Louis Armstrong
Read pages 68-73.
Listen to "West End Blues" in JCC, "Sobbin' Hearted Blues" in CGC.
Supplement: "Hotter Than Hot," "Potato Head Blues," and "Struttin' With Some Barbecue" in SCCJ

The 1930's

Week 6

Monday: Duke Ellington
Read Chapter 7.
Listen to "Harlem Airshaft" and "Cottontail" in JCC.
Supplement: "Concerto for Cootie" and "In A Mellotone" in SCCJ
Note: Though these recordings were made in 1940, they represent the culmination of Ellington's work in the 1930's

Wednesday: Duke Ellington
Read Chapter 7.
Listen to "Transblucency" and "Prelude to a Kiss" in JCC, "I've Got It Bad" in CGC.

Friday: Coleman Hawkins, Roy Eldridge, Art Tatum
Read Chapter 6.
Listen to "Body and Soul," "Rockin' Chair," "Too Marvelous For Words," "Willow Weep For Me," and "I Can't Believe That You're In Love With Me" in SCCJ.

Week 7

Monday: Benny Goodman
Read Chapter 6.
Listen to "I've Got a New Baby," "Breakfast Feud," and "Body and Soul" in SCCJ.

Wednesday: Count Basie
Read Chapter 8.
Listen to "Taxi War Dance" and "Lester Leaps In" in JCC.

Friday: Lester Young
See Wednesday's assignment; listen to "Back in Your Own Back Yard" in CGC.

The 1940's

Week 8

Monday: Charlie Parker and Dizzy Gillespie
Read Chapter 9.
Listen to "Shaw Nuff" in JCC and follow listening guide.
Supplement: "Ko-ko" and "Things to Come" in CGC; Parker and Gillespie items in SCCJ

Wednesday: Thelonious Monk and Bud Powell
Read Chapter 9.
Listen to Monk and Powell items in SCCJ.

Friday: Stan Getz and Dexter Gordon
Read Chapter 9.
Listen to "No Figs" and "Four Brothers" in JCC.
Supplement: "Bikini" in SCCJ; "Dexter Digs In" in CGC

Week 9

Monday: Woody Herman's Bop band, Lennie Tristano, Lee Konitz
Read Chapters 9 and 10.
Listen to "Four Brothers" and "No Figs" in JCC.
Supplement: "Boplicity" and Tristano items in SCCJ; "Sax of a Kind" in CGC

Wednesday: Miles Davis
Read Chapter 9 and 10.
Listen to "Crazeology" ("Little Benny"), Klactoveesedstene," and "Boplicity" in SCCJ.

Friday: SECOND EXAM

The 1950's

Week 10

Monday: Gerry Mulligan and Dave Brubeck
Read Chapter 10.
Supplement: "Boplicity" in SCCJ and assorted recordings cited in endnotes of Chapter 10

Wednesday: Clifford Brown and Sonny Rollins
Read Chapter 11.
Listen to "Pent-Up House" and "Blue Seven" in SCCJ and "Get Happy" in CGC.

Friday: John Coltrane
Read Chapter 13.
Listen to "Flamenco Sketches" in JCC and "So What" in SCCJ, "Two Bass Hit" in CGC.

Week 11

Monday: Art Blakey
Read Chapter 11.
Supplement: assorted Blakey albums on Blue Note cited in endnotes of Chapter 11

Wednesday: Horace Silver and Cannonball Adderley
Read Chapter 11.
Listen to Adderley solos on "Flamenco Sketches" in JCC, "So What" in SCCJ, and "Two Bass Hit" in CGC.
Supplement: assorted Silver and Adderley albums cited in endnotes of Chapter 11

Friday: Miles Davis
Read Chapter 12.
Listen to "Flamenco Sketches," "Fishermen, Strawberry, Devil Crab" in JCC, "Blue in Green" in CGC, and "So What" and "Summertime" in SCCJ.

The 1960's

Week 12

Monday: Ornette Coleman and Cecil Taylor
Read Chapter 14.
Listen to "Jitney No. 2" in JCC.
Supplement: "Enter Evening," "Congeniality," and "Free Jazz" in SCCJ; "Cloning" in CGC

Wednesday: Bill Evans
Read Chapter 15.
Listen to "Flamenco Sketches" and "Solar" in JCC, "Blue in Green" in CGC, and "So What" in SCCJ.

Friday: John Coltrane
Read Chapter 13.
Listen to "Flamenco Sketches" and "The Promise" in JCC, "Two Bass Hit" and "Your Lady" in CGC, "Alabama" and "So What" in SCCJ.

Week 13

Monday: Bossa Nova
Supplement: assorted 1960's recordings of Antonio Carlos Jobim, Stan Getz, and Joao Gilberto

Wednesday: Charles Mingus, Sun Ra, AACM
Read Chapter 14.
Listen to Mingus selections in SCCJ.
Supplement: assorted recordings cited in chapter endnotes of Chapter 14

Friday: Herbie Hancock, Wayne Shorter, Freddie Hubbard
Read Chapters 12 and 15.
Listen to "Masqualero" in JCC.
Supplement: assorted recordings cited in endnotes of Chapters 12 and 15

The 1970's

Week 14

Monday: Weather Report
Read pages 338-346.
Listen to "Surucucu" in JCC, "Birdland" in CGC.

Wednesday: John McLaughlin
Read Chapter 16.
Supplement: assorted recordings cited in endnotes of Chapter 16

The 1980's

Friday: Fuzak and New Age
Read pages 346-348.
Supplement: assorted recordings on Windham Hill and Narada, plus popular recordings by Spyro Gyra, Kenny G, George Benson, Grover Washington, Earl Klugh, and other contemporary artists

Week 15

FINAL EXAM

15-WEEK INTRODUCTION TO JAZZ

(emphasizing elements of music and how to listen)

Tuesday-Thursday Schedule; Three Exams

Note: All selections accompanied by the JCC designation are represented by listening guides in the appropriate chapters and should be studied in conjunction with those guides. All references to JSDC are demonstrations available in the JAZZ STYLES DEMONSTRATION COMPACT DISC (available separately) and the demonstration cassette that accompanies both the one-cassette version and the two-cassette version of the JAZZ STYLES textbook.

Week 1

Tuesday: What is Jazz
Read Chapters 1 and 2.

Thursday: Elements of Music (rhythm)
Read pages 358-65.

Week 2

Tuesday: Elements of Music (instruments)
Read pages 388-91.
Listen to JSDC, side 2 (CD tracks 59-98).
Listen to "No Figs" and "Flamenco Sketches" in JCC for instrument identifications.

Thursday: Elements of Music (chords)
Read pages 365-77.
Listen to JSDC, side 1 (CD tracks 16-20).

Week 3

Tuesday: How to Listen (12-bar blues forms)
Read pages 372-378.
Listen to JSDC, side 1 (CD tracks 19, 28-30).
Listen to "West End Blues," "Frame for the Blues," and "Step" in JCC, "Sobbin' Hearted Blues" and "Two Bass Hit" in CGC.

Thursday: How to Listen (A-A-B-A forms)
Read pages 378-384.
Listen to JSDC, side 1 (CD track 33).
Listen to JCC for "Lester Leaps In," "Shaw Nuff," "Taxi War Dance," and "Four Brothers" and to CGC for "Dexter Digs In."

Week 4

Tuesday: How to Listen (instrument roles and jam session routines)
Read Chapter 3.
Listen to JSDC, side 1 (CD track 32).
Listen to "Masqualero" and "Flamenco Sketches."
First use layered listening approach; then follow listening guides in chapter 12.

Thursday: FIRST EXAM

Week 5

Tuesday: Origins of Jazz
Read Chapter 4.
Listen to first 7 selections in JCC.

Thursday: Origins of Jazz
Ready Chapter 4.
Listen to "Maple Leaf Rag" and "Dippermouth Blues" in SCCJ.

The 1920's

Week 6

Tuesday: ODJB and Jelly Roll Morton
Read Chapter 5.
Listen to "Dixie Jazz Band One-Step" in JCC and "Black Bottom Stomp" in SCCJ.

Thursday: James P. Johnson and Fats Waller
Read pages 64-66.
Listen to "You've Got To Be Modernistic" in JCC and "Carolina Shout" and "I Ain't Got Nobody" in SCCJ.

Week 7

Tuesday: Sidney Bechet and Louis Armstrong
Read pages 68-73 and 76-77.
Listen to "West End Blues" in JCC, "Sobbin' Hearted Blues" in CGC.
Supplement: "Cake Walkin' Babies From Home," "Weather Bird," "Hotter Than That," "Blue Horizon," "Potato Head Blues," and "Struttin' With Some Barbecue" in SCCJ.

The 1930's

Thursday: Duke Ellington
Read Chapter 7.
Listen to "Harlem Airshaft" and "Cottontail" in JCC.
Supplement: "Concerto for Cootie" and "In a Mellotone" in SCCJ
Note: These pieces were recorded in 1940 but they represent a culmination of Ellington's work in the 1930's.

Week 8

Tuesday: Duke Ellington
Read Chapter 7.
Listen to "Transbluency" and "Prelude to a Kiss" in JCC, "I've Got It Bad" in CGC.
Note: These pieces were written during the 1930's, but the JCC renditions were recorded later.

Thursday: Count Basie and Lester Young
Read Chapter 8.
Listen to "Taxi War Dance" and "Lester Leaps In" in JCC, "Back In Your Own Back Yard" in CGC.

Week 9

Tuesday: Benny Goodman, Roy Eldridge, Coleman Hawkins, Art Tatum
Read Chapter 6.
Listen to "Tiger Rag" in CGC, "I Found a New Baby," "Body and Soul," "Rockin' Chair," "Willow Weep For Me," "Too Marvelous For Words," "I Can't Believe That You're In Love With Me" in SCCJ.
Note: Though some of these selections were recorded after the 1930's, all their styles reflect the 1930's jazz.

Thursday: SECOND EXAM

The 1940's

Week 10

Tuesday: Charlie Parker, Dizzy Gillespie, Thelonious Monk, Bud Powell
Read Chapter 9.
Listen to "Shaw Nuff" in JCC, "Ko-Ko," "Dexter Digs In," and "Things to Come" in CGC.
Supplement: Parker, Gillespie, Monk, and Powell items in SCCJ

Thursday: Lennie Tristano, Lee Konitz, Miles Davis, Stan Getz
Read Chapter 10.
Listen to "No Figs" and "Four Brothers" in JCC, "Sax of a Kind" in CGC.
Supplement: "Boplicity" and Tristano items in SCCJ

The 1950's

Week 11

Tuesday: Gerry Mulligan and Dave Brubeck
Read Chapter 10.
Listen to "Boplicity" in SCCJ and albums cited in endnotes of Chapter 10.

Thursday: Clifford Brown and Sonny Rollins
Read Chapter 11.
Listen to "Get Happy" in CGC, "Pent-Up House" and "Blue Seven" in SCCJ.

Week 12

Tuesday: Horace Silver and Cannonball Adderley
Read Chapter 11.
Listen to "Flamenco Sketches" in JCC, "Two Bass Hit" in CGC, "So What" in SCCJ.
Supplement: assorted Silver and Adderley albums cited in endnotes of Chapter 11

Thursday: Miles Davis
Read Chapter 12.
Listen to "Fishermen, Strawberries, Devil Crab," "Flamenco Sketches," and "Masqualero" in JCC, "Blue In Green" in CGC.
Supplement: "So What" and "Summertime" in SCCJ

The 1960's

Week 13

Tuesday: John Coltrane
Read Chapter 13.
Listen to "Flamenco Sketches," "The Promise" in JCC, "Your Lady," "Two Bass Hit" and "Blue in Green" in CGC, "So What" and "Alabama" in SCCJ.

Thursday: Ornette Coleman and Cecil Taylor
Read Chapter 14.
Listen to "Jitney No. 2" in JCC and "Cloning" in CGC.
Supplement: "Enter Evening," "Lonely Woman," "Congeniality," and "Free Jazz" in SCCJ

The 1970's

Week 14

Tuesday: Weather Report and John McLaughlin
Read pages 338-46 and 335-337.
Listen to "Surucucu" in JCC and "Birdland" in CGC.
Supplement: assorted McLaughlin CBS albums cited in endnotes of Chapter 16

The 1980's

Thursday: Fuzak and New Age
Read pages 346-348.
Supplement: assorted recordings on Windham Hill and Narada, plus music by Kenny G, Earl Klugh, Grover Washington, George Benson, and other popular contemporary artists

Week 15 FINAL EXAM

10-WEEK "STRAIGHT HISTORY" OF JAZZ

(no introductory emphasis on elements of music or how to listen)

Monday-Wednesday-Friday Schedule; midterm and a final exam

Note: Selections accompanied by the JCC designation have corresponding listening guides in the appropriate chapters.

Week 1

Monday: What is Jazz?

Wednesday: Origins of Jazz
Read Chapters 1, 2, and 4.
Listen to first 6 selections in JCC.
Listen to JSCD side 2 for blue notes (CD tracks 50-58).
Supplement: "Maple Leaf Rag" in SCCJ

Friday: Same as Wednesday

The 1920's

Week 2

Monday: ODJB and Jelly Roll Morton
Read Chapter 5.
Listen to "Dixie Jazz Band One-Step" in JCC.
Supplement: "Dippermouth Blues" and "Black Bottom Stomp" in SCCJ

Wednesday: Sidney Bechet, Louis Armstrong, and Bix Beiderbecke
Read Chapter 5.
Listen to "West End Blues" in JCC, "Sobbin' Hearted Blues" in CGC.
Supplement: "Blue Horizon," "Cake Walkin' Babies From Home," "Singin' the Blues," "Potato Head Blues," "Weather Bird," and "Hotter Than That" in SCCJ

Friday: James P. Johnson and Fats Waller
Read Chapter 5.
Listen to "You've Got To Be Modernistic" in JCC.
Supplement: "Carolina Shout" and "I Ain't Got Nobody" in SCCJ

The 1930's

Week 3

Monday: Duke Ellington
Read Chapter 7.
Listen to "Harlem Airshaft" and "Cottontail" in JCC.
Supplement: "Concerto for Cootie" and "In A Mellotone" in SCCJ
Note: Though these recordings were made in 1940, they represent the culmination of work Ellington did during the 1930's.

Wednesday: Duke Ellington
Read Chapter 7.
Listen to "Transblucency" and "Prelude to a Kiss" in JCC, "I've Got It Bad" in CGC.
Note: These pieces were written during the 1930's, but the JCC renditions were recorded later.

Friday: Fletcher Henderson and Jimmie Lunceford
Read Chapter 6.
Listen to "Wrappin' It Up" and Lunceford selections in SCCJ.

Week 4

Monday: Benny Goodman, Coleman Hawkins, Roy Eldridge, and Art Tatum
Read Chapter 6.
Listen to "Tiger Rag" in CGC and "Body and Soul," "Rockin' Chair," "Willow Weep For Me," "Too Marvelous For Words," "I Found A New Baby," and "I Can't Believe That You're In Love With Me" in SCCJ.
Note: Some of these recordings were made after the 1930's, but all represent styles of the 1930's.

Wednesday: Count Basie and Lester Young
Read Chapter 8.
Listen to "Lester Leaps In" and "Taxi War Dance" in JCC, "Back In Your Own Back Yard" in CGC.

Friday: MIDTERM EXAM

The 1940's

Week 5

Monday: Charlie Parker
Read Chapter 9.
Listen to JSDC side 1 for bop drumming (CD tracks 1-8).
Listen to "Shaw Nuff" in JCC, "Ko-Ko" in CGC.
Supplement: Parker selections in SCCJ

Wednesday: Dizzy Gillespie
Read Chapter 9.
Listen to "Shaw Nuff" in JCC, "Things to Come" in CGC.
Supplement: Gillespie selections in SCCJ

Friday: Thelonious Monk and Bud Powell
Read Chapter 9.
Listen to Monk and Powell selections in SCCJ.

Week 6

Monday: Lennie Tristano, Lee Konitz, and Stan Getz
Read Chapter 10.
Listen to "No Figs" and "Four Brothers" in JCC and "Sax of a Kind" in CGC.
Supplement: Tristano selections in SCCJ

Wednesday: Miles Davis
Read Chapter 10.
Listen to "Boplicity," "Crazeology" ("Little Benny"), and "Klactoveesedstene" in SCCJ.

The 1950's

Friday: Gerry Mulligan and Dave Brubeck
Read Chapter 10.
Supplement: listen to albums cited in endnotes of Chapter 10

Week 7

Monday: Clifford Brown and Sonny Rollins
Read Chapter 11.
Listen to "Pent-Up House" and "Blue Seven" in SCCJ and "Get Happy" in CGC.

Wednesday: Miles Davis
Read Chapter 12.
Listen to "Flamenco Sketches" in JCC and "Blue in Green" in CGC.
Supplement: "Summertime" and "So What" in SCCJ

Friday: Horace Silver and Cannonball Adderley
Read Chapter 11.
Listen to "Two Bass Hit" in CGC, Adderley solos in "So What" in SCCJ, "Flamenco Sketches" in JCC, and assorted Silver and Adderley albums cited in endnotes of Chapter 11.

The 1960's

<u>Week 8</u>

Monday: Bill Evans
Read Chapter 15.
Listen to "Flamenco Sketches" and "Solar" in JCC, "Blue in Green" in CGC.
Supplement: "So What" in SCCJ

Wednesday: Ornette Coleman and Cecil Taylor
Read Chapter 14.
Listen to "Jitney No. 2" in JCC, "Cloning" in CGC.
Supplement: "Congeniality," "Free Jazz," "Lonely Woman," and "Enter Evening" in SCCJ

Friday: John Coltrane
Read Chapter 13.
Listen to "Flamenco Sketches" and "The Promise" in JCC, and "Two Bass Hit, "Blue in Green," and "Your Lady" in CGC.
Supplement: "So What" and "Alabama" in SCCJ

<u>Week 9</u>

Monday: Wayne Shorter, Herbie Hancock, and Freddie Hubbard
Read Chapter 12 and 15.
Listen to "Masqualero" in JCC.
Supplement: assorted Blue Note albums cited in endnotes of Chapters 12 and 15

The 1970's and 1980's

Wednesday: Chick Corea and Keith Jarrett
Read Chapter 15.
Listen to "Steps" in JCC.
Supplement: assorted Corea and Jarrett albums cited in endnotes of Chapter 15

Friday: Weather Report, New Age, and Fuzak
Read Chapter 16.
Listen to "Surucucu" in JCC and "Birdland" in CGC.
Supplement: assorted recordings on Windham Hill and Narada, plus music by Kenny G, Grover Washington, George Benson, Earl Klugh, and other popular contemporary artists

<u>Week 10</u>

FINAL EXAM

10-WEEK "STRAIGHT HISTORY" OF JAZZ

(without emphasis on elements of music or how to listen)

Tuesday-Thursday Schedule; midterm and final

Note: Selections accompanied by the JCC designation have corresponding listening guides in the appropriate chapters.

Week 1

Tuesday: What is Jazz
Read Chapters 1 and 2.

Thursday: Origins of Jazz
Read Chapter 4.
Listen to JSDC for blue notes (CD tracks 50-58).
Listen to first 7 selections in JCC.
Supplement: "Maple Leaf Rag" in SCCJ

Week 2

Tuesday: Early Jazz: ODJB, Louis Armstrong, and James P. Johnson
Read Chapter 5.
Listen to "Dixie Jazz Band One-Step," "You've Got To Be Modernistic," and "West End Blues" in JCC.
Supplement: "Sobbin' Hearted Blues" in CGC; "Dippermouth Blues," "Cake Walkin' Babies From Home," "Carolina Shout," "Potato Head Blues," "Weather Bird," "Singin' the Blues," and "Hotter Than That" in SCCJ

Swing

Thursday: Count Basie and Lester Young
Read Chapter 6 and 8.
Listen to "Lester Leaps In" and "Taxi War Dance" in JCC, and "Back In Your Own Back Yard" in CGC.

Week 3

Tuesday: Duke Ellington
Read Chapter 7.
Listen to "Harlem Airshaft," "Cottontail," "Transblucency," and "Prelude To A Kiss" in JCC, "I've Got It Bad" in CGC, and "East St. Louis Toodle-o," "In a Mellotone," and "Concerto for Cootie" in SCCJ.

Thursday: FIRST EXAM

Week 4

Bop

Tuesday: Charlie Parker and Dizzy Gillespie
Read Chapter 9.
Listen to JSDC for bop drumming (CD tracks 1-8).
Listen to "Shaw Nuff" in JCC, and "Ko-Ko" and "Things to Come" in CGC.
Supplement: Parker and Gillespie selections in SCCJ

Thursday: Thelonious Monk and Bud Powell
Ready Chapter 9.
Listen to Monk and Powell selections in SCCJ.

Week 5

Cool

Tuesday: Lennie Tristano and Lee Konitz
Read Chapter 10.
Listen to "No Figs" in JCC and "Sax of a Kind" in CGC.
Supplement: "Boplicity" and Tristano selections in SCCJ

Thursday: Dave Brubeck and Gerry Mulligan
Read Chapter 10.
Listen to albums cited in endnotes of Chapter 10.

Hard Bop

Week 6

Tuesday: Clifford Brown and Sonny Rollins
Read Chapter 11.
Listen to "Pent-Up House" and "Blue Seven" in SCCJ, and "Get Happy" on CGC.

Thursday: Miles Davis and John Coltrane
Read Chapters 12 and 13.
Listen to "Flamenco Sketches," "The Promise," and "Masqualero" in JCC.
Supplement: "So What," "Alabama," "Summertime" in SCCJ; "Two Bass Hit" and "Blue in Green" in CGG

Free Jazz

Week 7

Tuesday: Ornette Coleman and Cecil Taylor
Read Chapter 14.
Listen to "Jitney No. 2" in JCC and "Cloning" in CGC.
Supplement: "Enter Evening," "Congeniality," "Lonely Woman," and "Free Jazz" in SCCJ

1960's Innovations

Thursday: Bill Evans
Read Chapter 15.
Listen to "Flamenco Sketches" and "Solar" in JCC, "Blue in Green" in CGC.
Supplement: "So What" in SCCJ

Week 8

Tuesday: Herbie Hancock, Wayne Shorter, and Freddie Hubbard
Read Chapter 12 and 15.
Listen to "Masqualero" in JCC.
Supplement: Blue Note albums cited in endnotes of Chapters 12 and 15

Thursday: Charles Mingus, Sun Ra, and the AACM
Read Chapter 14.
Listen to Mingus selections in SCCJ and Sun Ra/AACM albums cited in endnotes of Chapter 14.

1970's and 1980's

Week 9

Tuesday: Weather Report and John McLaughlin
Read Chapter 16.
Listen to "Surucucu" in JCC and "Birdland" in CGC.
Supplement: recordings cited in endnotes of Chapter 16

Thursday: Fuzak and New Age
Read pages 346-348.
Listen to recordings on Windham Hill and Narada, and study the music of Kenny G, Grover Washington, Earl Klugh, George Benson, Spyro Gyra and other popular contemporary musicians.

Week 10

FINAL EXAM

10-WEEK INTRODUCTION TO JAZZ
(with introductory emphasis on elements of music and how to listen)

Monday-Wednesday-Friday Schedule; three exams

Note: Selections accompanied by the JCC designation have corresponding listening guides in the appropriate chapters. These guides should be used whenever studying a given selection. The CGC designation is for selections in the cassette and compact disc that accompany the CONCISE GUIDE TO JAZZ textbook. Listening guides for those selections are in the 16-page booklet that accompanies the CD and in the textbook itself. Citations for JSDC indicate demonstrations found on the JAZZ STYLES DEMONSTRATION CASSETTE that accompanies both the one-cassette version and the two-cassette version of the JAZZ STYLES textbook. These demonstrations are also available separately on the JAZZ STYLES DEMONSTRATION COMPACT DISC.

Week 1

Monday: What is Jazz
Read Chapters 1 and 2.

Wednesday: Elements of Music (rhythm)
Read pages 358-365.

Friday: Elements of Music (instruments)
Read pages 388-391.
Listen to JSDC, side 2 (CD tracks 1-15, 59-98).
Listen to "No Figs" and "Flamenco Sketches" in JCC for instrument identifications.

Week 2

Monday: Elements of Music (chords)
Read pages 365-377.
Listen to JSDC, side 1 (CD tracks 16-19).

Wednesday: How To Listen (song forms)
Read pages 377-388.
Listen to JSDC, side 1 (CD tracks 16-20, 33-36).

Friday: How To Listen (instrument roles)
Read Chapter 3.
Listen to JSDC, all (CD tracks 19-32).

Week 3

Monday: Layered Listening Approach
Listen and follow the listening guides for "Harlem Airshaft" and "Masqualero" in JCC.

Wednesday: Blues vs. A-A-B-A
Listen and follow the listening guides for "West End Blues," "Frame For The Blues," "Lester Leaps In," "Taxi War Dance," "Cottontail," "Steps," "Four Brothers," and "Shaw Nuff" in JCC, and "Sobbin' Hearted Blues," "Two Bass Hit," and "Dexter Digs In" in CGC.

Friday: FIRST EXAM

Week 4

Monday: The Origins of Jazz
Read Chapter 4.
Listen to JSDC side 2 (CD tracks 50-58).
Listen to the first 7 selections in JCC.
Supplement: "Maple Leaf Rag" in SCCJ

Wednesday: Origins of Jazz
same assignment as Monday

Friday: Early Jazz (ODJB, James P. Johnson)
Read Chapter 5.
Listen to "Dixie Jazz Band One-Step," "You've Got To Be Modernistic," and "West End Blues" in JCC, and "Sobbin' Hearted Blues" in CGC.
Supplement: "Carolina Shout" and "Dippermouth Blues" in SCCJ

Week 5

Monday: Early Jazz (Louis Armstrong and Earl Hines)
Read pages 62-74.
Listen to "West End Blues" in JCC.
Supplement: "Weather Bird," "Cake Walkin' Babies From Home," "Potato Head Blues," and "Hotter Than That" in SCCJ

Wednesday: Swing (Benny Goodman, Coleman Hawkins, Roy Eldridge)
Read Chapter 6.
Listen to "Body and Soul," "Rockin' Chair," "I Found a New Baby," and "I Can't Believe That You're In Love With Me" in SCCJ.

Friday: Count Basie and Lester Young
Read Chapter 8.
Listen to "Taxi War Dance" and "Lester Leaps In" in JCC, and "Back In Your Own Back Yard" in CGC.

Week 6

Monday: Duke Ellington
Read Chapter 7.
Listen to "Harlem Airshaft" and "Cottontail" in JCC.
Supplement: "Concerto for Cootie" and "In A Mellotone" in SCCJ

Wednesday: Duke Ellington
Read Chapter 7.
Listen to "Transblucency" and "Prelude To A Kiss" in JCC, and "I've Got It Bad" in CGC.
Supplement: "Ko-Ko" and "East St. Louis Toodle-o" in SCCJ

Friday: Bop (Charlie Parker and Dizzy Gillespie)
Read Chapter 9.
Listen to "Shaw Nuff" in JCC and "Ko-Ko" and "Things to Come" in CGC.
Supplement: Parker and Gillespie selections in SCCJ

Week 7

Monday: Bop (Thelonious Monk and Bud Powell)
Read Chapter 9.
Listen to Monk and Powell selections in SCCJ and "Dexter Digs In" in CGC.

Wednesday: Cool (Lennie Tristano, Lee Konitz)
Read Chapter 10.
Listen to "No Figs" in JCC and "Sax of a Kind" in CGC.
Supplement: "Boplicity" and Tristano selections in SCCJ

Friday: SECOND EXAM

Week 8

Monday: Hard Bop (Clifford Brown and Sonny Rollins)
Read Chapter 11.
Listen to "Frame For The Blues" in JCC, "Get Happy" in CGC, and "Pent-Up House" and "Blue Seven" in SCCJ.

Wednesday: Miles Davis and John Coltrane
Read Chapters 12 and 13.
Listen to "Flamenco Sketches," "Masqualero," and "The Promise" in JCC.
Supplement: "So What" and "Alabama" in SCCJ; "Two Bass Hit," "Blue in Green," and "Your Lady" in CGC

Friday: Free Jazz (Ornette Coleman and Cecil Taylor)
Read Chapter 14.
Listen to "Jitney No. 2" in JCC and "Cloning" in CGC.
Supplement: "Enter Evening," "Congeniality," "Lonely Woman," and "Free Jazz" in SCCJ

Week 9

Monday: Bill Evans, Herbie Hancock, and Chick Corea
Read Chapters 12 and 15.
Listen to "Flamenco Sketches," "Solar," "Masqualero," and "Steps" in JCC, "Blue in Green" in CGC, and "So What" in SCCJ.

Wednesday: Fusion (Weather Report)
Read Chapter 16.
Listen to "Surucucu" in JCC and "Birdland" in CGC.

Friday: Fuzak and New Age
Read pages 346-348.
Listen to albums on Windham Hill and Narada, and study the music of Kenny G, Grover Washington, Earl Klugh, George Benson, Spyro Gyra and other popular contemporary musicians.

Week 10

FINAL EXAM

10-WEEK INTRODUCTION TO JAZZ
(with introductory emphasis on elements of music and how to listen)

Tuesday-Thursday Schedule; three exams

Note: Selections accompanied by the JCC designation have corresponding listening guides in the appropriate chapters. These guides should be used whenever studying a given selection. The CGC designation is for selections in the cassette and compact disc that accompany the CONCISE GUIDE TO JAZZ textbook. Listening guides for those selections are in the 16-page booklet that accompanies the CD and in the textbook itself. Citations for JSDC indicate demonstrations found on the JAZZ STYLES DEMONSTRATION CASSETTE that accompanies both the one-cassette version and the two-cassette version of the JAZZ STYLES textbook. These demonstrations are also available separately on the JAZZ STYLES DEMONSTRATION COMPACT DISC.

Week 1

Tuesday: What is Jazz
Read Chapters 1 and 2.

Thursday: Elements of Music To Listen For
Read pages 358-365 (rhythm).

Week 2

Tuesday: Elements of Music (Instruments)
Read 388-391.
Listen to JSDC, side 2 (CD tracks 1-15, 59-98).
Listen to "No Figs" and "Flamenco Sketches" in JCC for instrument identifications.

Thursday: Elements of Music (chords)
Read pages 365-374.
Listen to JSDC, side 1 (CD tracks 16-20).

Week 3

Tuesday: How To Listen (song form routines and instrument roles)
Read chapter 3 and pages 374-388.
Listen to JSDC side 1 (CD tracks 19-37).
Listen to identify blues and A-A-B-A forms on "West End Blues," "Frame for the Blues," "Cottontail," "Shaw Nuff," "Steps," and "Taxi War Dance" in JCC, and "Sobbin' Hearted Blues," "Two Bass Hit," and "Dexter Digs In" in CGC.

Thursday: FIRST EXAM

Week 4

Tuesday: Origins of Jazz
Read Chapter 4.
Listen to first 7 examples in JCC.
Listen to blue notes and pitch bends in JSDC, side 2 (CD tracks 50-58).
Listen to "Maple Leaf Rag" in SCCJ.

Thursday: Early Jazz
Read Chapter 5.
Listen to "Dixie Jazz Band One-Step" and "You've Got To Be Modernistic" in JCC, and "Carolina Shout" in SCCJ.

Week 5

Tuesday: Early Jazz
Read pages 62-73.
Listen to "West End Blues" in JCC and "Sobbin' Hearted Blues" in CGC.
Supplement: "Weather Bird," "Cake Walkin' Babies From Home," "Potato Head Blues," and "Hotter Than That" in SCCJ

Thursday: Swing
Read Chapter 6 and 8.
Listen to "Lester Leaps In" and "Taxi War Dance" in JCC, and "Back in You Own Back Yard" in CGC.

Week 6

Tuesday: Duke Ellington
Read Chapter 7.
Listen to "Cottontail," "Harlem Airshaft," "Prelude to a Kiss," and "Transblucency" in JCC, "I've Got It Bad" in CGC, and "Concerto for Cootie" and "In a Mellotone" in SCCJ.

Thursday: SECOND EXAM

Week 7

Tuesday: Bop
Read Chapter 9.
Listen to "Shaw Nuff" and "Four Brothers" in JCC, and "Ko-Ko," "Things to Come," and "Dexter Digs In" in CGC.
Supplement: Parker and Gillespie items in SCCJ

Thursday: Cool
Read Chapter 10.
Listen to "No Figs" in JCC, "Sax of a Kind" in CGC.
Supplement: "Boplicity" and Tristano items in SCCJ

Week 8

Tuesday: Hard Bop and Miles Davis
Read Chapters 11 & 12.
Listen to "Frame for the Blues" and "Flamenco Sketches" in JCC.
Supplement: "Two Bass Hit," "Blue in Green, and "Get Happy" in CGC; "Pent-Up House," "Blue Seven, "So What," and "Summertime" in SCCJ

Thursday: John Coltrane and Cecil Taylor
Read Chapters 13 and 14.
Listen to "The Promise" and "Jitney No. 2" in JCC, "Your Lady," "Two Bass Hit," "Flamenco Sketches," "Blue in Green," and "Cloning" in CGC, and "Enter Evening," "Lonely Woman," "Free Jazz," "Alabama," and "Congeniality" in SCCJ.

Week 9

Tuesday: Bill Evans, Chick Corea, Herbie Hancock, and Wayne Shorter
Read Chapters 12 and 15.
Listen to "Flamenco Sketches," "Solar," "Masqualero," and "Steps" in JCC, "Blue in Green" in CGC, and "So What" in SCCJ.

Thursday: Fusion
Read Chapter 16.
Listen to "Surucucu" in JCC and "Birdland" in CGC.

Week 10

FINAL EXAM

JAZZ STYLES DEMONSTRATION CASSETTE CONTENTS

SIDE ONE

1. bass drum
2. high-hat cymbal
3. high-hat struck in open position
4. high-hat struck in semi-open position
5. high-hat struck in closed position
6. ride rhythm played on opening and closing high-hat
7. ride rhythm on ride cymbal
8. crash cymbal
9. snare drum
10. ride cymbal vs. crash cymbal
11. small tom-tom
12. large tom-tom
13. combining the drums and cymbals
14. snare drum rhythm of early jazz
15. wood block rhythm of early jazz
16. wire brushes stirring soup on snare drum
17. wire brushes striking ride cymbal
18. drum stick striking ride cymbal
19. mallets striking drums
20. mallets striking cymbals
21. chord definition and demonstration
22. I-chord explanation and demonstration in C
23. I-chord in F#
24. I-chord in Bb
25. I-chord in the key of C
26. II-chord in the key of C
27. III-chord in the key of C
28. IV-chord in the key of C
29. V-chord in the key C
30. VI-chord in the key of C
31. VII-chord in the key of C
32. definition of chord change and example of I-II progression
33. I-IV progression
34. IV-I progression
35. I-V-I progression
36. I-IV-I-V-I blues progression, keyed to diagram on page 374
37. chord voicing examples on page 375
38. definition of syncopation and comping; demonstration contrasting chording in unsyncopated manner with
39. chording in syncopated manner
40. bass played by bow (arco)
41. bass played by plucking (pizzicato)
42. definition and demonstration of walking bass
43. embellished walking style
44. 12-bar blues played by walking bass
45. right-hand horn-like piano lines accompanied by walking bass demonstrating blues without chord accompaniment
46. horn-like pizzicato bass improvisation
47. non-repetitive style bass playing with piano improvisation
48. walking bass combined with piano comping on 12-bar blues
49. definition of chorus, demonstrated in two choruses of 12-bar blues played by walking bass
50. piano, bass and drums accompaniment for 12-bar blues
51. tenor sax accompanied by piano, bass and drums
52. sax accompanied by piano and drums
53. sax accompanied by piano, bass and drums
54. sax accompanied by bass and drums
55. sax accompanied by piano, bass and drums
56. sax accompanied by piano and bass
57. sax accompanied by drums
58. sax accompanied piano, bass and drums
59. sax accompanied by piano
60. sax accompanied by bass
61. sax accompanied by piano, bass and drums
62. explanation and demonstration of A-A-B-A: first A-section of "(Meet The) Flintstones"

63. second A-section of "(Meet The) Flintstones"
64. bridge of "(Meet The) Flintstones"
65. final A-section of "(Meet The) Flintstones"
66. demonstration of how chords guide improvisation: Flintstones theme played by flute while pianist improvises, guided by accompaniment chords
67. piano improvisations on Flintstones progression without using the aid of melody sounded by flute
68. stop-time solo break explanation and demonstration

SIDE TWO

69. double-timing explanation and demonstration
70. half-time explanation and demonstration
71. left-hand comping on piano
72. right-hand horn-like melody lines on piano accompanied by left hand comping
73. right-hand horn-like piano lines without accompaniment
74. stride-style explanation and demonstration
75. stride-style left hand accompaniment with right-hand melody
76. walking tenths
77. horn-like piano lines
78. octave-voiced piano lines
79. tremolo
80. swing eighth-note pattern
81. legato
82. staccato
83. tone with no vibrato
84. tone with regular vibrato (slow)
85. tone with regular vibrato (fast)
86. tone with terminal vibrato
87. drop (fall-off)
88. scoop
89. smear
90. doit
91. C scale without blue notes
92. C scale with the flat third blue note
93. trombone playing C scale
94. trombone playing C scale with flat third
95. trombone playing major scale, sliding down to neutral third
96. trombone playing major scale, sliding up to neutral third
97. trumpet
98. trumpet with no vibrato
99. trumpet with vibrato
100. fluegelhorn
101. trumpet vs. fluegelhorn
102. fluegelhorn identification quiz
103. cup muted trumpet
104. Harmon mute with stem
105. Harmon mute without stem
106. straight mute
107. plunger mute
108. trumpet
109. fluegelhorn
110. cup-muted trumpet
111. Harmon mute with stem
112. Harmon mute without stem
113. straight mute
114. plunger mute and growl
115. clarinet
116. clarinet with no vibrato
117. clarinet with vibrato
118. soprano sax
119. soprano sax with no vibrato
120. soprano sax with vibrato
121. clarinet vs. soprano sax
122. alto sax
123. alto sax with no vibrato
124. alto sax with vibrato
125. tenor sax
126. tenor sax with no vibrato

127. tenor sax with vibrato
128. baritone sax
129. baritone sax with no vibrato
130. baritone sax with vibrato
131. flute
132. flute with no vibrato
133. flute with vibrato
134. flute vs. clarinet
135. tenor sax vs. soprano sax
136. tenor sax vs. soprano sax
137. trombone
138. trombone with no vibrato
139. trombone with vibrato
140. cup-muted trombone
141. straight-muted trombone
142. plunger-muted trombone with buzz mute
143. trumpet-fluegelhorn-trombone comparison
144. soprano sax, alto sax, tenor sax, baritone sax, flute & clarinet
145. hollow-body guitar, unamplified, played pizzicato with pick
146. hollow-body guitar, amplified, played pizzicato with pick
147. hollow-body guitar, amplified, plucked with thumb
148. finger-plucked octaves on hollow-body guitar, amplified
149. rhythm guitar style played with pick
150. comping by guitar, played with pick
151. reverberated electric guitar tone
152. banjo solo line
153. banjo chords played in rhythm style
154. banjo vs. guitar
155. amplified guitar plucked vs. picked vs. octave-voiced
156. reverberated electric guitar
157. vibraharp
158. tenor sax playing blues
159. trumpet playing blues
160. trombone playing blues
161. alto sax playing blues
162. flute playing blues
163. soprano sax playing blues
164. trumpet with Harmon mute with no stem playing blues
165. fluegelhorn playing blues
166. trombone with plunger mute playing blues
167. trumpet with plunger mute playing blues
168. baritone sax playing blues
169. trombone with cup mute playing blues
170. trumpet with cup mute playing blues
171. clarinet playing blues

Complete Contents of the JAZZ CLASSICS CASSETTE/CD

Available only with the TWO-CASSETTE VERSION of Gridley, JAZZ STYLES (Prentice-Hall ISBN 0-13-17969-8) or CD alone (Prentice-Hall ISBN 0-13-174475-5)

SIDE ONE

1. Afro-American Pitch Bending Illustrations

   A. "Street Cries of Charleston" (excerpt); no recording date, composer or performer credits are known; this is owned by Fantasy Records, originally issued by Riverside Records; reissued as RIVERSIDE HISTORY OF CLASSIC JAZZ, Fantasy: RB-005; volume 1, side 1, track 2.

   B. "Fisherman, Strawberry, Devil Crab" (excerpt); recorded July 29, 1958; first issued on the album, Miles Davis, PORGY AND BESS, Columbia CS 8085, side 2, track 3; composer: George Gershwin; arranger: Gil Evans; trumpet soloist: Miles Davis.

2. Afro-American Retentions Sequence

   A. "Hunter's Dance" (30 second excerpt); this is a West African field recording made by Gilbert Rouget; no composer or performer credits are known; owned by Vogue, which is a French company and by Everest, which is an American record company; originally available on the French LP, MUSIQUE D' AFRIQUE OCCIDENTALE, Vogue LVLX 193; later issued on ANTHOLOGY OF MUSIC OF BLACK AFRICA, Everest SDBR 3254, 3LP set; available as AFRICAN TRIBAL MUSIC AND DANCE: MUSIC OF THE MALINKE; MUSIC OF THE BAOULE AND OTHERS, Tradition: 2223, AC; or AFRICAN TRIBAL MUSIC AND DANCES, Legacy International: CD 328, CD.

   B. "One Day" (30 second excerpt); performed by the Angelic Gospel Singers, Dixie Hummingbirds and a pianist; recorded in 1951; reissued on side 3, track 1 of THE GOSPEL SOUND, Columbia: G 31086, 2LP set.

   C. "One O'Clock Jump" (30 second excerpt); composed and performed by Count Basie; recorded January 21, 1942; matrix CO 32274; first issued on Okeh 6634; owned by Columbia; trumpets: Harry Edison, Al Kilian, Buck Clayton, Ed Lewis; trombones: Robert Scott, Eli Robertson, Dicky Wells; saxes: Earl Warren, Tab Smith, Buddy Tate, Don Byas, Jack Washington; rhythm section: Count Basie, Freddy Green, Walter Page, Jo Jones.

   D. "Birdland" (30 second excerpt); composed by Josef Zawinul; recorded in 1977 in North Hollywood, California; performed by Josef Zawinul, Wayne Shorter, Jaco Pastorius, Alex Acuna & Manolo Badrena; first available on Weather Report, HEAVY WEATHER, Columbia: 34418.

3. "Dixie Jazz Band One-Step" (2:35); performed by The Original Dixieland Jazz Band: Nick LaRocca (cornet), Larry Shields (clarinet), Eddie Edwards (trombone), Henry Ragas (piano); February 26, 1917; matrix B-19332-3; clearances: ASCAP, Victor.

4. "West End Blues" (3:16); recorded June 6, 1928; composed by Joe Oliver and Clarence Williams; performed by Louis Armstrong, Earl Hines, Fred Robinson, Jimmy Strong, Mancy Cara and Zutty Singleton; originally issued by Okeh, owned by CBS; matrix number 400967B.

5. "You've Got To Be Modernistic" (3:10); recorded January 21, 1930; composed and performed as piano solo by James P. Johnson; Brunswick 4762; matrix E-31958; owned by MCA.

6. "Cottontail" (3:08); composer: Duke Ellington; publisher clearances: ASCAP; recorded May 4, 1940 in Hollywood, California; trumpets: Wallace Jones, Cootie Williams, Rex Stewart; trombones: Joe Nanton, Lawrence Brown, Juan Tizol; saxophones: Barney Bigard, Otto Hardwicke, Johnny Hodges, Ben Webster, Harry Carney; rhythm section: Ellington (piano), Freddy Guy (guitar), Jimmy Blanton (bass), Sonny Greer (drums); matrix 049655-1; issued as Victor 26610; owned by RCA.

7. "Harlem Airshaft" (2:57); composer: Duke Ellington; publisher clearances: ASCAP; recorded July 22, 1940 in New York; performed by same musicians as "Cottontail"; matrix 054606-1; issued as Victor 26731; owned by RCA.

8. "Transblucency" (2:58); composed by Lawrence Brown and Duke Ellington; licensed by ASCAP; recorded July 9, 1946 by Kay Davis (vocal), Jimmy Hamilton (clarinet), Lawrence Brown (muted trombone), Duke Ellington (piano), Oscar Pettiford (bass); saxophones (one chorus only): Russell Procope, Johnny Hodges, Al Sears, Harry Carney; matrix D6VB2095; owned by RCA.

9. "Prelude to a Kiss" (1:30 excerpt); composed by Duke Ellington; recorded October 1, 1957; featuring Johnny Hodges (alto sax); Ellington band with Duke Ellington (piano), Jimmy Woode (bass), Sam Woodyard (drums); matrix CO59897; first issued on ELLINGTON INDIGOS, Columbia CL 1085;

10. "Taxi War Dance" (2:47); composed by Count Basie and Lester Young on the chord progression of "Willow Weep For Me"; arranged by Buck Clayton; recorded March 19, 1939; performed by trumpets: Buck Clayton, Shad Collins, Harry Edison, Ed Lewis; trombones: Dan Minor, Benny Morton, Dicky Wells; saxes: Earl Warren, Jack Washington, Buddy Tate, Lester Young; Count Basie (piano), Freddie Green (guitar), Walter Page (bass), Jo Jones (drums); originally issued as Vocalion 4748 (matrix 24242-1); owned by Columbia.

11. "Lester Leaps In" (3:11); composed by Lester Young over the chord progression of "I Got Rhythm"; recorded September 5, 1939 in New York; performed by the Count Basie's Kansas City Six: Lester Young, Buck Clayton, Dicky Wells, Count Basie, Walter Page, Jo Jones; matrix 25297-1; originally issued as Vocalion 5118; owned by Columbia. NOT ON CD FORMAT.

12. "Shaw 'Nuff" (2:56); composed by Dizzy Gillespie and Charlie Parker; recorded May 11, 1945 by Dizzy Gillespie, Charlie Parker, Al Haig, Curley Russell & Sid Catlett; first issued on Guild 1002 (matrix 566); owned by Trend Record Corporation.

13. "Four Brothers" (3:16); composed by Jimmy Giuffre; licensed by ASCAP; recorded by Woody Herman band, December 27, 1947 in Los Angeles; owned by Columbia; Woody Herman (clarinet); trumpets: Ernie Royal, Bernie Glow, Stan Fishelson, Shorty Rogers, Marky Markowitz; trombones: Earl Swope, Ollie Wilson, Bob Swift; saxes: Herbie Steward, Zoot Sims, Stan Getz, Serge Chaloff; Fred Otis (piano), Gene Sargent (guitar), Walt Yoder (bass), Don Lamond (drums); matrix HCO.3061-1; first issued as Columbia 38304. NOT ON CD FORMAT.

14. "No Figs" (2:51); recorded by the Metronome All-Stars; composed and arranged by Lennie Tristano, conducted by Pete Rugolo; clearances: BMI; recorded January 10, 1950 by Kai Winding (trombone), Buddy DeFranco (clarinet), Lee Konitz (alto sax), Stan Getz (tenor sax), Serge Chaloff (baritone sax), Billy Bauer (guitar), Lennie Tristano (piano), Eddie Safranski (bass), Max Roach (drums); Columbia 38734; matrix CO 42630-1; this is an edited version; the original additionally has a Dizzy Gillespie solo and a second Getz solo.

15. "Frame for the Blues" (excerpt first 2:25 only); composed by Slide Hampton; published by Second Floor Music; licensed by BMI; recorded by Maynard Ferguson band, May, 1958 in New York; owned by Roulette (EMI); originally issued on Maynard Ferguson, A MESSAGE FROM NEWPORT (Roulette: 52050); trumpets: Ferguson, Joe Slaney, Jr., Clyde Reasinger, Bill Chase; trombones: Slide Hampton, Don Sebesky; saxes: Jimmie Ford (alto), Willie Maiden, Carmen Leggio (tenor), Jay Cameron (bari); rhythm section John Bunch (piano), Jimmy Rowser (bass), Jake Hanna (drums). NOT ON CD FORMAT.

SIDE TWO

16. "Flamenco Sketches" (9:25); recorded by Miles Davis (trumpet), Cannonball Adderley (alto sax), John Coltrane (tenor sax), Bill Evans (piano), Paul Chambers (bass), and Jimmy Cobb (drums), April 22, 1959; issued on Miles Davis, KIND OF BLUE, Columbia: PC 8163; side 2, track 2; composer credits: Miles Davis; licensing: BMI.

17. "Solar." (excerpt first 4:00 only); recorded June 25, 1961; composer: Chuck Wayne, though wrongly credited to Miles Davis; publisher: Prestige Music; licensing: BMI; performers: Bill Evans, Scott LaFaro, Paul Motian; owned by Fantasy Records; originally issued as Bill Evans, SUNDAY AT THE VILLAGE VANGUARD (Riverside: 376).

18. "The Promise" (8:04); composed by John Coltrane; published by Jowcol Music; publisher clearances: BMI; performed by John Coltrane, McCoy Tyner, Jimmy Garrison & Elvin Jones; recorded October 8, 1963 at Birdland, in New York; owned by MCA; originally issued on John Coltrane, COLTRANE LIVE AT BIRDLAND, Impulse: A-50.

19. "Jitney No. 2" (3:21); composed, arranged and performed by Cecil Taylor; recorded July 2, 1974 at the Montreux Jazz Festival in Switzerland; first issued on Cecil Taylor, SILENT TONGUES, Arista AL 1005 (Arista/Black Lion/Freedom); licensed by BMI; published by Unit Core.

20. "Masqualero" (8:53); performed by Miles Davis (trumpet), Wayne Shorter (tenor sax), Herbie Hancock (piano), Ron Carter (bass), Tony Williams (drums); May 17, 1967; composer: Wayne Shorter; licensing: BMI; issued on Miles Davis, SORCERER, side 1, track 3 (Columbia CS 9532).

21. "Steps" (5:02); recorded June 1968; composer: Chick Corea; publisher: Litha Music; licensing: ASCAP; originally issued as Chick Corea, NOW HE SINGS, NOW HE SOBS, Solid State: 18039; currently owned by Liberty Records (Transamerica); performers: Chick Corea, Miroslav Vitous, Roy Haynes.

22. "Surucucu" (first 4:10 only); recorded January 13, 1972 in Shibuya Kokaido Hall, Tokyo, Japan; composer: Wayne Shorter; licensing: BMI; performed by Weather Report (Joseph Zawinul, Wayne Shorter, Miroslav Vitous, Eric Gravatt & Dom Um Romao); originally issued on Weather Report, I SING THE BODY ELECTRIC, Columbia: KC 31352.

TEACHING THE ORIGINS OF JAZZ: ISSUES, BIBLIOGRAPHIES & DISCOGRAPHIES

Teaching the origins of jazz presents several problems for the instructor in a course devoted to American music or jazz. First of all, to do justice to African music alone requires at least a semester-long, ethnomusicologically-oriented course. To do justice to ragtime, blues or blackface minstrel traditions also requires far more than a week-long slice. In other words, to do the topic justice requires far more time than most semesters provide, especially if a substantial portion of the semester is allocated to teaching listening skills and part of the semester introduces recent styles of jazz. A second problem is that no one knows how jazz originated, and this means that teachers are speculating in public whenever they lecture on the origins of jazz. Third is the problem that, though many of us assume jazz to have African roots, we can find little or no jazz that sounds like any African music available (though a solution is outlined in the chapter called "An Easy Way to Demonstrate Connections Between Jazz and African Music" of **HOW TO TEACH JAZZ HISTORY**, 200 pages, by Mark Gridley, published by IAJE Press, Box 724, Manhattan, Kansas 66502; phone 913-776-8744). A brief, but effective solution is available in the listening guide and accompanying recordings at the end of the Chapter 4: Origins of Jazz (tracks 3-6 of JAZZ CLASSICS CASSETTE/CD). All the recordings in the sequence prominently exhibit the kind of rhythmic groove that is called "swinging" (or, as Duke Ellington defined it, "a lilting buoyant feeling"). All of them also use considerable syncopation, extensive repetition of brief patterns, and overlapping call-and-response format.

One solution to these problems is to skip the origins of jazz and devote your semester to developing listening skills and to introducing jazz styles instead. A less extreme solution is, **FIRST**, to tell students that jazz has roots in ragtime, blues, work songs, marches, and nineteenth century dance music, **SECOND**, tell them that we do not know what weights to attach to any of those likely sources, then, **THIRD**, go directly into your coverage of New Orleans and Chicago styles of jazz. This is precisely what I did in the 1978 edition of JAZZ STYLES, also my design for ten years of teaching "History and Styles of Jazz" to nonmusicians at Case Western Reserve University. However, the most popular solution is to play brief examples for each of these sources, then move directly to early jazz. But the connections between jazz and its "roots" might not be apparent to your students if you approach the problem that way. That catch is one reason behind the element-by-element format used in Chapter 4 of JAZZ STYLES. There is still another catch, too. And that is the rarity of recorded examples to illustrate the points you will want to make. So, because of this, what follows is a guide through currently-available source materials that are appropriate for illustrating and researching the origins of jazz.

No one knows exactly how jazz originated. But we can find clues by comparing the characteristics of the earliest jazz with characteristics of other kinds of music that existed near the same time and place as the earliest jazz. Throughout this discussion, however, we must remember that similarity alone is not sufficient to prove a cause and effect relationship. In fact, it is dangerous to reason that whatever two styles have in common indicates the influence that one style had upon another. A few examples should make this more clear. Call and response format is common in European music and in African music, though it is found somewhat more often in African music. Therefore, instances of call and response format in jazz should not be assumed to reflect African influence, even if jazz musicians have African ancestry. Here is another example. Just because both jazz and African music are highly syncopated does not necessarily prove that African music influenced jazz. There is syncopation in European music, too, though it is less prominent than it is in jazz and African music.

Jazz has several characteristics in common with African music. Both kinds of music are

1. highly percussive, even in the manner of playing wind instruments
2. filled with a wide range of rough and colorful timbres
3. characterized by much rhythmic variety in terms of off-beat accents, the simultaneous presence of contrasting rhythms, displacement of phrase structures, syncopations, multimeters, polyrhythms
4. characterized by pitch flexibility deviating from well-tempered intonation
5. improvised, at least somewhat
6. dependent upon short-term repetition and brief, cyclic forms
7. capable of eliciting a rhythmic feeling ("groove") in the listener that is distinctive and frequently identified with jazz and African music.

All these similarities are evident in the examples on the "African-American Retentions Sequence" (tracks 3-6 of JAZZ CLASSICS CASSETTE/CD). But none of these similarities necessarily proves African roots for jazz. Mere similarity is not sufficient for proving cause.

A nagging problem that pervades our search for the roots of jazz is that the almost continuous back and forth borrowing of characteristics and repertory that exists within the evolution of American musical styles makes it impossible to determine the relative strength of influence exerted by any given source and to assign proper credit to the primary innovations. For instance, with respect to Negro spirituals, trying to distinguish the relative contributions of European hymns from those of African repertory and singing practices continues to puzzle historians (see readings list for references concerned with spirituals).

Another problem that plagues our quest for the origins of jazz is that the term jazz has a narrower meaning today than it had during the 1920's. Yet, before we can say **HOW** jazz originated, we must say **WHAT** jazz is and **WHEN** there first was music that qualifies by that definition. If we call almost all its roots (ragtime, blues, etc.) "jazz," then what qualifies some music for the "roots" category and other music for the "jazz" category? An illustration will make this problem clearer. For the sake of argument, let's define jazz as highly syncopated American music that is improvised, and let's define improvisation as spontaneously composing fresh melody lines during each performance. By those constraints, then it would follow that much New Orleans combo music recorded between 1917 and 1927 is not jazz because it was worked out in advance, with little spontaneous variation from performance to performance. (Alternate renditions, by the same musicians, of the "Dixie Jazz Band One-Step" and "You've Got to Be Modernistic" differ only slightly from the versions heard in the JAZZ CLASSICS CASSETTE/CD.) Much 1917-24 music SOUNDS spontaneous, though such an impression is deceiving, and this is clearly a credit to the skills of those pioneers. The impression of spontaneity has been prized in jazz as one component of its spirited nature. However, it is problematic to apply such a definition here because, knowing that only toward the late 1920's did much syncopated American music exhibit improvisation in this sense of the term, we might no longer be justified in saying jazz originated in New Orleans. We would be forced to say that jazz did not begin until at least the mid-1920's, and then, only within the playing of a few musicians. And our search for the roots of jazz improvisation would be expanded beyond New Orleans.

We also must recognize that, not only at the time the first jazz was described, but recently, too, musicians have referred to ragtime and jazz just as **WAYS** of playing music rather than identifiable bodies of music themselves. To "jazz it" was to vary the rhythms of a piece and make it sound more lively and make the pitches and timbres more flexible. In other words, then, as today, "how you play" was the key to extracting the peculiar feeling we associate with jazz. Almost any type of music--polkas, marches, ballads--could be altered in performance to sound more lively and swinging. Jazz performance practice reflects a departure from accepted ways of playing professional dance music and allows a greater latitude for individuality of performance, though we still cannot tell whether this reflects African tradition or a combination of traditions that existed in folk music and popular music of Italian, German, Irish as well as African background. (The answer might be "none of the above.")

Among turn-of-the-century New Orleans musicians, the improvisational creativity of the players was directed at piecing together ensemble routines that were effective. Some routines were spontaneously devised during performances, thereby qualifying as improvised, though they were repeated from memory thereafter. Commercially published stock arrangements often provided the basis for band routines, but the players may have done much without referring to written scores. However, the absence of notation should not be taken as evidence of improvisation any more than we would consider "improvised" the music of today's wedding bands and lounge acts that sometimes play fresh routines and do so without notation. At this point, it is relevant to mention how common the practice of reading music was. Karl Koenig's research has shown that most of the early New Orleans jazz musicians could read music. Some could not read music, however, and most chose not to read pieces once they had been learned. There is no question that at one time, and perhaps for the first few run-through's in the early jazz combo pieces, many of the parts were not fixed. Trombone counterlines, clarinet obbligatos, trumpet variations of the melody were invented and performed spontaneously. Accompaniments were improvised and varied by the more adventurous and creative of the players, but a striving for improvisation during that era was not as central to a jazz aesthetic as it has become, though there was a striving for personalization that did not necessarily require spontaneously devised parts. But after a suitable set of parts had been worked out, frequently the musicians remained relatively loyal to them. Much of this we have deciphered by comparing alternate takes of recorded jazz pieces such as the material of The Original Dixieland Jazz Band from 1917 to 1919 and the Joe Oliver band's "Dippermouth Blues," and by studying the evolution of routines used on such pieces as "Weather Bird" in successive recordings by Joe Oliver and Louis Armstrong. Some of these conclusions also stem from thinking about the requirements for the commercial situations these musicians found themselves in playing for dancers and for crowds who needed predictability and who wanted to hear the same material again and again in order to coordinate their movements. This resembles today's situation and the intolerance for improvisation from a public that wants music to sound just like the recorded version--as though to say, "too many surprises are no fun." But somehow these tendencies expanded by the late 1920's, and practices evolved into the extent of improvisation we ordinarily expect from most jazz today. Unfortunately, we will never know whether this occurred out of boredom with fixed routines, a need to learn new material without recourse to sheet music, a greater interest in bravura solo excursions, a continuation of European and/or African traditions for spontaneous alteration, or simply an unbridled creativity.

Jazz originated in the blends of folk music, popular music and light classical music that were current near the beginning of the twentieth century, especially in New Orleans. Collections that are useful for illustrating these styles include:

EARLY BAND RAGTIME, Smithsonian/Folkways: RBF 38, AC, [1979].

JAZZ, vol. 1: THE SOUTH, Smithsonian/Folkways: 2801, AC, [1950].

JAZZ, vol. 2: THE BLUES, Smithsonian/Folkways: 2802, AC, 1923-48.

RIVERSIDE HISTORY OF CLASSIC JAZZ, Riverside/Fantasy: RB-005, 5LP set, ca. 1900-1956; volume 1 only.

THAT'S MY RABBIT, MY DOG CAUGHT IT: TRADITIONAL SOUTHERN INSTRUMENTAL STYLES, New World: NW 226, LP, 1925-77.

COME AND TRIP IT: INSTRUMENTAL DANCE MUSIC 1780-1920's, New World: NW 293, LP, [1978].

THE SOUSA AND PRYOR BANDS: ORIGINAL RECORDINGS, 1901-1926, New World: NW 282, LP, [1976].

STEPPIN' ON THE GAS: RAGS TO JAZZ, New World: NW 269, LP, 1913-27. side 1 only.

JAZZ: SOME BEGINNINGS, Smithsonian/Folkways: RF 31, AC, 1914-1926. side 1 only.

NOTE: New World Records (Recorded Anthology of American Music) may be found in many college libraries; the Rockefeller Foundation donated sets to many educational institutions. Folkways records are in many music libraries. See page 78 of this manual for where to order recordings.

Americans with African ancestry are disproportionately represented throughout jazz history, and jazz shares several characteristics with African music. However, early jazz did not derive its similarities to African music directly from contact with African music. It acquired these tendencies through other music that had been devised itself by contact with African musical practices in the New World. For instance, some of the syncopation in jazz probably derived from music played during the 18th and 19th centuries on the banjo, an instrument invented in the New World by musicians who had African ancestry (see references list for Dena Epstein's article, "The Folk Banjo: A Documentary History"). This is because banjo music, in combination with European march music, influenced the formation of popular piano styles that by the 1890's were being called ragtime, which, in turn, influenced jazz. (Listen to EARLY BAND RAGTIME, Folkways: RBF 38, AC, 1979; and then listen for similarities in KING OLIVER'S JAZZ BAND: 1923, Smithsonian: 2001, 2LP set, 1975.)

Bluesy approaches to pitch and timbre among jazz hornmen are not in direct imitation of African singing. The ornamentations in jazz hornwork might stem instead from imitation of wide-ranging, imaginative sounds found in New World vocal idioms such as Negro field hollers, work songs, cries of street vendors, and the blues (as exemplified in STREET CRIES AND CREOLE SONGS OF NEW ORLEANS, Smithsonian/Folkways: 2202, AC, 1956, side 2; ROOTS OF THE BLUES, New World: 80252-2, CD; THE RIVERSIDE HISTORY OF CLASSIC JAZZ, Riverside/Fantasy: RB-005, 5LP set, 1956, volume 1, side 1; and AFRICAN JOURNEY: A SEARCH FOR THE ROOTS OF THE BLUES, Vanguard: SRV 73014/5, 2LP set, 1975). Listen to the "Street Cries of Charleston" (track 1 of JAZZ CLASSICS CASSETTE/CD) and then to Miles Davis's instrumentalized version (track 2 of JAZZ CLASSICS CASSETTE/CD). African singing is far less varied in these respects than jazz hornwork, and not all non-African folk music found in the New World is smooth and unvaried in its timbre. The sharp line drawn by Europeans between speech and lyric singing is less clear in much West African music. It is possible that a preference for rough, varied timbres was retained by Afro-Americans in the New World, and it was manifested by the cultivation of rough and highly varied timbres in jazz. Listen to the male singer on "One Day" (track 4 of the JAZZ CLASSICS CASSETTE/CD). Some of this was perpetuated in the hokum style used by minstrel show musicians and activated in novelty effects such as the imitation barnyard sounds heard in the Original Dixieland Band's 1917 recording of "Livery Stable Blues." Listen to the pitch bends of the clarinetist on "Dixie Jazz Band One-Step" (track 7 of the JAZZ CLASSICS CASSETTE/CD). The tendency to playfully vary the sounds of instruments might stem in part from African traditions, but similar musical traditions were also available as models in other ethnic groups in New Orleans at the same time, for example, the Scotch-Irish, who had a tradition for pitch flexibility, leading to what we might identify as "blue notes" (see reference list for William Tallmadge's article "Blue Notes and Blue Tonality"). Therefore we cannot say that such practices reflect exclusively Afro-American sources.

Summary

Sometimes we need to be reminded that jazz did not come from Africa. Only the ancestors for some of its originators did. Jazz originated in America, and, despite all the other areas of the world to which Africans have been moved, America is the only region in which jazz emerged. Note that jazz emerged only in **OUR** part of the New World and only where African practices were applied to a peculiar mix of non-African music. We must also remember that, as Karl Koenig has found in his research, about half the early New Orleans jazz musicians were white (though to be entirely accurate, by comparison with distribution in the population at large, blacks are overrepresented as musicians). This means that jazz was not the exclusive province of Afro-Americans, though at the same time this does not necessarily prove that **BOTH** races were equally involved in its creation. (White musicians **COULD** have imitated black musicians and soon outnumbered them as players of an originally black style.) Intermingling of styles in America has resulted in fresh styles. Remember also that the earliest jazz did not sound like African music so much as it sounded like band ragtime, which was the pop music of the day. And only a portion of the earliest band repertories was blues. The bulk of most band repertories was pop music, show tunes, and well-known songs.

The arguments outlined above constitute only a taste of what you're likely to get mired in if you choose to do a respectable job on the origins of jazz, and African retentions in particular. However, if you remain undeterred after all that preface, here is a list of the leading texts in the area. This is nowhere near an exhaustive listing. For a beginning, consult Donald Kennington and Danny L. Read, THE LITERATURE OF JAZZ: A CRITICAL GUIDE, 2nd ed. rev., American Library Association, 1980; and the bibliography at the end of Barry Kernfeld, ed., THE NEW GROVE DICTIONARY OF JAZZ, Macmillan, 1988. Remember that, like textbook assignments, these readings will mean next to nothing unless you and your students **HEAR** the music that they describe. Therefore the discography here is more valuable than the bibliography.

BASIC TEXTS ON AFRICAN MUSIC

(the most useful texts for a jazz course are listed first)

Nketia, J.H. Kwabena. THE MUSIC OF AFRICA. Norton, 1974.

Nketia, J.H. Kwabena and Jacqueline Coggell DjeDje, eds. SELECTED REPORTS IN ETHNOMUSICOLOGY, vol. 5: STUDIES IN AFRICAN MUSIC. Los Angeles, CA: Program in Ethnomusicology, Department of Music, University of California, 1984.

Bebey, Francis. AFRICAN MUSIC: A PEOPLE'S ART. L. Hill, 1975.

Kebede, Ashenafi. ROOTS OF BLACK MUSIC: THE VOCAL, INSTRUMENTAL, AND DANCE HERITAGE OF AFRICA AND BLACK AMERICA. Prentice-Hall, 1982.

Jones, A.M. STUDIES IN AFRICAN MUSIC. vol. 1 & 2. Oxford University Press, 1959.

Roberts, John Storm. BLACK MUSIC OF TWO WORLDS. Praeger; Tivoli, NY: Original Music, 1972.
Accompanying audio cassettes: BLACK MUSIC OF TWO WORLDS, Smithsonian/Folkways: 4602, 3AC set.

Oliver, Paul. SAVANNAH SYNCOPATORS: AFRICAN RETENTIONS IN THE BLUES. Stein and Day, 1970.
Accompanying 2-LP set: SAVANNAH SYNCOPATORS, CBS (UK): 52799.

Chernoff, John Miller. AFRICAN RHYTHM AND SENSIBILITY: AESTHETICS AND SOCIAL ACTION IN AFRICAN MUSICAL IDIOMS. University of Chicago Press, 1979, 1981.
With accompanying audio cassette examples.

Gayle, Addison. THE BLACK AESTHETIC. Doubleday, 1971.

Many important insights and much of the most solid research data never find their way into full-length textbooks. Much scholarly thinking and data gathering is available only in papers read at professional conferences, rewritten for professional journals. A few of such works are included below. If your library does not carry these journals, ask your reference librarian to request the article via inter-library loan. Frequently a copy can be sent to you for a small fee from a library that holds the journal you seek.

IMPORTANT SCHOLARLY PAPERS ABOUT AFRICAN MUSIC

(the most useful papers for a jazz course are listed first)

Waterman, Richard A. "Hot Rhythm In Negro Music." JOURNAL OF THE AMERICAN MUSICOLOGICAL SOCIETY, vol. 1 (1948): pages 24-37.
Based on a paper delivered December 28, 1943.

________. "African Influence On The Music Of The Americas." In ANTHROPOLOGY AND ART: READINGS IN CROSS CULTURAL AESTHETICS. Edited by Charlotte M. Otten, 227-44. University of Texas Press, 1976. Reprinted from ACCULTURATION IN THE AMERICAS: PROCEEDINGS AND SELECTED PAPERS OF THE XXIX INTERNATIONAL CONGRESS OF AMERICANISTS, edited by Sol Tax, University of Chicago Press, 1952.
A paper delivered in 1951.

________. "On Flogging A Dead Horse: Lessons Learned From The Africanisms Controversy." ETHNOMUSICOLOGY, vol. 7, no. 2 (1963): pages 83-87.

Evans, David. "African Elements in Twentieth Century United States Black Folk Music." In INTERNATIONAL MUSICOLOGICAL SOCIETY, REPORT OF THE TWELFTH CONGRESS, BERKELEY, 1977, pages 54-66. Kassel: Barenreiter, 1981.

Tallmadge, William. "Blue Notes and Blue Tonality." THE BLACK PERSPECTIVE IN MUSIC, vol. 12, no. 2 (1984): pages 155-65.

Kaufman, Robert. "African Rhythm: A Reassessment" ETHNOMUSICOLOGY, vol. 24 (1980): pages 393-415.

Epstein, Dena J. "The Folk Banjo." ETHNOMUSICOLOGY, vol. 19 (1975): pages 347-372.

Gridley, Mark C., and Wallace Rave. "Towards Identification of African Traits in Early Jazz." THE BLACK PERSPECTIVE IN MUSIC, vol. 12, no. 1 (1984): pages 44-56.

Wilson, Olly. "The Significance of the Relationship Between Afro-American Music and West African Music." THE BLACK PERSPECTIVE IN MUSIC, vol. 2 (1974): pages 3-23.

________. "Black Music As An Art Form." BLACK MUSIC RESEARCH JOURNAL (1983): pages 1-22.
Note: BLACK MUSIC RESEARCH JOURNAL is published by Center For Black Music Research, Columbia College Chicago, 600 South Michigan Ave, Chicago, Illinois 60605-1996.

Williams-Jones, Pearl. "Afro-American Gospel Music: A Crystallization of the Black Aesthetic." ETHNOMUSICOLOGY, vol. 19 (1975): pages 373-86.

Floyd, Samuel A., Jr., and Martha J. Reisser. "The Sources And Resources of Classic Ragtime Music." BLACK MUSIC RESEARCH JOURNAL (1984): pages 22-59.
See above address for Center For Black Music Research.

Epstein, Dena. "Black Spirituals: Their Emergence Into Public Knowledge." BLACK MUSIC RESEARCH NEWSLETTER, vol. 8, no. 2 (1986): pages 5-8.
See above for address of Center For Black Music Research.

Cronbach, Lee. "Structural Polytonality in Contemporary Afro-American Music." BLACK MUSIC RESEARCH JOURNAL, vol. 2 (1981-2): pages 15-33.

Koetting, James. "What Do We Know About African Rhythm?" ETHNOMUSICOLOGY, vol. 30, no. 1 (1986): pages 58-63.

Stone, Ruth. "The Value of Local Ideas In Understanding West African Rhythm." ETHNOMUSICOLOGY, vol. 30, no. 1 (1986): pages 54-57.

REFERENCES FOR EARLY AFRO-AMERICAN CULTURE AND NEW ORLEANS

(the most useful items for a jazz course are listed first)

Epstein, Dena. "A White Origin for the Black Spiritual? An Invalid Theory and How It Grew." AMERICAN MUSIC, vol. 1, no. 2 (1983): pages 53-59.

Lomax, Alan. MISTER JELLY ROLL: THE FORTUNES OF JELLY ROLL MORTON, NEW ORLEANS CREOLE AND "INVENTOR OF JAZZ." University of California Press, 1950; Pantheon, 1993.

Berlin, Edward A. REFLECTIONS AND RESEARCH ON RAGTIME. I.S.A.M. Monographs; no. 24. Brooklyn, NY: Institute for Studies in American Music, Conservatory of Music, Brooklyn College, 1987.

Garst, John F. "Mutual Reinforcement and the Origins of Spirituals." AMERICAN MUSIC, vol. 4, no. 4 (1986): pages 390-406.

Foster, George M. POPS FOSTER: THE AUTOBIOGRAPHY OF A NEW ORLEANS JAZZMAN AS TOLD TO TOM STOPPARD. University of California Press, 1971.

Shapiro, Nat, and Nat Hentoff, eds. HEAR ME TALKIN' TO YA: THE STORY OF JAZZ BY THE MEN WHO MADE IT. Reinhart, 1955; Dover, 1966.

Marquis, Donald M. IN SEARCH OF BUDDY BOLDEN: FIRST MAN OF JAZZ. Louisiana State University Press, 1978, 1993.

Southern, Eileen. THE MUSIC OF BLACK AMERICANS: A HISTORY, 2nd ed. Norton, 1983.

Epstein, Dena J. SINFUL TUNES AND SPIRITUALS: BLACK FOLK MUSIC TO THE CIVIL WAR. University of Illinois Press, 1977.

Blassingame, John W. THE SLAVE COMMUNITY: PLANTATION LIFE IN THE ANTEBELLUM SOUTH. 2nd rev. enl. ed. Oxford University Press, 1979.

Koenig, Karl. "The Plantation Belt Brass Bands and Musicians." THE SECOND LINE, vol. 33 (1981): pages 24-40.
Note: THE SECOND LINE is published at Suite 265, 828 Royal Street, New Orleans, La 70116.

________. "Professor James B. Humphrey." THE SECOND LINE, vol. 34 (1982): pages 15-19.

________."Chris Kelly, Blues King of New Orleans." THE SECOND LINE, vol. 35 (spring 1983): pages 4-26.

________."Louisiana Brass Bands and History in Relation to Jazz History." THE SECOND LINE, vol. 35 (summer 1983): pages 7-15.

________."John Philip Sousa's Impact on Jazz." THE SECOND LINE, vol. 35 (winter 1983): pages 39-41.

________."Jack Laine 'Papa'." THE MISSISSIPPI RAG (March 1984): pages 1-6.
Note: THE MISSISSIPPI RAG is published at 5644 Morgan Ave. S., Minneapolis, Minnesota 55419.

Note: Informative summaries and bibliographies are included in H. Wiley Hitchcock and Stanley Sadie, eds., THE NEW GROVE DICTIONARY OF AMERICAN MUSIC, Macmillan, 1986. See entries for New Orleans, Blues, Traditional Jazz, Spirituals, and Ragtime, as well as the entries for particular musicians.

ALBUM LINER NOTES THAT SUMMARIZE PRE-JAZZ AND EARLY JAZZ RESEARCH

(annotator's name is in parentheses)

(the most useful items for a jazz course are listed first)

THE RIVERSIDE HISTORY OF CLASSIC JAZZ (Charles Edward Smith). Riverside/Fantasy: RB-005, 5LP set, 1956.

THE ROOTS OF THE BLUES (Alan Lomax). New World: 80252-2, CD, 1977.

STEPPIN' ON THE GAS: RAGS TO JAZZ 1913-1927 (Lawrence Gushee). New World: NW 269, LP, 1977.

Oliver, Joe "King." KING OLIVER'S JAZZ BAND, 1923 (Lawrence Gushee). Smithsonian: 2001, 2LP set, 1975.

Keppard, Freddie. LEGENDARY NEW ORLEANS CORNET (Lawrence Gushee). Smithsonian: 2020, LP, 1979?.

ROOTS OF BLACK MUSIC IN AMERICA (Samuel Charters). Smithsonian/Folkways: 2694, 2AC set, 1972.

COME AND TRIP IT: INSTRUMENTAL DANCE MUSIC 1780-1920's (Thorton Hagert). New World: NW 293, LP, 1978.

GEORGIA SEA ISLAND SONGS (Alan Lomax). New World: 80278-2, CD, 1977.

SOUND RECORDINGS TO AID IN UNDERSTANDING AFRICAN MUSIC

The following list is a brief compilation of available works that are relevant to connecting jazz and African music. It is far from definitive, but it could get you started if you need materials for an ethnomusicologically oriented course in jazz or Afro-American music. In pursuing the items on this list, note that ordinary record stores and most mail order houses do not sell these records, but you can get them from specialty houses and importers. Frequently it is best to order directly from mail order services (see attached addresses and phone numbers and page 78 of this manual; to obtain the French Ocora records, write Harmonia Mundi USA, 3364 S. Robertson Blvd., Los Angeles, CA 90034). If a large music library exists near you, it may be helpful to contact the reference librarian there for the names and addresses of dealers that service the library's ethnomusicology needs.

Many of the best recordings of African music and pre-jazz have been out of print for ages and are not listed here, though you might find them in libraries. One that is particularly worth seeking is ANTHOLOGY OF MUSIC OF BLACK AFRICA (Everest 3254/3, 2LP set), half of which was originally issued as MUSIQUE D' AFRIQUE OCCIDENTALE (French Vogue LVLX 193), and **currently** available as AFRICAN TRIBAL MUSIC AND DANCE: MUSIC OF THE MALINKE; MUSIC OF THE BAOULE AND OTHERS, Tradition: 2223, AC; or **AFRICAN TRIBAL MUSIC AND DANCES**, Legacy International: CD 328, CD.

> **NOTE**: If you choose illustrations not listed here, keep in mind that the music of Africa is very diverse, and that music from West Africa is the most relevant for your purposes. Try to stick to Gambia, Senegal, Guinea, Ivory Coast, Ghana, and Nigeria. Otherwise, you risk generalizing from music that may have had little or no influence on jazz because the culture that produced it contributed few slaves to America.

These records are all interesting, and most contain informative notes:

AFRICA, SOUTH OF THE SAHARA, Smithsonian/Folkways: 4503, 2AC set, 1957.
Compilation by Harold Courlander of numerous cultures, with richly detailed notes prepared by the eminent Africanist Alan P. Merriam; note that only some examples are from West Africa.

AFRICAN JOURNEY: A SEARCH FOR THE ROOTS OF THE BLUES, Vanguard: SRV 73014/5, 2LP set, 1975.
Compilation of various West African cultures visited by Samuel Charters and described in his travelogue: Charters, THE ROOTS OF THE BLUES: AN AFRICAN SEARCH, Salem, NH: Marion Boyars, 1981; Perigee, 1981.

BLACK MUSIC OF TWO WORLDS, Smithsonian/Folkways: 4602, 3AC set, 1977.
Contains music of Ghana, Sierra Leone, Liberia, as well as music from many areas of the New World; accompanies the book: John Storm Roberts, BLACK MUSIC OF TWO WORLDS, Praeger; Tivoli, NY: Original Music, 1972.

COTE D'IVOIRE: MUSIQUE DES BAOULE-KODE, Ocora: OCR 34, LP/AC, [1982].
The Baule people of the Ivory Coast.

GAMBIA'S MUSIC. Vol. 1, Smithsonian/Folkways: 4521, 2AC set, 1978.

THE GRIOTS: MINISTERS OF THE SPOKEN WORD, Smithsonian/Folkways: 4178, 2AC set, 1975.
Vocal music of Gambia, Senegal and Mali collected by Samuel Charters.

MASQUES DAN, Ocora: OCR 52, LP, 1965, 1967.
Music from Ivory Coast; French import distributed by Harmonia Mundi USA.

THE MUSIC OF NIGERIA: HAUSA MUSIC, UNESCO COLLECTION, ANTHOLOGY OF AFRICAN MUSIC, v. 6, Barenreiter Musicaphon: BM 30 L 2306, LP, [1965?].
The Hausa people of Nigeria.

MUSIC OF THE CAMEROONS, Folkways: 4372, AC, 1959.

THE MUSIC OF THE DAN, UNESCO COLLECTION, ANTHOLOGY OF AFRICAN MUSIC, v. 1, Barenreiter Musicaphon: BM 30 L 2301, LP, [1966].
People of Ivory Coast and Liberia.

THE MUSIC OF THE SENUFO, UNESCO COLLECTION, ANTHOLOGY OF AFRICAN MUSIC, v. 8, Barenreiter Musicaphon: BM 30 L 2308, LP, [1965].
People of Ivory Coast, Upper Volta & Mali.

MUSIQUES DU CAMEROUN, Ocora: OCR 25, LP/AC, 1965.
People of the Cameroons.

DRUMS OF WEST AFRICA: RITUAL MUSIC OF GHANA, Lyrichord: LLCT 7307, AC, 1974-76.
Music of the Ewe people; order from Lyrichord Discs, Inc., 141 Perry Street, New York, NY 10014; phone: 212-929-8234.

ROOTS OF BLACK MUSIC IN AMERICA, Smithsonian/Folkways: 2694, 2AC set, 1972.
Wide range of African and Afro-American music with lengthy and well-documented notes by Samuel Charters.

SONGS OF WAR AND DEATH FROM THE SLAVE COAST: ABUTIA KLOE, EWE, GHANA, Smithsonian/Folkways: 4258/4259, 2AC set, 1982.
Music of the Ewe people of Ghana.

TOGO: MUSIC FROM WEST AFRICA, Rounder: CD 5004, CD, 1978.
Music of the Ewe people; order from Rounder Records, One Camp Street, Cambridge, MA 02140; 617-354-0700.

WOLOF MUSIC OF SENEGAL AND THE GAMBIA, Smithsonian/Folkways: 4462, AC, 1955.

INDEX OF RECORDINGS CITED IN JAZZ STYLES

What follows is information to help you find recordings that are cited in JAZZ STYLES: HISTORY AND ANALYSIS. Music discussed in the text that is contained in THE SMITHSONIAN COLLECTION OF CLASSIC JAZZ is not covered in as much detail here because it is described within the *SCCJ* set. And there are few citations for many musicians whose work is available in *SCCJ*, especially those for whom *SCCJ* was the only citation in the text.

This is not a list of recommended "essential" albums, though most are indeed excellent. That "basic" list appears on page 1 in the text itself. What lies here is simply information that would not fit in the textbook itself and/or would be more convenient if compiled separately. **THE APPORTIONMENT OF CONTENTS HERE SHOULD NOT BE CONSTRUED AS AN INDEX FOR THE RELATIVE IMPORTANCE OF ANY MUSICIANS.** The entries for Duke Ellington, Miles Davis, and Stan Kenton, for example, far outnumber those for other players who are equally important. Frequently, as with Ellington, Davis and Kenton, the number of entries listed for a particular musician reflects only the number of selections cited in the text passages devoted to those particular musicians, and some text passages have more record citations per page than other text passages have. Consequently there are more albums listed here for the musicians treated in those passages than for musicians treated in other passages. Some entries represent my own self-imposed, but not entirely adhered to, requirement to try to recommend at least one representative work for each musician or band that is mentioned in the text. And some selections are merely updated entries for recordings cited in the first edition of JAZZ STYLES, even though they are not cited in this current edition. Such updating is for the convenience of those listeners who are still seeking recordings that were mentioned in the first edition and have since been reissued in altered form. Current catalog numbers and reissues have been added to or substituted for older ones that were listed in the first edition's discography.

An additional feature of this discography is the inclusion of album lists under a major player's name which illustrate his stylistic development in the context of albums under other bandleaders' names. For example, the John Coltrane section cites a Dizzy Gillespie album that features an early Coltrane solo; the Chick Corea section contains Herbie Mann albums that feature early Corea solos.

For the convenience of readers who are interested in big band arranging, Count Basie and Stan Kenton albums are organized by arrangers. Note that as we went to press, many Stan Kenton albums on Creative World were still available by mail from GNP Crescendo Records, 8400 Sunset Blvd., Hollywood, CA 90069; phone: 1-800-654-7029; 213-656-2614.

All the albums listed in this discography are available to anyone willing to seek out quality record stores or contact the mail order firms listed below. The author knows several individuals who bought the first edition of JAZZ STYLES in 1978, and, by now, have acquired every album they wanted that was mentioned in that book's discography. They watched for reissues, followed auction lists and corresponded with the mail order firms that were listed in the text's Guide To Record Buying. Record dealers and importers are listed on page 78. For out-of-print recordings contact the rare record dealers and auction lists on page 399 of your text and page 78 of this manual with your want list and be persistent.

I am very grateful for the professional effort of William E. Anderson in updating and editing this discography. Bill's advice and assistance have been indispensable in the preparation of all editions of JAZZ STYLES as well as this teachers' manual.

Regarding Asterisked Recordings

Throughout JAZZ STYLES: HISTORY AND ANALYSIS, it is sometimes necessary to cite out-of-print recordings. One reason is that many historically significant recordings were not in print at press time. Another reason is that recommending only current issues would be an unintentional disservice to the musician who has no work in print at press time or whose best work is yet to be reissued. Given a choice between an out-of-print record representing a player's best work and a current one which does not do the player justice, the out-of-print one has been listed. Then personnel, tune titles, and recording dates are included so that if the item is reissued, you can recognize it. You can look for the original copy in libraries, used record stores, rare record dealers, and the cut-out bins which sometimes appear in record stores and other stores. (It is very helpful to subscribe to jazz magazines that run record sales and list auctions and rare record finding services. Two good ones are CODA, Box 87, Station J, Toronto, Ontario, M4J 4X8, Canada; and CADENCE, Cadence Building, Redwood, New York 13679-9612.) For helpful strategies in obtaining jazz albums, especially out-of-print items, consult the Guide to Album Buying which appears on pages 392-399 of JAZZ STYLES (5th edition). Also see the list of importers and record dealers on page 78 of this manual.

For information about the availability of recordings, the following may be useful:

Spectrum (published quarterly by Schwann Publications, P.O. Box 55442, Boulder, CO 80322, 1-800-234-3373, and available at some record stores, newsstands, and libraries)

Phonolog (published by Trade Service Corp., 10996 Torreyana Rd., San Diego, CA 92121-1192, 619-457-5920; available in some record stores and libraries).

Some of the records listed here might be out-of-print by the time you read this, so the details attached to the entries constitute your key to finding them in reissued form. Chances are good that, within a few years of your reading this, some important works that were out-of-print -- denoted by an asterisk (*) -- will have been reissued. In the following discography, the most recent issue number is listed first. Original and/or alternate release numbers are listed in parentheses. **See the Key on page 79.**

INFORMATION FOR MAIL ORDER LABELS

Smithsonian Recordings
P.O. Box 2071
Colchester, VT 05449-2071
1-800-669-1559

Creative World (Kenton)
c/o GNP Crescendo Records
8400 Sunset Blvd.
Hollywood, CA 90069
1-800-654-7029

Mosaic Records
35 Melrose Place
Stamford, CT 06902-7533
tel: 203-327-7111
fax: 203-323-3526

Mobile Fidelity
P.O. Box 1657
Sebastopol, CA 95472-1657
1-800-423-5759

Smithsonian/Folkways Recordings (for Folkways label)
414 Hungerford Drive; Suite 444
Rockville, MD 20850
tel: 301-443-2314
fax: 301-443-1819

New World Records
701 Seventh Avenue
NYC, NY 10036
tel: 212-302-0460
fax: 212-944-1922

The Recorded Anthology of American Music on New World Records has been distributed to many libraries. Some titles can still be ordered from this address.

MAIL ORDER SOURCES FOR JAZZ RECORDINGS (INCLUDING IMPORTS)

Cadence
Cadence Building
Redwood, NY 13679-9612
tel: 315-287-2852
fax: 315-287-2860

Roundup Records
One Camp Street
Cambridge, MA 02140-1194
tel: 617-661-6308
fax: 617-868-8769

Roots & Rhythm
6921 Stockton Ave.
El Cerrito, CA 94530
tel: 510-525-1494
fax: 510-525-2904

"Double-Time" Jazz
P.O. Box 1244
New Albany, IN 47151
tel: 1-800-293-8528
fax: 812-949-2006

Stash-Daybreak M.O.
140 W. 22nd Street, 12th Floor Front
New York, NY 10011
tel: 1-800-666-JASS
fax: 212-243-4483

LIBRARIES AND INSTITUTIONS ONLY

Audio Buff Co., Inc.
P.O. Box 2628
Athens, OH 45701-5428
tel: 614-593-3014
fax: 614-592-6693

Harmonia Mundi USA, Inc.
3364 S. Robertson Blvd.
Los Angeles, CA 90034
tel: 310-559-0802
fax: 310-837-4150

KOCH International Corp.
177 Cantiague Rock Road
Westbury, NY 11590
tel: 516-938-8080
fax: 516-938-8055

FOR OUT-OF-PRINT RECORDINGS AND AUCTION LISTS

The Record Finder
P.O. Box 1047
Glen Allen, VA 23060

Jazz Etc.
P.O.Box 393
Bergenfield, NJ 07621

RECORD RESEARCH (magazine)
65 Grand Ave.
Brooklyn, NY 11205
718-857-7003

International Association of Jazz Record Collectors
P.O. Box 800
Grand Central Station
New York, NY 10163

KEY TO INFORMATION IN DISCOGRAPHY

artist **title** **alternate title** **label & current catalog number** **original issue number**

CANNONBALL ADDERLEY

* CANNONBALL & COLTRANE(QUINTET IN CHICAGO), Mercury: 834588-2 (MG-20449), CD, 1959; with John Coltrane, Wynton Kelly, Paul Chambers, and Jimmy Cobb: Limehouse Blues, Stars Fell on Alabama, Grand Central.

year recorded

format available
CD = compact disc
LP = long-playing record
AC = audio cassette

personnel

selected tunes from session

*** = out of print (1993)**

CANNONBALL ADDERLEY (ALTO SAX)

CANNONBALL & COLTRANE (QUINTET IN CHICAGO), Emarcy: 834588-2 (MG-20449), CD, 1959.
with John Coltrane, Wynton Kelly, Paul Chambers, and Jimmy Cobb: Limehouse Blues, Stars Fell on Alabama, Grand Central, etc.

THEM DIRTY BLUES, Landmark: 1301 (Riverside RLP 322), CD/LP/AC, 1960.
with Nat Adderley, Barry Harris or Bobby Timmons, Sam Jones, and Louis Hayes: Jeannine, Dat Dere, and Del Sasser.

CANNONBALL IN EUROPE, Landmark: 1307 (Riverside RLP-499), CD/LP/AC, 1962.
with Nat Adderley, Yusef Lateef, Joe Zawinul, Sam Jones, and Louis Hayes.

* MERCY, MERCY, MERCY, Capitol: 16153 (ST 2663), 1966.
(live) with Nat Adderley, Joe Zawinul, Victor Gaskin, and Roy McCurdy; recommended not for its popular title track, Mercy, Mercy, Mercy, but for some blazing solos and driving rhythm section on Fun that seems to show roots in both the hard bop style of the 1950's and Coltrane's methods of the 1960's.

see MILES DAVIS - BASIC MILES, MILES AND COLTRANE, MILESTONES, '58 SESSIONS, and KIND OF BLUE
see ANTHOLOGIES - THE SMITHSONIAN COLLECTION OF CLASSIC JAZZ

HENRY RED ALLEN (TRUMPET)

* HENRY RED ALLEN AND COLEMAN HAWKINS, Smithsonian: 2022, 1933.

1933-1935, Classics: 551, CD, 1933-1935. (import - see page 78)
Body and Soul, etc.

see FLETCHER HENDERSON
see LUIS RUSSELL
see ANTHOLOGIES - TRUMPETER'S HOLIDAY

GENE AMMONS (TENOR SAX)

Gene Ammons/Sonny Stitt - BOSS TENORS (PRIME CUTS), Verve: 837440-2 (2V6S-8812/MGV 8426), CD, 1961.
Blues Up and Down, etc.

LOUIS ARMSTRONG (TRUMPET)

* LOUIS ARMSTRONG & SIDNEY BECHET IN NEW YORK, Smithsonian: 2026, 1923-25.
Wild Cat Blues, Cake Walkin' Babies, etc.

THE HOT FIVES, VOL. 1, Columbia: 44049, CD/AC, 1925-26.
THE HOT FIVES & HOT SEVENS, VOL. 2, Columbia: 44253, CD/AC, 1926-27.
THE HOT FIVES & HOT SEVENS, VOL. 3, Columbia: 44422, CD/AC, 1927-28.
LOUIS ARMSTRONG & EARL HINES, VOL. 4, Columbia: 45142, CD/AC, 1928.
1: Heebie Jeebies, Cornet Chop Suey, and King of the Zulus; 2: Big Butter & Egg Man, Wild Man Blues, Alligator Crawl, Potato Head Blues, and Twelfth Street Rag; 3: S.O.L. Blues, Struttin' with Some Barbecue, I'm Not Rough, Hotter Than That, Fireworks, Skip the Gutter, and Monday Date; 4: West End Blues, Weatherbird, Muggles, etc.

* LOUIS ARMSTRONG STORY VOLS. 1-4, Columbia: CL 851/854, 1926-31.

* LOUIS ARMSTRONG AND EARL HINES, Smithsonian: 2002, 1928.

LAUGHIN' LOUIE, RCA Bluebird: 9759 (AXM2-5515), CD/AC, 1932-33.

see KING OLIVER
see BESSIE SMITH
see ANTHOLOGIES - THE SMITHSONIAN COLLECTION OF CLASSIC JAZZ

ART ENSEMBLE OF CHICAGO

A JACKSON IN YOUR HOUSE, Affinity: 752 (AFF9/Actuel BYG 2), CD, 1969. (import - see page 78).
with Roscoe Mitchell, Joseph Jarman, Lester Bowie, and Malachi Favors.

PEOPLE IN SORROW, Nessa: N-3, LP, 1969.

NICE GUYS, ECM: 827876 (1126), CD/AC, 1978.

URBAN BUSHMEN, ECM: 829394-2 (2-1211), 2CD set, 1980 concert.

ALBERT AYLER (TENOR SAX)

* MY NAME IS ALBERT AYLER, Fantasy: 86016, 1963.
with Neils Bronsted, Neils-Henning Orsted Pedersen, and Ronnie Gardiner: Billie's Bounce.

SPIRITUAL UNITY, ESP-DISK: 1002, 1964.
with Gary Peacock and Sunny Murray: Ghosts, The Wizard, and Spirits; all tunes composed by Ayler.

CHET BAKER (TRUMPET)

* SMOKIN' WITH THE CHET BAKER QUINTET, Prestige: 7449, 1965.

see GERRY MULLIGAN - BEST and COMPLETE PACIFIC JAZZ RECORDINGS
see ART PEPPER - COMPLETE PACIFIC JAZZ

COUNT BASIE (PIANO/BIG BAND)

THE COMPLETE DECCA RECORDINGS, Decca Jazz/GRP: GRD3-611, 3CD set, 1937-39.
One O'Clock Jump, Jumpin' at Woodside, Topsy, Jive at Five, Cherokee, etc.

ONE O'CLOCK JUMP, Decca Jazz/MCA: 42324, CD/AC/LP, 1937.
One O'Clock Jump, Topsy, etc.

BEST OF COUNT BASIE, MCA: MCAC2-4050 (Decca DXSB 7170), 2AC set, 1937-39.
big band: One O'Clock Jump, Jumpin' at the Woodside, Topsy, Jive at Five, Cherokee, etc.

THE ESSENTIAL COUNT BASIE, VOL. 1, Columbia: 40608, CD/AC, 1936-39.
THE ESSENTIAL COUNT BASIE, VOL. 2, Columbia: 40835, CD/AC, 1939-40.
Lady Be Good, Taxi War Dance (v. 1); and Lester Leaps In (v. 2).

THE COMPLETE ROULETTE STUDIO RECORDINGS OF COUNT BASIE AND HIS ORCHESTRA, Mosaic: MD10-149/10CD set, MQ15-149/15LP set, 1957-61.
includes all of the following albums listed on the next page: KANSAS CITY SUITE, THE LEGEND, BASIE, BASIE PLAYS HEFTI, ONE MORE TIME, and CHAIRMAN OF THE BOARD. (mail order - see page 78)

see LESTER YOUNG - STORY
see ANTHOLOGIES - ANTHOLOGY OF BIG BAND SWING, BIG BAND JAZZ, JAZZ PIANO, JIVE AT FIVE, and SMITHSONIAN COLLECTION OF CLASSIC JAZZ

(the following list of Basie recordings is organized by arranger)

BILLY BYERS

- * MORE HITS OF THE 50s AND 60s, Verve: V-8563, 1963.
  The Second Time Around, I'll Never Smile Again, In the Wee Small Hours, Come Fly with Me, etc.

- * BASIE LAND, Verve: V-8597, 1963.
  Basie Land, Rabble Rouser, Instant Blues, etc.

BENNY CARTER

- KANSAS CITY SUITE, Roulette: 94575 (52056/RE-124), CD, 1960.
  Vine Street Rumble, Katy Do, The Wiggle Walk, etc.

- * THE LEGEND, Roulette: 59038 (52086/RE-118), 1961.
  The Swizzle, The Trot, The Legend, etc.

NEAL HEFTI

- * BASIE (ATOMIC BASIE), Roulette: 52003, 1957.
  Fantail, Lil' Darlin', etc.

- * BASIE PLAYS HEFTI, Roulette: 52011, 1958.
  Cute, Ponytail, Sloofoot, etc.

- * ON MY WAY AND SHOUTIN' AGAIN, Verve: V-8511, 1962.
  I'm Shoutin' Again, Jump for Johnny, Skippin' with Skitch, Ducky Bumps, etc.

QUINCY JONES

- ONE MORE TIME, Roulette: 97271 (52024), CD, 1958-59.
  For Lena and Lennie, Jessica's Day, The Midnight Sun Will Never Set, etc.

- LI'L OL' GROOVEMAKER, Verve: 821799-2 (V-8549), CD, 1963.
  Li'l Ol' Groovemaker, Nasty Magnus, Count 'Em, etc.

THAD JONES

- * CHAIRMAN OF THE BOARD, Roulette: 52032, 1959.
  Thad Jones wrote The Deacon, Mutt and Jeff, Speaking of Sounds, and Her Royal Highness.

SAMMY NESTICO

- * STRAIGHT AHEAD, MCA: 29004 (Dot 25902), 1967.
  Basie-Straight Ahead, Switch in Time, and The Queen Bee.

- * HAVE A NICE DAY, Emarcy: 824867 (Daybreak 2005), 1971.
  Have a Nice Day, Scott's Place, You 'n' Me, etc.

ERNIE WILKINS

- DANCE SESSIONS, Verve: 314 521648-2 (MGC-626/MGC-647), CD, 1953-54.
  Sixteen Men Swingin' and She's Just My Size.

- * HALL OF FAME, Verve: MGV 8291, 1956.
  Blues Inside Out, Big Red, Trick or Treat, and Flute Juice.

SIDNEY BECHET (CLARINET/SOPRANO SAX)

LEGENDARY SIDNEY BECHET, RCA Bluebird: 6590, CD/AC, 1932-41.
I've Found a New Baby, Weary Blues, and Maple Leaf Rag with Willie The Lion Smith; When It's Sleepy Time Down South with Gus Aiken and Sandy Williams; The Sheik of Araby, with Bechet playing every instrument (clarinet, soprano sax, tenor sax, piano, bass, and drums).

THE VICTOR SESSIONS/MASTER TAKES, RCA Bluebird: 2402, 3CD/3AC set, 1932-43.

* THE COMPLETE BLUE NOTE RECORDINGS OF SIDNEY BECHET, Mosaic: MD4-110/ 4CD set, MR6-110/6LP set, 1939-53.
* SIDNEY BECHET JAZZ CLASSICS, Vol. 1, Blue Note: 81201, 1939-46.
Milenberg Joys (1945) with Bunk Johnson and Pops Foster; Summertime (1939) with Meade Lux Lewis, Teddy Bunn, Sid Catlett, etc.

see LOUIS ARMSTRONG - ARMSTRONG & BECHET IN NEW YORK
see EARL HINES - PIANO MAN

BIX BEIDERBECKE (CORNET)

BIX BEIDERBECKE, VOL. 1: SINGIN' THE BLUES, Columbia: 45450 (CL 845), CD/AC.
1927-28 sessions by Beiderbecke with Frankie Trumbauer, Joe Venuti, Eddie Lang, and others: Singin' the Blues, etc.

BIX BEIDERBECKE, VOL. 2: AT THE JAZZ BAND BALL, Columbia: 46175, CD/AC, 1927-1928.
A Good Man Is Hard to Find, Mississippi Mud, etc.

* THE BIX BEIDERBECKE STORY, VOL. 3: WHITEMAN DAYS, Columbia: CL 846.
sessions of Bix with the 1928-29 Paul Whiteman Orchestra: Sweet Sue and China Boy; a piano solo by Beiderbecke called In a Mist; and 1928-29 combo dates including Margie with Frankie Trumbauer.

BIX LIVES!, RCA Bluebird: 6845, CD/AC, 1927-30.
with Jean Goldkette, Paul Whiteman, and own groups.

see ANTHOLOGIES - THE SMITHSONIAN COLLECTION OF CLASSIC JAZZ, BIG BAND JAZZ

BUNNY BERIGAN (TRUMPET)

* COMPLETE BUNNY BERIGAN, VOL. 1, RCA Bluebird: 5584, 1937.
I Can't Get Started and Caravan with Berigan's big band.

see TOMMY DORSEY - THIS IS

ART BLAKEY (DRUMS/BANDLEADER)

A NIGHT AT BIRDLAND, VOLS. 1 & 2, Blue Note: 46519/46520 (81521/22), CD, 1954. live recordings with Clifford Brown, Lou Donaldson, Horace Silver, and Curly Russell: Split Kick, Confirmation, Once in a While, Night in Tunisia, Quicksilver, etc.; some volatile moments in Blakey's drum style. Silver's piano style is more Bud Powell-like here than the leaner conception Silver employed later.

* JAZZ MESSENGERS, Columbia: PC 37021 (CL 897), 1956.
with Donald Byrd, Hank Mobley, and Horace Silver; excellent Byrd work and two Silver compositions. This LP is recommended for some of the most well-constructed solos of Hank Mobley's career: Ecaroh, Nica's Dream (both by Silver); Carol's Interlude, Hank's Symphony, and Infra-Rae (all by Mobley).

THE JAZZ MESSENGER, Columbia: 47118, CD/AC, 1956.
compilation which includes all of the above except Nica's Dream.

COMPLETE BLUE NOTE RECORDINGS OF ART BLAKEY'S 1960 JAZZ MESSENGERS, Mosaic: MD6-141/6CD set, MR10-141/10LP set, 1960-61. (mail order - see page 78)
with Lee Morgan, Wayne Shorter, and Bobby Timmons.

A NIGHT IN TUNISIA, Blue Note: 84049, CD, 1960.
with Morgan, Shorter, and Timmons.

MOSAIC, Blue Note: 46523 (84090), CD, 1961.
with Freddie Hubbard, Curtis Fuller, Wayne Shorter, and Cedar Walton.

THREE BLIND MICE, VOLS. 1 & 2, Blue Note: 84451/84452, 2CDs, 1962.
with Hubbard, Fuller, Shorter, and Cedar Walton.

CARAVAN, Fantasy: OJC-038 (Riverside RLP-9438), CD/LP/AC, 1962.
UGETSU, Fantasy: OJC-090 (RLP-9464), CD/LP/AC, 1963.
live recordings with Hubbard, Fuller, and Shorter.

INDESTRUCTIBLE, Blue Note: 46429 (84193), CD, 1964.
with Lee Morgan, Wayne Shorter, and Curtis Fuller.

see HORACE SILVER AND THE JAZZ MESSENGERS
see ANTHOLOGIES - NICA'S DREAM

PAUL BLEY (PIANO)

* PAUL BLEY AT THE HILLCREST CLUB, Inner City: 1007, 1958.
with Ornette Coleman, Don Cherry, Charlie Haden, and Billy Higgins; includes Charlie Parker's Klactoveesedstene.

TURNING POINT, Improvising Artists: 123841-2 (373841), CD, 1964.
* TURNS, Savoy: 1192 (2235), 1964.
with John Gilmore, Gary Peacock, and Paul Motian.

see JIMMY GIUFFRE - 1961 and FREE FALL
see ANTHOLOGIES - MASTERS OF THE MODERN PIANO

BLOOD SWEAT AND TEARS

* CHILD IS FATHER TO THE MAN, Columbia: 9619, 1967.
BLOOD SWEAT AND TEARS, Columbia: 9720, CD/LP/AC, 1968.

ANTHONY BRAXTON (ALTO SAX, MULTI-INSTRUMENTALIST)

THREE COMPOSITIONS OF NEW JAZZ, Delmark: 415, CD/LP, 1968.
with Leo Smith, Leroy Jenkins, and Richard Abrams.

FOR ALTO, Delmark: DS-420/421, 2LP set, 1968, solo.

* FIVE PIECES 1975, Arista: 4064, 1975.

CREATIVE ORCHESTRA MUSIC, RCA Bluebird: 6579-2-RB (Arista 4080), CD, 1976.

* FOR 4 ORCHESTRAS, Arista: 8900, 1978, four orchestras at Oberlin.

see DAVE HOLLAND - CONFERENCE OF THE BIRDS

MICHAEL AND RANDY BRECKER (TENOR SAX/TRUMPET)

see HORACE SILVER - IN PURSUIT OF THE 27TH MAN

BOB BROOKMEYER (TROMBONE)

see JIMMY GIUFFRE - TRAVELIN' LIGHT and WESTERN SUITE
see THAD JONES - PRESENTING THAD JONES-MEL LEWIS AND THE JAZZ ORCHESTRA
see GERRY MULLIGAN - CONCERT JAZZ BAND
see ZOOT SIMS - ONE TO BLOW ON

CLIFFORD BROWN (TRUMPET)

* COMPLETE BLUE NOTE AND PACIFIC JAZZ RECORDINGS OF CLIFFORD BROWN, Mosaic: MR5-104, 5LP set, 1953-54.

BROWNIE/THE COMPLETE EMARCY RECORDINGS OF CLIFFORD BROWN, Emarcy: 838306-2, 10CD set, 1954-56.

CLIFFORD BROWN AND MAX ROACH, Emarcy: 814645-2 (MG-36036), CD, 1954.
with Harold Land, Richie Powell, and George Morrow: What Am I Here For? (Ellington), Delilah (Victor Young), Jordu (Duke Jordan), Parisian Thoroughfare (Powell), and Brown's Daahoud, Joy Spring, and Blues Walk.

CLIFFORD BROWN AND MAX ROACH AT BASIN STREET, Emarcy: 814648-2 (MG-36070), CD, 1956.
with Sonny Rollins: What Is This Thing Called Love.

see ART BLAKEY - A NIGHT AT BIRDLAND
see J.J. JOHNSON - EMINENT
see SONNY ROLLINS - PLUS FOUR
see ANTHOLOGIES - BEBOP

JAMES BROWN (R&B-FUNK BAND)

STAR TIME, Polydor: 849108, 4CD/4AC set, 1956-1974.
20 ALL TIME GREATEST HITS, Polydor: 314 511326, CD/AC, 1956-74.
* THE CD OF JB II, Polydor: 831700-2, 1959-76.
all of the above include Cold Sweat (1967).

DAVE BRUBECK (PIANO)

THE DAVE BRUBECK OCTET, Fantasy: OJC-101 (Fantasy 3-239), CD/LP/AC, 1946-49.
with Dick Collins, Bob Collins, Paul Desmond, Bob Cummings, Dave Van Kriedt, Bill Smith, Dave Brubeck, Ron Crotty, and Cal Tjader: The Way You Look Tonight, Love Walked In, What Is This Thing Called Love?, September in the Rain, Prelude, Fugue on Bop Themes, Let's Fall in Love, IPCA, How High the Moon, Serenades Suite, Playland-at-the-Beach, Prisoner's Song, Schizophrenic Scherzo, Rondo, I Hear a Rhapsody, You Go to My Head, Laura, and Closing Theme; some of these arrangements sound like the BIRTH OF THE COOL arrangements, historically interesting in light of the fact that these were made before the Miles Davis Nonet recorded.

JAZZ AT OBERLIN, Fantasy: OJC-046 (Fantasy 3-245), CD/LP/AC, 1953.
concert with Paul Desmond: These Foolish Things, Perdido, and How High the Moon.

GONE WITH THE WIND, Columbia: 40627 (CL 1347), CD/AC, 1959.
with Desmond, Gene Wright, and Joe Morello: Georgia on My Mind and Basin Street Blues;

TIME OUT, Columbia: 40585 (CL 1397), CD/AC, 1959.
with Desmond and Morello: Take Five and Blue Rondo Ala Turk.

TIME FURTHER OUT, Columbia: 8490 (CL 1690), AC, 1961.

MILT BUCKNER (PIANO)

see LIONEL HAMPTON - STEPPIN' OUT, FLYING HOME, and MIDNIGHT SUN.

KENNY BURRELL (GUITAR)

KENNY BURRELL & JOHN COLTRANE, Fantasy: OJC-300 (NJ 8276), CD/LP/AC, 1958.
with Tommy Flanagan, Paul Chambers, and Jimmy Cobb: Lyresto, Big Paul, etc.

see THAD JONES - DETROIT-N.Y. JUNCTION
see JIMMY SMITH - MIDNIGHT SPECIAL

GARY BURTON (VIBRAHARP)

* DUSTER, RCA: LSP-3835, 1967.
with Larry Coryell, Steve Swallow, and Roy Haynes.

* LOFTY FAKE ANAGRAM, RCA: LSP-3901, 1967.
with Coryell, Swallow, and Bob Moses.

* ARTIST'S CHOICE, RCA Bluebird: 6280-2-RB, 1963-68.

CRYSTAL SILENCE, ECM: 831331 (1024), CD/AC, 1972.
duets with Chick Corea.

RING, ECM: 829191-2 (1051), CD, 1974.
with Mick Goodrick, Pat Metheny, and Eberhard Weber.

DREAMS SO REAL, ECM: 833329-2 (1072), CD, 1975.
with Goodrick and Metheny; compositions of Carla Bley.

DON BYAS (TENOR SAX)

see DIZZY GILLESPIE - DIZZIEST
see ANTHOLOGIES - THE BEBOP REVOLUTION and THE SMITHSONIAN COLLECTION OF CLASSIC JAZZ

DONALD BYRD (TRUMPET)

see ART BLAKEY - JAZZ MESSENGER

CAB CALLOWAY (SINGER/BANDLEADER)

* 16 CAB CALLOWAY CLASSICS, CBS (France): 62950, 1939-41.
includes Dizzy Gillespie's solo on Pickin' the Cabbage and Milt Hinton's solo on Pluckin' the Bass.

BEST OF THE BIG BANDS, Columbia: 45336, CD/AC, 1932-42.
includes Pickin' the Cabbage.

CONTE CANDOLI (TRUMPET)

see STAN KENTON - NEW CONCEPTS OF ARTISTRY IN RHYTHM

BENNY CARTER (ALTO SAX/ARRANGER)

BENNY CARTER-OSCAR PETERSON, Verve: 314 521673-2 (MGV8226), CD, 1952, 1954.
included for Carter solos which get my vote for his best on record: Poinciana and A Foggy Day.

JAZZ GIANT, Fantasy: OJC-167 (Contemporary 7555), CD/LP/AC, 1957-58.
with Ben Webster, Frank Rosolino, and Shelley Manne.

FURTHER DEFINITIONS, MCA/Impulse: MCAD-5651 (A-12), CD, 1961.
with Phil Woods, Coleman Hawkins, Charlie Rouse, etc.

see COUNT BASIE - list of Basie arrangers - BENNY CARTER
see COLEMAN HAWKINS - GIANTS OF THE TENOR SAX
see ANTHOLOGIES - ALTO SAXES, BIG BAND JAZZ, SMITHSONIAN COLLECTION OF CLASSIC JAZZ, and THREE GREAT SWING SAXOPHONISTS

RON CARTER (BASS)

see MILES DAVIS - SEVEN STEPS TO HEAVEN, IN EUROPE, COMPLETE CONCERT 1964, HEARD 'ROUND THE WORLD, E.S.P., MILES SMILES, SORCERER, NEFERTITI, MILES IN THE SKY, and FILLES DE KILIMANJARO
see ERIC DOLPHY - FAR CRY
see HERBIE HANCOCK - EMPYREAN ISLES and MAIDEN VOYAGE
see JOE HENDERSON - TETRAGON and POWER TO THE PEOPLE
see WAYNE SHORTER - SPEAK NO EVIL

PAUL CHAMBERS (BASS)

see CANNONBALL ADDERLEY - CANNONBALL & COLTRANE
see KENNY BURRELL - KENNY BURRELL & JOHN COLTRANE
see JOHN COLTRANE - BLUE TRAIN, TRANEING IN, SOULTRANE, and GIANT STEPS
see MILES DAVIS - COLLECTOR'S ITEMS, NEW QUINTET, WORKIN', STEAMIN', COOKIN', RELAXIN', ROUND ABOUT MIDNIGHT, BASIC MILES, MILES AND COLTRANE, MILESTONES, '58 SESSIONS, KIND OF BLUE, SOMEDAY MY PRINCE WILL COME, FRIDAY NIGHT, SATURDAY NIGHT, and AT CARNEGIE HALL

DON CHERRY (TRUMPET)

THE COMPLETE BLUE NOTE RECORDINGS OF DON CHERRY, Mosaic: MD2-145/2CD set, MQ3-145/3LP set, 1965-66. (mail order - see page 78)

* COMPLETE COMMUNION, Blue Note: 84226, 1965.
with Gato Barbieri, Henry Grimes, and Ed Blackwell: Complete Communion, Elephantasy, etc. COMPLETE COMMUNION is recommended for Cherry's compositions and his work as a leader, and for some of tenor saxophonist Gato Barbieri's best playing on record. The Mosaic set also includes SYMPHONY FOR IMPROVISERS and WHERE IS BROOKLYN?.

* ETERNAL NOW, Antilles: 7034, 1973.

see ORNETTE COLEMAN - SOMETHING ELSE, BEAUTY IS A RARE THING, THE SHAPE OF JAZZ TO COME, CHANGE OF THE CENTURY, and FREE JAZZ
see SONNY ROLLINS - ON THE OUTSIDE
see ANTHOLOGIES - THE SMITHSONIAN COLLECTION OF CLASSIC JAZZ

CHICAGO

CHICAGO TRANSIT AUTHORITY, Columbia: 8, CD/AC, 1969.
CHICAGO'S GREATEST HITS, Columbia: 33900, CD/AC, 1969-1975.

CHARLIE CHRISTIAN (GUITAR)

GENIUS OF THE ELECTRIC GUITAR, Columbia: 40846 (CL 652), CD/AC, 1939-41.
performances by guitarist Charlie Christian in the context of the Benny Goodman big band and small groups.

CHARLIE CHRISTIAN & DIZZY GILLESPIE (LIVE SESSIONS), Vogue: 600135 or Jazz Anthology: 550012 (Everest 219), CD, 1941.
LIVE: 1939-41, Music Memoria: 34009, CD, 1939-41.
SWING TO BOP, Natasha: 4020, CD, 1941.
(imports - see page 78)
Note: The above all contain the 1941 Minton's Playhouse jam session in New York City featuring Charlie Christian, Dizzy Gillespie, Thelonious Monk, and Kenny Clarke.

HOT LIPS PAGE AND JOE GUY: TRUMPET BATTLE AT MINTON'S, Xanadu: 107, LP, 1941; with Charlie Christian and Thelonious Monk.

see BENNY GOODMAN - SEXTET FEATURING CHRISTIAN
see ANTHOLOGIES - SMITHSONIAN COLLECTION OF CLASSIC JAZZ

KENNY CLARKE (DRUMS)

see MILES DAVIS - BIRTH OF THE COOL, WALKIN', BAG'S GROOVE, and MODERN JAZZ GIANTS
see DIZZY GILLESPIE - SHAW NUFF
see J.J. JOHNSON - EMINENT
see MODERN JAZZ QUARTET - DJANGO
see ANTHOLOGIES - THE BEBOP REVOLUTION, JAZZ IN REVOLUTION, and SMITHSONIAN COLLECTION OF CLASSIC JAZZ

JOHN COATES (PIANO)

* THE PIANO SOUND OF JOHN COATES, Omnisound: 1004, 1974.
influence on Keith Jarrett.

JIMMY COBB (DRUMS)

see CANNONBALL ADDERLEY - CANNONBALL & COLTRANE
see KENNY BURRELL - KENNY BURRELL & JOHN COLTRANE
see MILES DAVIS - MILES AND COLTRANE, '58 SESSIONS, KIND OF BLUE, SOMEDAY MY PRINCE WILL COME, FRIDAY NIGHT, SATURDAY NIGHT, and AT CARNEGIE HALL

NAT COLE (PIANO)

HIT THAT JIVE, JACK: THE EARLIEST RECORDINGS, Decca Jazz/MCA: 42350, CD/AC, 1940-41.
trio with Oscar Moore and Wesley Prince.

THE COMPLETE CAPITOL RECORDINGS OF THE NAT KING COLE TRIO, Mosaic: MD18-138/18CD set, MR27-138/27LP set, 1942-61. (mail order - see page 78)

BEST OF THE NAT KING COLE TRIO: INSTRUMENTAL CLASSICS, Capitol: 98288 (11033), CD/AC, 1944-49.
1944-47: Oscar Moore & Johnny Miller; 1949: Irving Ashby & Joe Comfort.

see ANTHOLOGIES - JAZZ PIANO

ORNETTE COLEMAN (ALTO SAX)

SOMETHING ELSE!, Fantasy: OJC-163 (Contemporary 7551), CD/LP/AC, 1958.
with Don Cherry, Walter Norris, Don Payne, and Billy Higgins; all tunes composed by Coleman: Invisible, The Blessing, When Will the Blues Leave?, etc.

BEAUTY IS A RARE THING: THE COMPLETE ATLANTIC RECORDINGS, Rhino/Atlantic: R2 71410, 6CD set, 1959-61.

THE SHAPE OF JAZZ TO COME, Atlantic: 1317 (19238), CD/AC, 1959.
with Don Cherry, Charlie Haden, and Billy Higgins: Lonely Woman, Congeniality, and Peace.

CHANGE OF THE CENTURY, Atlantic: 81341 (1327), CD/AC, 1959.
with Cherry, Haden and Higgins: Ramblin', etc.

FREE JAZZ, Atlantic: 1364, CD/AC, 1960.
recording of one, uninterrupted, collective improvisation employing very little preset structure; with Ornette Coleman, Eric Dolphy, Don Cherry, Freddie Hubbard, Scott LaFaro, Charlie Haden, Billy Higgins, and Ed Blackwell.

AT THE GOLDEN CIRCLE, VOL. 1, Blue Note: 84224, CD, 1965.
concert by Coleman, David Izenzon, and Charles Moffett: Faces and Places, European Echoes, Dee Dee, and Dawn.

FORMS & SOUNDS: THE MUSIC OF ORNETTE COLEMAN, RCA Bluebird: 6561-2-RB (LSC-2982), CD, 1968.
includes Coleman's Forms and Sounds, played by the Philadelphia Woodwind Quintet, trumpet interludes played by Coleman; and Saints and Soldiers and Space Flight played by the Chamber Symphony of Philadelphia Quartet.

* SKIES OF AMERICA, Columbia: 31562 (33669), 1972.
Coleman's writing performed by the London Symphony Orchestra, conducted by David Measham with Coleman on saxophone: Skies of American, Native Americans, The Good Life, Birthdays and Funerals, Dreams, Sounds of Sculpture, Holiday for Heroes, All of My Life, Dancers, The Soul Within Woman, The Artist in America, The New Anthem, Place in Space, Foreigner in a Free Land, Silver Screen, Poetry, The Men Who Live in the White House, Love Life, Military, Jam Session, and Sunday in America.

* DANCING IN YOUR HEAD, A&M/Horizon: 0807-2 (SP-722), 1976.
electric band.

OF HUMAN FEELINGS, Antilles: 2001, CD/LP, 1979.
electric band.

see PAUL BLEY AT THE HILLCREST CLUB
see PAT METHENY - SONG X
see ANTHOLOGIES - SMITHSONIAN COLLECTION OF CLASSIC JAZZ

JOHN COLTRANE (SOPRANO & TENOR SAX)

Note: Personnel and significance for albums not given here can be determined by referring to the John Coltrane coverage in the JAZZ STYLES text.

THE LAST GIANT: THE JOHN COLTRANE ANTHOLOGY, Rhino: 71255, 2CD/2AC set, 1946-67.
includes early solos with Dizzy Gillespie, Gay Crosse, and Johnny Hodges plus a selection of Blue Note and Atlantic recordings.

BLUE TRAIN, Blue Note: 46095 (81577), CD/AC, 1957.
with Lee Morgan, Curtis Fuller, Paul Chambers, and Philly Joe Jones.

THE PRESTIGE RECORDINGS, Prestige: 16PCD-4405-2, 16CD set, 1956-58.

TRANEING IN, Fantasy: OJC-189 (Prestige 7123), CD/LP/AC, 1957.
with Red Garland, Paul Chambers, and Art Taylor.

SOULTRANE, Fantasy: OJC-021 (Prestige 7142), CD/LP/AC, 1958.
with Garland, Chambers, and Taylor: Good Bait, Theme for Ernie, I Want to Talk About You, etc.

GIANT STEPS, Atlantic: 1311, CD/AC, 1959.

COLTRANE JAZZ, Atlantic: 1354, CD/AC, 1959.

MY FAVORITE THINGS, Atlantic: 1361, CD/AC, 1960.

COLTRANE PLAYS THE BLUES, Atlantic: 1382, CD/AC, 1960.

AVANT-GARDE, Atlantic 90041-2 (1451), CD, 1960.

OLE COLTRANE, Atlantic: 1373, CD/AC, 1961.

AFRICA/BRASS, MCA/Impulse: MCAD-42001/CD, MCAC-42231/AC (Impulse 6), 1961.

LIVE AT THE VILLAGE VANGUARD, MCA/Impulse: 39136 (Impulse 10), CD/LP/AC, 1961.

* THE OTHER VILLAGE VANGUARD TAPES, MCA: MCA2-4137 (Impulse 9325), 1961.
with Eric Dolphy, McCoy Tyner, Jimmy Garrison, Reggie Workman, Elvin Jones, etc.

IMPRESSIONS, MCA/Impulse: 5887 (Impulse 42), CD/AC, 1961-63.

COLTRANE, MCA/Impulse: 5883 (Impulse 21), CD/AC, 1962.

LIVE AT BIRDLAND, MCA/Impulse: 33109 (Impulse 50), CD/LP/AC, 1963.

CRESCENT, MCA/Impulse: 5889 (Impulse 66), CD/AC, 1964.

A LOVE SUPREME, MCA/Impulse: 5660 (Impulse 77), CD/LP/AC, 1964.

THE MAJOR WORKS OF JOHN COLTRANE, Impulse/GRP: GRD2-113, 2CD set, 1965.
includes Ascension - editions I & II (Impulse 95) and Kulu Se Mama (Impulse 9106).

MEDITATIONS, MCA/Impulse: 39139 (Impulse 9110), CD/AC, 1965.

TRANSITION, Impulse/GRP: GRD-124 (Impulse 9195), CD, 1965.

* LIVE IN SEATTLE, MCA: MCA2-4134 (Impulse 9202), 1965.

* SUN SHIP, MCA: 29028 (Impulse 9211), 1965.

INTERSTELLAR SPACE, Impulse/GRP: GRD-110 (Impulse 9277), CD, 1967.

EXPRESSION, Impulse/GRP: GRD-131 (Impulse 9120), CD, 1967.

see CANNONBALL ADDERLEY - CANNONBALL & COLTRANE
see KENNY BURRELL AND JOHN COLTRANE
see TADD DAMERON - MATING CALL
see MILES DAVIS - NEW QUINTET, COOKIN', RELAXIN', WORKIN', STEAMIN', 'ROUND ABOUT MIDNIGHT, MILES AND COLTRANE, MILESTONES, '58 SESSIONS, and KIND OF BLUE
see ANTHOLOGIES - THE SMITHSONIAN COLLECTION OF CLASSIC JAZZ

FOR EXAMPLES OF EARLY COLTRANE SOLOS:

see THE LAST GIANT (above)

* GREAT MOMENTS IN JAZZ, VOL. 2: ALTO MASTERS, Swing Treasury: 109.
  includes 1954 Coltrane solo with Johnny Hodges combo.

see DIZZY GILLESPIE - SCHOOL DAYS

CHICK COREA (KEYBOARDS)

INNER SPACE, Atlantic: 305-2 (Vortex 2004), CD, 1966.
Tones for Joan's Bones and Litha.

NOW HE SINGS, NOW HE SOBS, Blue Note: 90055 (Solid State 18039), CD, 1968.
with Miroslav Vitous and Roy Haynes: Matrix, Steps-What Was, and Now He Sings, Now He Sobs.

SONG OF SINGING, Blue Note: 84353, CD, 1970.
with Dave Holland and Barry Altschul.

A.R.C., ECM: 833678-2 (1009), CD, 1971.
with Dave Holland and Barry Altschul: Nefertiti, Ballad for Tillie, Thanatos, etc.

PIANO IMPROVISATIONS, VOLS. 1 & 2, ECM: 811979 (1014) and ECM: 829190 (1020), CD/AC, 1971.
solo piano; all tunes written by Corea except Thelonious Monk's Trinkle Tinkle and Wayne Shorter's Masqualero.

RETURN TO FOREVER, ECM: 811978 (1022), CD/AC, 1972.
with Stanley Clarke, Airto Moreira, Flora Purim, and Joe Farrell; all tunes composed by Corea: Return to Forever, Crystal Silence, What Game Shall We Play Today?, and Some Time Ago - La Fiesta.

RETURN TO FOREVER - LIGHT AS A FEATHER, Polydor: 827148 (5525), CD/AC, 1972.
with Joe Farrell, Stanley Clarke, Airto, and Flora Purim.

RETURN TO FOREVER - HYMN TO THE SEVENTH GALAXY, Polydor: 825336 (5536), CD/AC, 1973.

RETURN TO FOREVER - WHERE HAVE I KNOWN YOU BEFORE?, Polydor: 825206 (6509), CD/AC, 1974.
with Al DiMeola, Stanley Clarke, Lenny White.

RETURN TO FOREVER - NO MYSTERY, Polydor: 827149 (PD 6512), CD/AC, 1975.
with Chick Corea (acoustic and electric piano, clavinet, Yamaha organ, synthesizers, snare drum, marimba, and vocal), Al Dimeola (electric and acoustic guitar), Stanley Clarke (acoustic and electric bass, Yamaha organ, synthesizer and vocal), and Lenny White (drums, marimba, conga, and percussion); Spanish "flamenco" and rock are the idioms, not primarily jazz, with little soft material, mostly hard feel; includes Dayride (Clarke), Jungle Waterfall (Corea-Clarke), Flight of the Newborn (Dimeola), Excerpt from the Movement of Heavy Metal (entire band), No Mystery (Corea), Interplay (Corea-Clarke), Celebration Suite I and II (Corea). This recording is cited to illustrate the mixture of acoustic and electric, jazz and rock styles, which typified Corea concerts of the mid-1970's.

TRIO MUSIC, ECM: 827702 (2-1232), 2CD/2AC set, 1981.
with Miroslav Vitous and Roy Haynes.

CHICK COREA as Sideman

BLUE MITCHELL - THE THING TO DO, Blue Note: 84178, CD, 1964.
with Chick Corea, Junior Cook, Gene Taylor, Al Foster (basically Horace Silver's band with Corea taking Silver's place): Chick's Tune, Step Lightly, The Thing to Do, Mona's Mood, Fungi Mama; includes some Bud Powell-influenced Corea solos.

* HERBIE MANN PLAYS THE ROAR OF THE GREASEPAINT - THE SMELL OF THE CROWD, Atlantic: 1437, 1965.
  with Chick Corea, Dave Pike, Potato Valdez, Earl May, and Bruno Carr: The Joker, Feeling Good, Who Can I Turn To?, and On a Wonderful Day Like Today; contains good examples of early Corea.

* HERBIE MANN - STANDING OVATION AT NEWPORT, Atlantic: 1445, 1965.
  with Corea, Pike, Valdez, May and Carr: Potato?, Stolen Moments, Mushi Mushi, and Comin' Home Baby; good examples of early Corea.

* HERBIE MANN - MONDAY NIGHT AT THE VILLAGE GATE, Atlantic: 1462, 1965.
  with Corea, Pike, Valdez, May, and Carr: Away From The Crowd, Motherless Child, In Escambrum, The Young Turks, and You're Gonna Make It With Me; good examples of early Corea.

* BLUE MITCHELL - BOSS HORN, Blue Note: 84257, 1966.
  with Chick Corea, Julian Priester, Junior Cook, Pepper Adams, Gene Taylor, and Mickey Roker: Tones for Joan's Bones, Straight Up and Down, etc.: includes some Bud Powell-influenced Corea solos.

* CAL TJADER - SOUL BURST, Verve: 8637, 1966.
  with Chick Corea, Jerome Richardson, Jerry Dodgion, Seldon Powell, Richard Davis, and Grady Tate: Oran, Curacao, My Ship, Manteca, and Soul Burst; includes some McCoy Tyner-influenced Corea soloing.

STAN GETZ - SWEET RAIN, Verve: 815054-2 (V 8693), CD, 1967.
with Corea, Ron Carter, and Grady Tate: Litha, Windows, and Con Alma.

see GARY BURTON - CRYSTAL SILENCE
see MILES DAVIS - BLACK BEAUTY
see ANTHOLOGIES - JAZZ PIANO

LARRY CORYELL (GUITAR)

* FREE SPIRITS, ABC: 593, 1966.
  with Jim Pepper, Chris Hills, Steve Marcus, and Bob Moses.

* LADY CORYELL, Vanguard: 6509, 1968.
  with Jimmy Garrison, Bob Moses, and Elvin Jones.

SPACES, Vanguard: 79345 (6558), CD, 1970.
with John McLaughlin, Chick Corea, Miroslav Vitous, and Billy Cobham.

INTRODUCING THE ELEVENTH HOUSE, Vanguard: 79342, CD/AC, 1972.

THE ESSENTIAL LARRY CORYELL, Vanguard: VCD-75/76, CD, 1968-72.

see GARY BURTON - DUSTER, LOFTY FAKE ANAGRAM, and ARTIST'S CHOICE

TADD DAMERON (PIANO/ARRANGER)

MATING CALL, Fantasy: OJC-212 (Prestige 7070), CD/LP/AC, 1956.
quartet with John Coltrane: Mating Call, Soultrane, etc.

see DEXTER GORDON - DEXTER RIDES AGAIN
see FATS NAVARRO - NOSTALGIA, MEMORIAL, and FABULOUS
see ANTHOLOGIES - BEBOP and SMITHSONIAN COLLECTION OF CLASSIC JAZZ

MILES DAVIS (TRUMPET)

Note: Personnel and significance for albums not given here can be determined by referring to the Miles Davis coverage in the JAZZ STYLES text itself.

BIRTH OF THE COOL, Capitol: 92862 (T 762), CD, 1949-50.
sessions arranged by Johnny Carisi, John Lewis, Miles Davis, Gerry Mulligan, and Gil Evans; with soloists Davis, Mulligan, Lee Konitz, etc.: Jeru, Boplicity, Budo, Moon Dreams, etc. Instrumentation consists of trumpet, alto sax, baritone sax, trombone, French horn, tuba, piano, bass, and drums; often called the Miles Davis Nonet.

CHRONICLE: THE COMPLETE PRESTIGE RECORDINGS, Prestige: 8PCD-012-2, 8CD set, 1951-56.

DIG, Fantasy: OJC-005 (Prestige 7012), CD/LP/AC, 1951.
with Sonny Rollins, Jackie McLean, Walter Bishop, Jr., Tommy Potter, and Art Blakey: George Shearing's Conception, McLean's Dig (also called Donna, based on the chord progressions of Sweet Georgia Brown), Denial (based on the chord changes of Charlie Parker's Confirmation), Bluing, Out of the Blue, and It's Only a Paper Moon.

COLLECTOR'S ITEMS, Fantasy: OJC-071 (P-7044), CD/LP/AC, 1953 & 1956.
1956; with Sonny Rollins, Tommy Flanagan, Paul Chambers, and Art Taylor: Dave Brubeck's In Your Own Sweet Way and Davis' Vierd Blues and No Line; also contains a 1953 session with Sonny Rollins, Charlie Parker (playing tenor and identified as Charlie Chan), Walter Bishop, Jr., Percy Heath, and Philly Joe Jones: Compulsion, 'Round Midnight, and two takes of The Serpent's Tooth.

WALKIN', Fantasy: OJC-213 (P-7076), CD/LP/AC, 1954.
with Horace Silver, J.J. Johnson, Kenny Clarke, etc.

BAG'S GROOVE, Fantasy: OJC-245 (P-7109), CD/LP/AC, 1954.
with Milt Jackson, Thelonious Monk, Percy Heath, and Kenny Clarke: Bags' Groove; also a 1954 session with Sonny Rollins, Horace Silver, Percy Heath, and Kenny Clarke, including the Rollins compositions Oleo, Doxy, and Airegin, and But Not For Me (Gershwin).

MILES DAVIS & THE MODERN JAZZ GIANTS, OJC-347 (P-7150), CD/LP/AC, 1954.
with Jackson, Monk, Heath, and Clarke: The Man I Love, Swing Spring, and Bemsha Swing.

NEW QUINTET, Fantasy: OJC-006 (P-7014), CD/LP/AC, 1955.
with John Coltrane, Red Garland, Paul Chambers, and Philly Jo Jones.

COOKIN', OJC-128 (P-7094), CD/LP/AC, 1956.
RELAXIN', OJC-190 (P-7129), CD/LP/AC, 1956.
WORKIN', OJC-296 (P-7166), CD/LP/AC, 1956.
STEAMIN', OJC-391 (P-7200), CD/LP/AC, 1956.
with Coltrane, Garland, Chambers, and Jones: Oleo, If I Were a Bell, You're My Everything, I Could Write a Book, It Could Happen to You, Woody 'n' You, My Funny Valentine, Blues by Five, Airegin, Tune Up, When Lights Are Low, It Never Entered My Mind, Four, In Your Own Sweet Way, The Theme (Takes #1 and #2), Trane's Blues, Ahmad's Blues, and Half Nelson.

'ROUND ABOUT MIDNIGHT, Columbia: 40610 (CL 949), CD/AC, 1955-56.

BASIC MILES, Columbia: PCT 32025, AC, 1955-61.
includes Budo (1955).

MILES AND COLTRANE, Columbia: 44052, CD/AC, 1955, 1958.
includes 1958 Newport performance with John Coltrane, Cannonball Adderley, Bill Evans, Paul Chambers, and Jimmy Cobb.

MILES AHEAD, Columbia: 53225 (CL1041), CD/AC, 1957 (Gil Evans).
Note: the previous Columbia reissue (40784) uses alternate takes and does not contain the same music as the above.

MILESTONES, Columbia: 40837 (CL1193), CD/AC, 1958.

PORGY AND BESS, Columbia: 40647 (CL1274), CD/AC, 1958 (Gil Evans).

'58 SESSIONS, Columbia: 46835, CD/AC, 1958.
* JAZZ AT THE PLAZA, Columbia: 32470, 1958 live.
with Coltrane, Adderley, Bill Evans, Chambers, and Cobb.

KIND OF BLUE, Columbia: 40579 (8163/CL1355), CD/AC, 1959.
Note: Sony has also issued KIND OF BLUE in their MASTERSOUND series (CK 52861) with superior sound and a speed correction for two tracks; it does not include an available alternate take.

SKETCHES OF SPAIN, Columbia: 40578 (CL1480), CD/AC, 1959-60 (Gil Evans).

SOMEDAY MY PRINCE WILL COME, Columbia: 40947 (8456/CL1656), CD/AC, 1961.

FRIDAY NIGHT AT THE BLACKHAWK, Columbia: 44257 (CL1669), CD/AC, 1961.
SATURDAY NIGHT AT THE BLACKHAWK, Columbia: 44425 (CL1670), CD/AC, 1961.

AT CARNEGIE HALL, Columbia: PCT 8612 (CL1812), AC, 1961.

SEVEN STEPS TO HEAVEN, Columbia: 48827 (CS8851/CL2051), CD/AC, 1963.

* IN EUROPE, Columbia: 8983 (CL2183), 1963.

THE COMPLETE CONCERT 1964, Columbia: 48821, 2CD/2AC set, 1964.
includes MY FUNNY VALENTINE (CS9106/CL2306) and FOUR AND MORE (CS9253/CL2453).

* HEARD ROUND THE WORLD, Columbia: C2 38506, 1964.
concert in Berlin with Wayne Shorter, Herbie Hancock, Ron Carter, and Tony Williams: Milestones, Autumn Leaves, So What, Walkin ; plus concert in Tokyo with Sam Rivers, Hancock, Carter, and Williams: If I Were a Bell, My Funny Valentine, So What, Walkin, and All of You.

E.S.P., Columbia: 46863 (9150/CL2350), CD/AC, 1965.

* LIVE AT THE PLUGGED NICKEL, Columbia: C2 38266, 1965.
COOKIN' AT THE PLUGGED NICKEL, Columbia: 40645, CD/AC, 1965.

MILES SMILES, Columbia: 48849 (9401/CL2601), CD/AC, 1966.

SORCERER, Columbia: 52974 (9532/CL2732), CD/AC, 1967.

NEFERTITI, Columbia: 46113 (9594), CD/AC, 1967.

MILES IN THE SKY, Columbia: 48954 (9628), CD/AC, 1968.

FILLES DE KILIMANJARO, Columbia: 46116 (9750), CD/AC, 1968.

IN A SILENT WAY, Columbia: 40580 (9875), CD/AC, 1969.

BITCHES BREW, Columbia: 40577 (GP 26), 2CD/2AC set, 1969.

AT THE FILLMORE, Columbia: CGT 30038, AC, 1970.

A TRIBUTE TO JACK JOHNSON, Columbia: 47036 (30455), CD/AC, 1970.

LIVE-EVIL, Columbia: CGT 30954, AC, 1970.

* BIG FUN, Columbia: PC 32866, 1969 72.

BLACK BEAUTY: MILES DAVIS AT THE FILLMORE WEST, Sony (Japan): SRCS 5717/8 (CBS/Sony: SOPJ 39-40), 2CD set, 1970. (import - see page 78)
live with Steve Grossman, Chick Corea, Michael Henderson, Jack DeJohnette, and Airto Moreira. In the author's opinion, this set is superior to BIG FUN, AT THE FILLMORE, IN CONCERT, JACK JOHNSON, ON THE CORNER, and GET UP WITH IT. It provides the only recorded examples of extended improvisation by Chick Corea while he was with Davis, and might be the most exciting recorded playing of Corea's career. The concert was one of those nights when everything seemed to fall into place and forge ahead with blistering intensity.

ON THE CORNER, Columbia: 53579 (PC 31906), CD/AC, 1972.

* IN CONCERT, Columbia: PG 32092, 1972.

* GET UP WITH IT, Columbia: PG 33236, 1970-74.

AGHARTA, Columbia: 46799 (PG 33967), 2CD/2AC set, 1975.

PANGAEA, Columbia: 46115 (CBS/Sony: 50DP 239-40), 2CD/2AC set, 1975.

see FATS NAVARRO FABULOUS, VOL. 1
see CHARLIE PARKER - SAVOY and DIAL recordings
see ANTHOLOGIES - BEBOP, JAZZ COMPOSITIONS, and SMITHSONIAN COLLECTION OF CLASSIC JAZZ

MILES DAVIS - 1960's RHYTHM SECTION STYLE AS AN INFLUENCE - EXAMPLES:

JACKIE MCLEAN - RIGHT NOW, Blue Note: 84215, CD, 1965.

JOE HENDERSON - THE KICKER, Fantasy: OJC-465 (Milestone 9008), CD/LP/AC, 1967.
with Mike Lawrence, Grachan Moncur, Kenny Barron, Ron Carter, and Louis Hayes: Mamacita, The Kicker, Chelsea Bridge, Nardis, Without A Song, O Amor En Paz, and Mo' Joe.

* JOE HENDERSON - IF YOU'RE NOT PART OF THE SOLUTION, YOU'RE PART OF THE PROBLEM, Milestone: 9028, 1970.
with Woody Shaw, George Cables, Ron McClure, and Lenny White: Caribbean Fire Dance, 'Round Midnight, Mode for Joe, and Blue Bossa.

* JOE HENDERSON - IN PURSUIT OF BLACKNESS, Milestone: 9034, 1971.
with Curtis Fuller, Pete Yellin, George Cables, Stanley Clarke, and Lenny White: No Me Esqueca, Invitation, A Shade of Jade, Gazelle, and Mind Over Matter.

* KENNY COX & THE CONTEMPORARY JAZZ QUINTET - MULTIDIRECTION, Blue Note: 84339, 1969.
with Charles Moore, Leon Henderson, Kenny Cox, Ron Brooks, and Danny Spencer: Spellbound, Snuck In, Multidirection, What Other One, and Gravity Point.

JOE FARRELL QUARTET, CTI/CBS: ZK 40694 (6003), CD, 1970.

* ART LANDE - RUBISA PATROL, ECM: 1081, 1976.

WYNTON MARSALIS, Columbia: 37574, CD/AC, 1982.
WYNTON MARSALIS - THINK OF ONE, Columbia: 38641, CD/AC, 1983.
WYNTON MARSALIS - BLACK CODES (FROM THE UNDERGROUND), Columbia: 40009, CD/AC, 1985.

PAUL DESMOND (ALTO SAX)

LATE LAMENT (DESMOND BLUE), RCA Bluebird: 5778 (LSP 2438), CD/AC, 1961-62.
with strings; Jim Hall on some selections.

TWO OF A MIND - PAUL DESMOND & GERRY MULLIGAN, RCA Bluebird: 9654 (LSP 2624), CD/LP/AC, 1962.
All the Things You Are, The Way You Look Tonight, etc.

see DAVE BRUBECK - THE DAVE BRUBECK OCTET, JAZZ AT OBERLIN, GONE WITH THE WIND, and TIME OUT

WARREN "BABY" DODDS (DRUMS)

FOOTNOTES TO JAZZ, VOL. 1: BABY DODDS, Folkways: 2290 (LP 30), AC, 1946.
available by special order from Smithsonian/Folkways Recordings, 414 Hungerford Drive; Suite 444, Rockville, MD 20850; tel: 301-443-2314; fax: 301-443-1819.

ERIC DOLPHY (ALTO SAX, FLUTE, BASS CLARINET)

FAR CRY, Fantasy: OJC-400 (New Jazz 8270), CD/LP/AC, 1961.
with Booker Little, Jaki Byard, Ron Carter, and Roy Haynes: Bird's Mother, Ode to Charlie Parker, Far Cry, Miss Ann, Left Alone, Tenderly, and It's Magic.

OUT TO LUNCH, Blue Note: 46524 (84163), CD, 1964.
with Freddie Hubbard, Bobby Hutcherson, Richard Davis, and Tony Williams.

LAST DATE, Fontana: 822226-2 (Limelight 86013), CD, 1964.
concert with Misja Mengelberg, Jacques Schols, and Han Bennink: Epistrophy, South Street Exit, Miss Ann, The Madrig Speaks, The Panther Walks, and You Don't Know What Love Is.

see ORNETTE COLEMAN - FREE JAZZ
see JOHN COLTRANE - OLE, LIVE AT THE VILLAGE VANGUARD, THE OTHER VILLAGE VANGUARD TAPES, and IMPRESSIONS
see CHICO HAMILTON - GONGS EAST
see CHARLES MINGUS - COMPLETE CANDID RECORDINGS and MINGUS PRESENTS MINGUS
see OLIVER NELSON - BLUES AND THE ABSTRACT TRUTH

JIMMY DORSEY (ALTO SAX)

see ANTHOLOGIES - THESAURUS OF CLASSIC JAZZ

TOMMY DORSEY (TROMBONE, BIG BAND)

THIS IS TOMMY DORSEY, VOL. 1, RCA Bluebird: PK-5097 (VPM 6038), AC, 1935-45.
THIS IS TOMMY DORSEY, VOL. 2, RCA Bluebird: PK-5121 (VPM 6064), AC, 1935-45.

YES INDEED!, RCA Bluebird: 9987, CD/AC 1939-45.
Sy Oliver arrangements: Well Get It!, Opus One, and Easy Does It.

BEST OF TOMMY DORSEY, MCA: MCAC2-4074, 2AC set, 1950-53.

see ANTHOLOGIES - BIG BAND JAZZ

ROY ELDRIDGE (TRUMPET)

LITTLE JAZZ, Columbia: CK 45275 (38033), CD, 1935-1940.
includes 1935 selection with Teddy Hill; four 1936 selections with Fletcher Henderson; four 1936 selections with Teddy Wilson: Blues in C# Minor; and a 1937 Eldridge band date: Wabash Stomp, Florida Stomp, Heckler's Hop, After You've Gone, etc.

ROY ELDRIDGE WITH THE GENE KRUPA ORCHESTRA, Columbia: CK 45448, CD, 1940-49.
1940-42 with Gene Krupa Orchestra and Anita O'Day: Green Eyes, Let Me Off Uptown, After You've Gone, Rockin' Chair, Harlem On Parade, The Marines' Hymn, That Drummer's Band, Massachusetts, Murder, He Says, etc.

AFTER YOU'VE GONE, Decca Jazz/GRP: GRD-605, CD, 1943-46.
1943: The Gasser; 1944: After You've Gone, I Can't Get Started; 1946: All the Cats Join In, Hi Ho Trailus Boot Whip, Yard Dog, and Rockin' Chair.

* ALL THE CATS JOIN IN, MCA: 1355, 1944-46.
1944: After You've Gone, I Can't Get Started; 1945: Little Jazz Boogie; 1946: All The Cats Join In, Ain't That A Shame, Hi Ho Trailus Boot Whip, Tippin' Out, Yard Dog, Les Bounce, and Rockin' Chair.

see COLEMAN HAWKINS - GIANTS OF THE TENOR SAX
see BILLIE HOLIDAY
see FLETCHER HENDERSON
see GENE KRUPA
see ARTIE SHAW - COMPLETE GRAMERCY FIVE
see ANTHOLOGIES - ANTHOLOGY OF BIG BAND SWING, THE 1930'S-THE SMALL COMBOS, SMITHSONIAN COLLECTION OF CLASSIC JAZZ, and TRUMPETER'S HOLIDAY

DUKE ELLINGTON (PIANO, BIG BAND)

* THIS IS DUKE ELLINGTON, RCA: VPM 6042, 1927-1946.
Creole Love Call (1927 with Bubber Miley); Mood Indigo (1930); Solitude (1934); Cottontail (with Ben Webster solo), Don't Get Around Much Anymore (Never No Lament), Sophisticated Lady, C-Jam Blues, Concerto for Cootie (all 1940); and Take the 'A' Train (1941 with Rex Stewart and Ray Nance solos).

EARLY ELLINGTON, RCA Bluebird: 6852, CD/AC, 1927-34.
includes Creole Love Call with Bubber Miley; and an early example of piano comping (first chorus of Hodges' alto solo on The Mooche).

JUNGLE NIGHTS IN HARLEM, RCA Bluebird: 2499, CD/AC, 1927-32.

JUBILEE STOMP, RCA Bluebird: 66038, CD/AC, 1928-34.

DUKE ELINGTON: THE BRUNSWICK ERA, VOL. 1, Decca Jazz/MCA: 42325, CD/AC, 1926-29.

THE JUNGLE BAND: THE BRUNSWICK ERA, VOL. 2, Decca Jazz/MCA: 42348, CD/AC, 1929-31.

THE OKEH ELLINGTON, Columbia: 46177, 2CD/2AC set, 1927-30.

* THE ELLINGTON ERA, VOL. 1, Columbia: C3L 27, 3LP set, 1927-40.
big band recordings originally made for Brunswick, Okeh, and Columbia; 1927: East St. Louis Toodle-Oo, Black and Tan Fantasy; 1928: The Mooche; 1930: Rockin' In Rhythm; 1932: Lightnin', It Don't Mean A Thing If It Ain't Got That Swing; 1934: Solitude; 1936: Clarinet Lament, Echoes of Harlem; 1937: Caravan; 1938: Mood Indigo, Prelude to a Kiss, Boy Meets Horn; 1940: Sophisticated Lady.

BRAGGIN' IN BRASS, Portrait/CBS: 44395, 2CD/AC set, 1938.

THE DUKE'S MEN: SMALL GROUPS, VOL. 1, Columbia: C2K 46995, 2CD set, 1934-38.
THE DUKE'S MEN: SMALL GROUPS. VOL. 2. Columbia: 48835. 2CD/2AC set, 1938-40.
groups of Johnny Hodges, Rex Stewart, Cootie Williams, & Barney Bigard.

SOLOS, DUETS & TRIOS, RCA Bluebird: 2178, CD/AC, 1932-1967.
includes 1940 duets with bassist Jimmy Blanton.

* DUKE ELLINGTON: 1938, Smithsonian: 2003.
* DUKE ELLINGTON: 1939, Smithsonian: 2010.
* DUKE ELLINGTON: 1940, Smithsonian: 2013.
* DUKE ELLINGTON: 1941, Smithsonian: 2027.
1938: I Let A Song Go Out of My Heart, Prelude To A Kiss, Boy Meets Horn; 1939: The Sergeant Was Shy, Sophisticated Lady; 1940: Jack the Bear, Ko-Ko, Morning Glory, Cotton Tail, Never No Lament, Bojangles, Harlem Airshaft, All Too Soon, In A Mellotone, Warm Valley, Pitter Panther Patter, and Sophisticated Lady; 1941: Take the 'A' Train, Blue Serge, Solitude, Bakiff, Just A-Settin' and A-Rockin', Chelsea Bridge, and Raincheck.

THE BLANTON-WEBSTER BAND, RCA Bluebird: 5659-2-RB, 3CD set, 1940-42.
includes the above 1940-1941 sessions and more from 1942 with unusually scholarly, accurate, informative liner notes about what was probably Ellington's best band: Johnny Hodges, Cootie Williams, Joe Nanton, Ben Webster, Jimmy Blanton, etc.

BLACK, BROWN AND BEIGE, RCA Bluebird: 6641, 3CD/3AC set, 1944-46.
includes Mercer Ellington's Things Ain't What They Used to Be with solos by Johnny Hodges, Lawrence Brown, and Taft Jordan; a 1945 version of Mood Indigo with a wordless vocal; the Perfume Suite; etc.

* THE WORLD OF DUKE ELLINGTON, Columbia: 32564, 1947.
big band with Lawrence Brown, Tyree Glenn, Ray Nance, Shorty Baker, Dud Bascomb, Jimmy Hamilton, Hodges, and Oscar Pettiford: Boogie Bop Blues (which has some great bass work), On A Turquoise Cloud (with a wordless vocal, clarinet and muted trumpet, violin, and bass clarinet), Sultry Serenade (with solos by Tyree Glenn and Hodges), and Golden Cress (featuring Lawrence Brown).

ELLINGTON UPTOWN, Columbia: 40836 (CL 830), CD/AC, 1951-52.
big band featuring Russell Procope and Jimmy Hamilton (The Mooch), Paul Gonsalves (Take the 'A' Train), and Louis Bellson (Skin Deep), etc.

* ELLINGTON SHOWCASE, Capitol: T 679, 1953-55.
big band including a feature for Harry Carney (Serious Serenade), a feature for Cat Anderson (La Virgen de la Macarena), and a new version of Harlem Airshaft (with Clark Terry soloing in the spots where Cootie Williams and Barney Bigard had soloed, Quentin Jackson taking what had been Tricky Sam Nanton's part on the original 1940 version, and other interesting differences that help cast light on the original), etc.

HISTORICALLY SPEAKING - THE DUKE, Bethlehem: BR-5013 (BCP-60), CD, 1956.
DUKE ELLINGTON PRESENTS, Bethlehem: BR-5019 (BCP-6005), CD, 1956.
big band featuring Jimmy Hamilton, Ray Nance, Johnny Hodges, Quentin Jackson, and Britt Woodman; the first includes a violin feature for Ray Nance (Lonesome Lullaby) and two Billy Strayhorn pieces (Midriff and Upper Manhattan Medical Group - mistakenly credited to Ellington); the second recording contains the Harry Carney feature, Frustration.

ELLINGTON AT NEWPORT, Columbia: 40587 (CL 934), CD/AC, 1956.

SUCH SWEET THUNDER, Columbia: COL 469140-2 (CL 1033), CD, 1956-57.
(import - see page 78)

ELLINGTON INDIGOS, Columbia: 44444 (CS 8053/CL 1085), CD/AC, 1957.
big band featuring Hodges, Gonsalves, Hamilton, and Harold Shorty Baker; high points are the Hodges solo on Prelude To A Kiss, the Gonsalves solo on Where Or When, and the Baker solo on Willow Weep for Me. The music on the mono copy (CL 1085) of this album is not identical to that on the stereo copy (CS 8053); several different improvisations and a few alterations in ensemble playing occur. The mono copy also contains an entire tune not on the stereo copy, although it is mistakenly listed on the stereo copy's album jacket. That tune, The Sky Fell Down, is one of the prettiest Ellington compositions on the mono album, and it contains a gorgeous Ray Nance trumpet solo. The reissue (44444) has a previously unissued All the Things You Are and an alternate take of Autumn Leaves but not The Sky Fell Down.

* COSMIC SCENE, Columbia: CL 1198, 1958.
recording with abbreviated instrumentation: Hamilton, Gonsalves, and Terry plus three trombones, piano, bass, and drums: includes Ralph Burns's Early Autumn, W.C. Handy's St. Louis Blues, Johnny Green's Body and Soul (featuring Gonsalves), Lionel Hampton's Midnight Sun, several originals by Ellington and his sidemen, plus reworkings of Perdido, Take the 'A' Train, and Avalon.

* NEWPORT 1958, Columbia: CS 8072 (CL 1245), 1958.
featuring Terry, Hamilton, Gonsalves, Nance, Carney, Gerry Mulligan, etc.

* FESTIVAL SESSION, Columbia: PC 36979 (CL 1400), 1959.
big band with Gonsalves, Terry, Hamilton, Hodges, Procope, and Nance: Idiom '59, Launching Pad, etc.

* DUKE ELLINGTON'S CONCERT OF SACRED MUSIC, RCA. LSP-3582, 1965.
In the Beginning God, The Lord's Prayer, Come Sunday, etc.

FAR EAST SUITE, RCA Bluebird: 7640 (LSP-3782), CD/AC, 1966.

SECOND SACRED CONCERT, Prestige: PCD-24045-2 (Fantasy 8407/8), CD, 1968.
The Shepherd (Who Watches Over the Night Flock), T.G.T.T., The Biggest and Busiest Intersection, etc.

LATIN AMERICAN SUITE, Fantasy: OJC-469 (8419), CD/LP/AC, 1968.

AFRO-EURASIAN ECLIPSE, Fantasy: OJC-645 (9498), CD/LP/AC, 1971.

THE ELLINGTON SUITES, Fantasy: OJC-446 (Pablo 2310-762), CD/LP/AC, 1959, 1971-72.
Queen's Suite, Goutelas Suite, and the UWIS Suite.

* DUKE ELLINGTON'S THIRD SACRED CONCERT, RCA: APL1-0785, 1973.

see ANTHOLOGIES - ANTHOLOGY OF BIG BAND SWING, BIG BAND JAZZ, THE GREATEST JAZZ CONCERT IN THE WORLD, JAZZ PIANO, JIVE AT FIVE, and THE SMITHSONIAN COLLECTION OF CLASSIC JAZZ

BILL EVANS (PIANO)

BILL EVANS: THE COMPLETE RIVERSIDE RECORDINGS, Riverside: RCD-018-2/12CD set, R-018/18LP set, 1956-63.

NEW JAZZ CONCEPTIONS, Fantasy: OJC-025 (R-223), CD/LP/AC, 1956.
with Teddy Kotick and Paul Motian: I Love You, Five, Easy Living, Displacement, Conception, Speak Low, Our Delight, My Romance, and I Got It Bad.

EVERYBODY DIGS BILL EVANS, Fantasy: OJC-068 (R-1129), CD/LP/AC, 1958.
with Sam Jones and Philly Joe Jones: Peace Piece, Young and Foolish, What Is There To Say?, etc. Evans considered this to be among his very best playing on record.

EXPLORATIONS, Fantasy: OJC-037 (R-351), CD/LP/AC, 1961.
with Scott LaFaro and Paul Motian.

AT THE VILLAGE VANGUARD, Riverside: FCD-60-017, CD, 1961; or
SUNDAY AT THE VILLAGE VANGUARD, Fantasy: OJC-140 (RLP-9376) and WALTZ FOR DEBBY, Fantasy: OJC-210 (RLP-9399), CD/LP/AC, 1961.
with LaFaro and Motian: My Foolish Heart, Waltz for Debby, Alice in Wonderland, Gloria's Step, Milestones, etc.

UNDERCURRENT, Blue Note: 90583 (UA 14003), CD/AC, 1962.
duets with Jim Hall.

INTERMODULATION, Verve: 833771-2 (V6-8655), CD, 1966.
duets with Jim Hall.

see MILES DAVIS - MILES AND COLTRANE, BASIC MILES, '58 SESSIONS, and KIND OF BLUE
see OLIVER NELSON - BLUES AND THE ABSTRACT TRUTH
see ANTHOLOGIES - JAZZ COMPOSITIONS, JAZZ PIANO, and SMITHSONIAN COLLECTION OF CLASSIC JAZZ (REVISED)

BILL EVANS AS AN INFLUENCE

* PIANO JAZZ IN CZECHOSLOVAKIA, Supraphon: SUA 15991, 1968.
(import - see page 78)
Czech import anthology. The Jan Hammer Trio selections, Responsibility and Autumn Leaves, display Evans influence.

* JAN HAMMER - THE FIRST SEVEN DAYS, Nemperor: 432, 1975.
Light/Sun and Fourth Day display Bill Evans influence.

GIL EVANS (COMPOSER/ARRANGER)

see MILES DAVIS - THE BIRTH OF THE COOL, MILES AHEAD, PORGY AND BESS, and SKETCHES OF SPAIN
see CLAUDE THORNHILL - MEMORABLE and BEST OF THE BIG BANDS
see ANTHOLOGIES - THE BEBOP ERA, BIG BAND JAZZ, and JAZZ IN REVOLUTION

ART FARMER (TRUMPET)

MEET THE JAZZTET, Chess: 91550 (Argo 664), CD/AC, 1960.
with Art Farmer, Benny Golson, Curtis Fuller, McCoy Tyner, Addison Farmer and Lex Humphries: I Remember Clifford, Killer Joe (the same Killer Joe that Quincy Jones later recorded), Blues March, and Park Avenue Petite (all Golson compositions).

* THE JAZZTET AT BIRDHOUSE, Argo: 688, 1961.
live recording of Art Farmer, Benny Golson, Tom McIntosh, Cedar Walton, Tommy Williams, and Al Heath: Junction, Farmer's Market, Darn That Dream, Shutterbug, Round Midnight, and November Afternoon. I think this LP contains the best recorded solos of Farmer and Golson and is representative of the Jazztet's tasteful, swinging style.

see ANTHOLOGIES - NICA'S DREAM

MAYNARD FERGUSON (TRUMPET/BIG BAND)

* MESSAGE FROM NEWPORT/NEWPORT SUITE, Roulette: RE 116, 1958, 1960.
  1958 recordings originally on MESSAGE FROM NEWPORT (52012), with Willie Maiden, Don Sebesky, Slide Hampton, Jake Hanna, and others: Three Little Foxes, Slide Hampton's Frame for the Blues, etc.; also includes 1960 recordings originally on NEWPORT SUITE (52053), with Willie Maiden, Frank Hitner, and others: Ol' Man River, Got the Spirit, etc.

* MAYNARD '62, Roulette: 52083, 1962.
  with Don Menza, Willie Maiden, Mike Abene, Rufus Jones, and others: Have You Met Miss Jones?, Lazy Afternoon, Don Sebesky's arrangement of Maria, etc.

M.F. HORN, Columbia: CGT 33660 (30466), AC, 1970.

CHAMELEON, Columbia: 46112 (33007), CD/AC, 1974.

CONQUISTADOR, Columbia: 34457, CD/AC, 1976.
  includes Rocky Theme: Gonna Fly Now.

see STAN KENTON - NEW CONCEPTS OF ARTISTRY IN RHYTHM
see SHORTY ROGERS - SHORTSTOPS

TOMMY FLANAGAN (PIANO)

see KENNY BURRELL - KENNY BURRELL & JOHN COLTRANE
see JOHN COLTRANE - GIANT STEPS
see MILES DAVIS - COLLECTORS ITEMS
see WES MONTGOMERY - INCREDIBLE JAZZ GUITAR
see SONNY ROLLINS - SAXOPHONE COLOSSUS
see ANTHOLOGIES - JAZZ PIANO

CARL FONTANA (TROMBONE)

THE GREAT FONTANA, Uptown: 27.28, CD, 1987.

see STAN KENTON - CUBAN FIRE

FOURTH WAY (FUSION BAND)

* THE SUN AND MOON HAVE COME TOGETHER, Capitol/Harvest: SKAO 423, 1969.
  with Mike Nock and Michael White.

CURTIS FULLER (TROMBONE)

see ART BLAKEY - MOSAIC, CARAVAN, UGETSU, and INDESTRUCTIBLE
see JOHN COLTRANE - BLUE TRANE
see ART FARMER - MEET THE JAZZTET

RED GARLAND (PIANO)

see JOHN COLTRANE - TRANEING IN and SOULTRANE
see MILES DAVIS - NEW QUINTET, RELAXIN', WORKIN', STEAMIN', COOKIN', ROUND ABOUT MIDNIGHT, and MILESTONES

ERROLL GARNER (PIANO)

CONCERT BY THE SEA, Columbia: 40589 (9821), CD/AC, 1955.
  concert with Eddie Calhoun and Denzil Best: I'll Remember April, Red Top, Autumn Leaves, Where or When, etc.

see ANTHOLOGIES - JAZZ PIANO

STAN GETZ (TENOR SAX)

OPUS DE BOP, Savoy/Denon: SV-0118 (12114), CD, 1946-47.
  And the Angels Swing, Running Water, and Don't Worry About Me.

QUARTETS, Fantasy: OJC-121 (Prestige 7002), CD/LP/AC, 1949-50.
  with Al Haig: There's a Small Hotel, Indian Summer, etc.

THE COMPLETE RECORDINGS OF THE STAN GETZ QUARTET WITH JIMMY RANEY, Mosaic: MD3-131/3CD set, MR4-131/4LP set, 1951-53.
with Al Haig, Horace Silver, Jimmy Raney, Roy Haynes, etc; (mail order - see page 78)

THE ROOST QUARTETS, Roulette Jazz: 96052, CD, 1950-51.
with Al Haig, Horace Silver, Tommy Potter, and Roy Haynes.

AT STORYVILLE, Roulette: 94507 (Roost), CD, 1951.
with Jimmy Raney, Al Haig: Rubber Neck, Mosquito Knees, Hershey Bar, etc.

STAN GETZ AND J.J. JOHNSON AT THE OPERA HOUSE, Verve: 831272-2 (MGV-8265), CD, 1957.
live concert recording by Stan Getz, J.J. Johnson, Oscar Peterson, Herb Ellis, Ray Brown, and Connie Kay: Billie's Bounce, My Funny Valentine, Crazy Rhythm, Yesterdays, It Never Entered My Mind, and Blues in the Closet. Note that the original stereo version (Verve 68490) was not the same music as in the mono version (V6-8265). The CD reissue includes both stereo and mono versions.

FOCUS, Verve: 314 521419-2 (V6-8412), CD, 1961.
Eddie Sauter string arrangements; Getz improvises with no preset melody or chord progressions, using only the string parts as his guide.

JAZZ SAMBA, Verve: 810061-2 (MGV-8432), CD, 1962.
with Charlie Byrd: Desafinado.

GETZ/GILBERTO, Verve: 314 521414-2 (V6-8545), CD, 1963.
with Antonio Carlos Jobim, Joao and Astrud Gilberto: Girl From Ipanema, Desafinado, etc.

see WOODY HERMAN - THUNDERING HERDS and KEEPER OF THE FLAME
see ANTHOLOGIES - THE BEBOP ERA

DIZZY GILLESPIE (TRUMPET)

* THE DEVELOPMENT OF AN AMERICAN ARTIST, Smithsonian: 2004, 1940-46.
Gillespie with his own groups and the bands of Les Hite, Cab Calloway, Coleman Hawkins, Billy Eckstine, Boyd Raeburn, and others.

SHAW NUFF, Musicraft: MVSCD-53 (MVS-2009/MVS-2010), CD, 1945-46.
combos and big bands; 1945: with Charlie Parker, Al Haig, Curly Russell and Sid Catlett (Salt Peanuts, Hot House, All the Things You Are, etc.). One of the 1946 big band tunes is Things To Come.

DIZZIEST, RCA Bluebird: 5785-4-RB, AC, 1946-1949.
four combo tracks from 1946 with Don Byas, Bill De Arango, Milt Jackson, Al Haig, Ray Brown, and J.C. Heard: Anthropology, 52nd St. Theme, Ol' Man Rebop, and Night in Tunisia; 1947 and 1949 big band dates include the Dizzy Gillespie-George Russell collaboration Cubano Be - Cubano Bop, Gillespie's Manteca (both featuring conga drummer Chano Pozo), Tadd Dameron's Good Bait, etc.

SCHOOL DAYS, Savoy/Denon: SV-0157 (Regent 6043), CD, 1951-52.
includes Gillespie combo's We Love to Boogie, which contains 1951 example of John Coltrane's solo style; also has Lady Be Good, Pop's Confessin, School Days, etc. (included here only as an example of early Coltrane).

DUETS, Verve: 835253-2 (MGV-8260), CD, 1957.
SONNY SIDE UP, Verve: 314 521426-2 (MGV-8262), CD, 1957.
recordings with Sonny Stitt, Sonny Rollins, Ray Bryant, Tom Bryant, and Charlie Persip: Eternal Triangle, I Know That You Know, etc.; contains some of the fastest, most fluent tenor sax playing on record; Rollins, Gillespie, and Stitt keep up with each other at their fiery best on Eternal Triangle; some authorities consider this to be the best Rollins on record.

DIZZY GILLESPIE AT NEWPORT, Verve: 314 513754-2 (V6-8830/MGV8242), CD, 1957.
live recording made by Gillespie big band at Newport Jazz Festival; with Lee Morgan, Al Grey, Benny Golson, Billy Mitchell, Wynton Kelly, etc.: I Remember Clifford, Dizzy's Blues, Manteca, etc. Gillespie considers his Dizzy's Blues solo to be one of his best on record.

see CAB CALLOWAY
see CHARLIE PARKER - SAVOY and DIAL recordings and BIRD AND DIZ
see ANTHOLOGIES - BEBOP, THE BEBOP REVOLUTION, BIG BAND JAZZ, and SMITHSONIAN COLLECTION OF CLASSIC JAZZ

JIMMY GIUFFRE (CLARINET/TENOR SAX, ETC.)

* THE JIMMY GIUFFRE CLARINET, Atlantic: 90144 (1238), 1956.
unaccompanied clarinet solo: So Low; clarinet and celeste: Deep Purple; The Sheepherder with Buddy Collete and Harry Klee; and Fascinatin' Rhythm with Jimmy Rowles and Shelly Manne.

* TRAVELIN' LIGHT, Atlantic: 1282, 1958.
with Bob Brookmeyer and Jim Hall; includes Travelin' Light, The Swamp People, California Here I Come, and The Lonely Time.

* WESTERN SUITE, Atlantic: 1330, 1958.
with Brookmeyer and Hall: Eddie Durham's Topsy, Thelonious Monk's Blue Monk, and Giuffre's Western Suite.

* JIMMY GIUFFRE: PIECE FOR CLARINET AND STRING ORCHESTRA/MOBILES, Verve: V6 8395, 1959.
compositions and clarinet solos by Giuffre.

1961, ECM: 849644-2, 2CD set, 1961.
with Paul Bley and Steve Swallow; includes FUSION (Verve: V-8397): Carla Bley's Jesus Maria, In the Mornings Out There; Giuffre's Scootin' About, Emphasis, Cry Want, Trudgin', Used To Be, Brief Hesitation, and Venture; and THESIS (V-8402).

* FREE FALL, Columbia: CS 8764 (CL 1964), 1962.
with Paul Bley and Steve Swallow; all tunes composed by Giuffre: Yggdrasill, Propulsion, The Five Ways, etc.

see WOODY HERMAN - THUNDERING HERDS
see SHELLY MANNE - THE THREE AND THE TWO
see SHORTY ROGERS - SHORTSTOPS and COLLABORATION: WEST
see ANTHOLOGIES - ATLANTIC JAZZ: WEST COAST and MASTERS OF THE MODERN PIANO

BENNY GOLSON (TENOR SAX)

see ART FARMER - THE JAZZTET

BENNY GOODMAN (CLARINET/BIG BAND)

B.G. & BIG TEA IN NYC, Decca Jazz/GRP: GRD-609, CD, 1928-34.
combos led by Red Nichols and Adrian Rollini; plus the 1931 Venuti-Lang Farewell Blues and Beale St. Blues, with Jack Teagarden, Frank Signorelli, Joe Tarto, and Neil Marshall.

* COMPLETE BENNY GOODMAN, VOL. 1, RCA: AXK2-5505, 1935.
including After You've Gone and Body and Soul by the Benny Goodman Trio (Goodman, Teddy Wilson, and Gene Krupa), and big band recordings including Fletcher Henderson's arrangements of Sometimes I'm Happy, King Porter Stomp, Japanese Sandman, and Blue Skies.

THE BIRTH OF SWING, RCA Bluebird: 61038, 3CD/3AC set, 1935-1936.

SING SING SING, RCA Bluebird: 5630, CD/AC, 1935-38.
big band recordings including King Porter Stomp, Down South Camp Meeting, and Sing Sing Sing.

AFTER YOU'VE GONE, RCA Bluebird: 5631, CD/AC, 1935-36.
AVALON: THE SMALL BANDS, VOL. 2, RCA Bluebird: 2273, CD/AC, 1937-39.
trio and quartet recordings with Teddy Wilson, Lionel Hampton, and Gene Krupa.

CARNEGIE HALL JAZZ CONCERT, Columbia: 40244 (OSL 160), 2CD/2AC set, 1938.
Don't Be That Way, One O'Clock Jump, Shine, etc. with Count Basie, Lester Young, Lionel Hampton, Harry James, Gene Krupa, Teddy Wilson, etc.; Avalon, Blue Reverie, Blue Room, etc. with Johnny Hodges, Teddy Wilson, Gene Krupa, Harry James, etc.

BENNY GOODMAN SEXTET FEATURING CHARLIE CHRISTIAN, Columbia: 45144, CD/AC, 1939-41.

see CHARLIE CHRISTIAN - GENIUS OF THE ELECTRIC GUITAR
see ANTHOLOGIES - BIG BAND JAZZ, JAZZ HOLIDAY, and SMITHSONIAN COLLECTION OF CLASSIC JAZZ

DEXTER GORDON (TENOR SAX)

DEXTER RIDES AGAIN, Savoy/Denon: SV-0120 (2211/1154), CD, 1945-47.
1945: Argonne Thornton, Gene Ramey, Ed Nicholson: Blow Mr. Gordon, Dexter's Deck, etc.; 1946: Leonard Hawkins, Bud Powell, Curly Russell, and Max Roach: Long Tall Dexter, Dexter Rides Again, etc.; 1947: Leo Parker, Tadd Dameron, Curly Russell, and Art Blakey: Settin' the Pace, Dexter's Riff, etc.

THE CHASE, Spotlite: 130 (Dial), LP, 1947. (import - see page 78)
with Red Callender, Chuck Thompson or Roy Porter, Charles Fox, Jimmy Rowles, Jimmy Bunn, Teddy Edwards, and Wardell Gray: Lullaby in Rhythm, The Chase, Sweet and Lovely, The Duel, etc.

see DIZZY GILLESPIE - SHAW NUFF
see HERBIE HANCOCK - TAKIN' OFF
see ANTHOLOGIES - JAZZ IN REVOLUTION and SMITHSONIAN COLLECTION OF CLASSIC JAZZ

CHARLIE HADEN (BASS)

* CLOSENESS, A&M/Horizon: 0808-2 (SP-710), 1976.
with Keith Jarrett.

see ORNETTE COLEMAN
see KEITH JARRETT
see ANTHOLOGIES - SMITHSONIAN COLLECTION OF CLASSIC JAZZ

AL HAIG (PIANO)

see STAN GETZ - QUARTETS, ROOST QUARTETS, and AT STORYVILLE
see DIZZY GILLESPIE - SHAW NUFF and DIZZIEST
see CHARLIE PARKER - NOW'S THE TIME
see ANTHOLOGIES - THE BEBOP REVOLUTION and JAZZ PIANO

JIM HALL (GUITAR)

see PAUL DESMOND - LATE LAMENT
see BILL EVANS - UNDERCURRENT and INTERMODULATION
see JIMMY GIUFFRE - TRAVELIN' LIGHT and WESTERN SUITE
see SONNY ROLLINS - QUARTETS

CHICO HAMILTON (DRUMS)

* SPECTACULAR!, World Pacific Jazz: ST-20143 (PJ-1209), 1955.
with Buddy Collette, Jim Hall, Fred Katz, and Carson Smith: My Funny Valentine and I Want To Be Happy arranged by Hamilton; Jim Hall's Spectacular; Fred Katz's The Sage; Hamilton's The Morning After arranged by Hall; Buddy Collette's A Nice Day, Blue Sands, and Buddy Boo; and Walking Carson Blues arranged by Carson Smith.

GONGS EAST, Discovery: DSCD-831 (Warner Bros. 1271), CD, 1958.
with Eric Dolphy.

* PASSIN' THRU, MCA: 29037 (Impulse 29), 1962.
  with Charles Lloyd and Gabor Szabo.

see GERRY MULLIGAN - BEST and COMPLETE PACIFIC JAZZ RECORDINGS

LIONEL HAMPTON (VIBRAHARP, BIG BAND)

* STEPPIN' OUT, MCA: 1315 (Decca 79244), 1942-44.
  included for good examples of the locked hands, block chording that pianist Milt Buckner popularized: Royal Family (1942) and Blues in the News (1942).

FLYING HOME, Decca Jazz/MCA: 42349, CD/AC, 1942-1945.
includes Royal Family.

MIDNIGHT SUN, Decca Jazz/GRP: GRD-625 (MCA 1331), CD, 1946-47.
with Milt Buckner and Charles Mingus (Mingus Fingers).

see BENNY GOODMAN - AFTER YOU'VE GONE, AVALON, and CARNEGIE HALL CONCERT
see ANTHOLOGIES - BIG BAND JAZZ and SMITHSONIAN COLLECTION OF CLASSIC JAZZ

HERBIE HANCOCK (KEYBOARDS)

BEST OF HERBIE HANCOCK, Blue Note: 91142 (89907), CD/AC, 1962-69.

TAKIN' OFF, Blue Note: 46506 (84109), CD/AC, 1962.
with Dexter Gordon, Freddie Hubbard, and Billy Higgins.

EMPYREAN ISLES, Blue Note: 84175, CD, 1964.
with Freddie Hubbard, Ron Carter, and Tony Williams.

MAIDEN VOYAGE, Blue Note: 46339 (84195), CD, 1965.
pianist-composer Hancock leading the Miles Davis group of 1963, with trumpeter Freddie Hubbard instead of Davis; with George Coleman, Ron Carter, and Tony Williams; all tunes composed by Hancock: Maiden Voyage, Dolphin Dance, Little One, etc. It contains some of Hubbard's best recorded solos, and it showcases Hancock's writing.

* THE PRISONER, Blue Note: 46845 (84321), 1969.
  with solos by Johnny Coles, Joe Henderson, Garnett Brown, and Hancock; the interplay between pianist Hancock, bassist Buster Williams, and drummer Al Heath on He Who Lives in Fear conceptually resembles the Bill Evans-Scott LaFaro-Paul Motian approaches.

* MWANDISHI, Warner Bros.: 1898, 1970.
* CROSSINGS, Warner Bros.: 2617, 1971.
  These are from his space music period that was post-hard bop, pre-jazz/rock.

* SEXTANT, Columbia: 32212, 1972.
  one of the precursors of the jazz/rock styles.

HEAD HUNTERS, Columbia: 47478 (32731), CD/AC, 1974.
Hancock's best-selling record prior to FUTURE SHOCK; a funk/jazz style: Chameleon and a new Watermelon Man.

* THRUST, Columbia: 32965, 1974.
  with Hancock (electric piano and synthesizers), Bennie Maupin (soprano and tenor sax, saxello, bass clarinet, alto flute), Paul Jackson (electric bass), Mike Clark (drums), and Bill Summers (auxiliary percussion); all compositions by Hancock: Spank A Lee, Butterfly, Actual Proof, Palm Grease. This recording is included as an example of Hancock's popular mid-1970's band, which was heavily influenced by Sly Stone and funk. Hancock has stated that, along with his playing on Miles Davis MY FUNNY VALENTINE, THRUST represents his best work.

* DEATH WISH, Columbia: 36825 (33199), 1974.
  film score by Hancock: Death Wish, Suite Revenge, Fill Your Hand, etc. Most arranged by Jerry Peters; this is included as an example of Hancock's versatility as a composer. The first three selections on its second side are beautiful, classical type pieces in the manner of Erik Satie and other early 20th century composers.

FUTURE SHOCK, Columbia: 38814, CD/AC, 1983.

see MILES DAVIS - SEVEN STEPS TO HEAVEN, IN EUROPE, COMPLETE CONCERT 1964, HEARD ROUND THE WORLD, E.S.P., PLUGGED NICKEL, MILES SMILES, SORCERER, NEFERTITI, MILES IN THE SKY, and FILLES DE KILIMANJARO
see JOE HENDERSON - POWER TO THE PEOPLE
see WAYNE SHORTER - SPEAK NO EVIL
see MIROSLAV VITOUS - INFINITE SEARCH
see ANTHOLOGIES - JAZZ PIANO

BILL HARRIS (TROMBONE)

see WOODY HERMAN

COLEMAN HAWKINS (TENOR SAX)

* COLEMAN HAWKINS AND BENNY CARTER, DRG/Swing: 8403, 1935-37.
  in Paris: Honeysuckle Rose and Crazy Rhythm with Django Reinhardt.

BODY AND SOUL, RCA Bluebird: 5717-2-RB/CD, 5658-4-RB/2LP set/AC (LPV 501), 1939-56.
samples a variety of recording sessions: 1939 Body and Soul and a 1947 bop date with Fats Navarro (Half Step Down, Please).

GIANTS OF THE TENOR SAX: COLEMAN HAWKINS/FRANK WESS, Commodore/Pair: 7003, CD/LP/AC, 1940-43.
with Benny Carter, Roy Eldridge, etc.

COMPLETE COLEMAN HAWKINS ON KEYNOTE, Mercury: 830960-2, 4CD set, 1944.
includes sessions with Teddy Wilson, Charlie Shavers, Billy Taylor, and Denzil Best: My Man and El Salon de Gutbucket.

see BENNY CARTER - FURTHER DEFINITIONS
see FLETCHER HENDERSON
see DJANGO REINHARDT - DJANGOLOGIE U.S.A.
see ANTHOLOGIES - CLASSIC TENORS, JIVE AT FIVE, SMITHSONIAN COLLECTION OF CLASSIC JAZZ, and THREE GREAT SWING SAXOPHONISTS

ROY HAYNES (DRUMS)

see GARY BURTON - DUSTER
see CHICK COREA - NOW HE SINGS, NOW HE SOBS and TRIO MUSIC
see ERIC DOLPHY - FAR CRY
see STAN GETZ - ROOST QUARTETS
see OLIVER NELSON - BLUES AND THE ABSTRACT TRUTH
see BUD POWELL - THE AMAZING BUD POWELL

FLETCHER HENDERSON (BIG BAND)

* DEVELOPING AN AMERICAN ORCHESTRA, Smithsonian: 2006, 1923-37.
  big band recordings: Sugar Foot Stomp (solos by Rex Stewart and Coleman Hawkins); King Porter Stomp (1928 with solos by Hawkins and Jimmy Harrison); and Christopher Columbus (1936 with solos by Roy Eldridge and Chu Berry).

HOCUS POCUS, RCA Bluebird: 9904 (AXM2-5507), CD/AC, 1927-36.
Sugar Foot Stomp (1931), Hocus Pocus (1934), Sing, Sing, Sing (1936).

* SWING'S THE THING, MCA: 1318, 1931-34.
  Wrappin' It Up, Down South Camp Meetin' (Henry Red Allen solos).

see BENNY GOODMAN - COMPLETE BENNY GOODMAN, VOL. 1 and SING SING SING
see ANTHOLOGIES - ANTHOLOGY OF BIG BAND SWING, BIG BAND JAZZ, EARLY BLACK SWING, and SMITHSONIAN COLLECTION OF CLASSIC JAZZ

JOE HENDERSON (TENOR SAX)

* TETRAGON, Milestone: 9017, 1967-68.
  with Kenny Barron or Don Friedman, Ron Carter, Louis Hayes or Jack DeJohnette: Invitation, Tetragon, etc.

* POWER TO THE PEOPLE, Milestone: 9024, 1969.
  with Herbie Hancock, Ron Carter, Jack DeJohnette, and, on two tunes, Mike Lawrence: Black Narcissus, Power to the People, Lazy Afternoon, etc. Four tunes are written by Henderson, one by Carter.

see HERBIE HANCOCK - THE PRISONER
see HORACE SILVER - SONG FOR MY FATHER and CAPE VERDEAN BLUES

JIMI HENDRIX (ROCK GUITAR)

* SMASH HITS, Reprise: 2276, 1967-69.
* KISS THE SKY, Warner Bros: 25119, 1967-70.

THE ULTIMATE EXPERIENCE, MCA: MCAD-10829, 1967-69.

WOODY HERMAN (BIG BAND)

THUNDERING HERDS, Columbia: 44108 (9291), CD/AC, 1945-47.
with Sonny Berman, Pete Candoli, Bill Harris, Flip Phillips, Stan Getz, Zoot Sims, Herbie Steward, and Serge Chaloff: Jimmy Giuffre's Four Brothers (1947 featuring Getz, Sims, Steward, and Chaloff); and Ralph Burns' Summer Sequence (featuring Getz).

KEEPER OF THE FLAME (EARLY AUTUMN), Capitol: 98453 (11034), CD, 1948-50.
with Stan Getz, Zoot Sims, Gene Ammons, Al Cohn, Serge Chaloff, Bill Harris, etc.: Ralph Burns' arrangement Early Autumn (1948), Shorty Rogers' arrangement Lollypop (1949), Neal Hefti's Great Lie, a Gene Ammons feature called More Moon, and the famous Lemon Drop.

see ANTHOLOGIES - BIG BAND JAZZ

EARL HINES (PIANO)

* A MONDAY DATE, Milestone: 2012 (QRS), 1928 solos.

PIANO MAN, RCA Bluebird: 6750, CD/AC, 1939-42.
solo and big band; includes Blues in Thirds with Sidney Bechet.

see LOUIS ARMSTRONG AND EARL HINES
see JIMMIE NOONE
see ANTHOLOGIES - JAZZ PIANO and SMITHSONIAN COLLECTION OF CLASSIC JAZZ

MILT HINTON (BASS)

see CAB CALLOWAY
see ANTHOLOGIES - JAMMIN' FOR THE JACKPOT

JOHNNY HODGES (ALTO SAX)

* HODGE PODGE, Columbia Special Products: JEE 22001, 1938-39.
  recordings made for Vocalion; with Otto Hardwicke, Cootie Williams, Lawrence Brown, Harry Carney, Duke Ellington or Billy Strayhorn, Billy Taylor (Jimmy Blanton is on one selection), and Sonny Greer: Jeep's Blues, Dream Blues, Empty Ballroom Blues, etc.

* THE COMPLETE JOHNNY HODGES SESSIONS, Mosaic: MR6-126, 6LP set, 1951-55.

USED TO BE DUKE, Verve: 849394-2, CD, 1954.

DUKE'S IN BED/NOT SO DUKISH, Verve: 314 521666-2, CD, 1956.
DUKES IN BED (MGV 8203): sidemen from Ellington band (Jimmy Hamilton, Harry Carney, Ray Nance, Clark Terry, Quentin Jackson, Billy Strayhorn, Jimmy Woode, and Sam Woodyard): A-Oddie-Oobie, Meet Mr. Rabbit, Duke's in Bed (also known as Cop Out and Cop Out Extension, an Ellington big band feature for Paul Gonsalves), Just Squeeze Me (by Ellington), Ballad for Very Tired and Very Sad Lotus Eaters (Strayhorn), Confab with Rab, It Had To Be You, Black and Tan Fantasy, and Take the 'A' Train.

see DUKE ELLINGTON - THIS IS DUKE ELLINGTON, EARLY ELLINGTON, DUKE'S MEN, 1938, 1939, 1940, 1941, BLANTON-WEBSTER BAND, BLACK BROWN & BEIGE, THE WORLD OF DUKE ELLINGTON, ELLINGTON AT NEWPORT, and ELLINGTON INDIGOS
see ANTHOLOGIES - THE GREATEST JAZZ CONCERT IN THE WORLD and JIVE AT FIVE

BILLIE HOLIDAY (SINGER)

THE QUINTESSENTIAL BILLIE HOLIDAY, VOL. 3, Columbia: 44048, CD/AC, 1936-37.
THE QUINTESSENTIAL BILLIE HOLIDAY, VOL. 4, Columbia: 44252, CD/AC, 1937.
THE QUINTESSENTIAL BILLIE HOLIDAY, VOL. 5, Columbia: 44423, CD/AC, 1937-38.
all with Lester Young, Buck Clayton, Teddy Wilson, Roy Eldridge, etc.

DAVE HOLLAND (BASS)

CONFERENCE OF THE BIRDS, ECM: 829373-2 (1027), CD, 1972.
with Anthony Braxton, Sam Rivers, and Barry Altschul.

see ANTHONY BRAXTON - FIVE PIECES
see CHICK COREA - SONG OF SINGING and A.R.C.
see MILES DAVIS - BITCHES BREW

FREDDIE HUBBARD (TRUMPET)

see ART BLAKEY - MOSAIC, THREE BLIND MICE, CARAVAN, and UGETSU
see ORNETTE COLEMAN - FREE JAZZ
see JOHN COLTRANE - OLE
see ERIC DOLPHY - OUT TO LUNCH
see HERBIE HANCOCK - MAIDEN VOYAGE and EMPYREAN ISLES for some of Hubbard's best recorded solos
see J.J. JOHNSON - J.J. INC.
see OLIVER NELSON - BLUES AND THE ABSTRACT TRUTH
see WAYNE SHORTER - SPEAK NO EVIL

MILT JACKSON (VIBES)

MILT JACKSON QUINTET, Blue Note: 81509, CD, 1948-52.
includes Thelonious Monk's Evidence, Epistrophy, and Misterioso.

see MILES DAVIS - MILES DAVIS AND THE MODERN JAZZ GIANTS and BAG'S GROOVE
see DIZZY GILLESPIE - DEVELOPMENT OF AN AMERICAN ARTIST and DIZZIEST
see MODERN JAZZ QUARTET
see THELONIOUS MONK - COMPLETE BLUE NOTE RECORDINGS
see ANTHOLOGIES - SMITHSONIAN COLLECTION OF CLASSIC JAZZ and THE BEBOP REVOLUTION

KEITH JARRETT (PIANO)

SOMEWHERE BEFORE, Atlantic: 8808-2 (Vortex 2012), CD, 1969.
with Charlie Haden and Paul Motian.

FACING YOU, ECM: 827132 (1017), CD/AC, 1971.
solo piano; all compositions by Jarrett: In Front, Ritooria, etc.

IN THE LIGHT, ECM: 835011-2 (1033/34), 2CD set, 1973.

* DEATH AND THE FLOWER, MCA: 29046 (Impulse 9301), 1974.
quartet with Dewey Redman, Charlie Haden, and Paul Motian.

* SHADES, Impulse: 9322, 1975.
quartet with Redman, Haden, and Motian.

* BACKHAND, Impulse: 9305, 1976.
  with Redman, Haden, Motian, and Guilherme Franco: In Flight, Kuum, Valpallia, and Backhand.

STAIRCASE, ECM: 827337-2 (2-1090), 2CD set, 1976.
solo piano.

EYES OF THE HEART, ECM: 825476 (1150), CD/AC, 1976.
quartet with Redman, Haden, and Motian.

SILENCE, GRP/Impulse: GRD-117-2, CD, 1977.
quartet with Redman, Haden, and Motian; includes BYABLUE (Impulse 9331) and BOP-BE (Impulse 9334).

see ANTHOLOGIES - JAZZ PIANO

KEITH JARRETT AS SIDEMAN

* Art Blakey BUTTERCORN LADY, Emarcy: 822471 (Limelight 82034), 1966.

* Charles Lloyd FOREST FLOWER, Atlantic: 1473, 1966.

Jan Garbarek/Keith Jarrett, BELONGING, ECM: 829115 (1050), CD/AC, 1974.
with Garbarek, Jarrett, Palle Danielsson, and Jon Christensen; all tunes by Jarrett: Spiral Dance, Blossom, Long As You Know, You're Living Yours, Belonging, The Windup, and Solstice.

see CHARLIE HADEN - CLOSENESS

KEITH JARRETT AS INFLUENCE

Art Lande/Jan Garbarek, RED LANTA, ECM: 829383-2 (1038), CD, 1973.
Lande's playing here suggests the work of Keith Jarrett.

* Dave Liebman, FORGOTTEN FANTASIES, A&M/Horizon: SP-709, 1975.
  with Richie Beirach; the piano work here suggests Jarrett.

JAMES P. JOHNSON (PIANO)

SNOWY MORNING BLUES, Decca Jazz/GRP: GRD-604, CD, 1930, 1944.
You've Got to Be Modernistic and Jingles (1930).

see ANTHOLOGIES - ENCYCLOPEDIA OF JAZZ ON RECORDS VOL. 1, JAZZ PIANO, PIANO IN STYLE, and SMITHSONIAN COLLECTION OF CLASSIC JAZZ

J. J. JOHNSON (TROMBONE)

JAZZ QUINTET, Savoy/Denon: SV-0151 (2232), CD, 1946-49.
Coppin' the Bop, Jay Jay, and Jay-bird.

THE EMINENT JAY JAY JOHNSON, VOL. 1 & 2, Blue Note: 81505/81506, CDs, 1953-55.
1953 with Clifford Brown, Jimmy Heath, John Lewis, Percy Heath, Kenny Clarke: Turnpike, Lover Man, Get Happy, Sketch 1, Capri, and It Could Happen To You; 1954 with Wynton Kelly, Charles Mingus, Kenny Clarke, and Sabu: Jay, Old Devil Moon; 1955 with Hank Mobley, Horace Silver, and Paul Chambers.

* FIRST PLACE, Columbia: CL 1030, 1957.
  with Tommy Flanagan, Paul Chambers, and Max Roach.

* BLUE TROMBONE, Columbia: CL 1303, 1957.
  with Bobby Jaspar, Tommy Flanagan, and Elvin Jones.

* J.J. INC., Columbia: 36808 (CL 1606), 1960.
  with Freddie Hubbard, Clifford Jordan, and Cedar Walton.

TROMBONE MASTER, Columbia: 44443, CD/AC, 1957-60.
compilation from various sessions.

see STAN GETZ - STAN GETZ AND J.J. JOHNSON AT THE OPERA HOUSE
see SONNY STITT - STITT/POWELL/JOHNSON
see ANTHOLOGIES - JAZZ COMPOSITIONS

ELVIN JONES (DRUMS)

see JOHN COLTRANE - most Atlantic and Impulse recordings
see SONNY ROLLINS - LIVE AT THE VILLAGE VANGUARD
see WAYNE SHORTER - NIGHT DREAMER and SPEAK NO EVIL

PHILLY JOE JONES (DRUMS)

see JOHN COLTRANE - BLUE TRAIN
see TADD DAMERON - MATING CALL
see MILES DAVIS - COLLECTORS ITEMS, NEW QUINTET, WORKIN', STEAMIN', COOKIN', RELAXIN', 'ROUND ABOUT MIDNIGHT, and MILESTONES
see BILL EVANS - EVERYBODY DIGS

SAM JONES (BASS)

see CANNONBALL ADDERLEY - THEM DIRTY BLUES and IN EUROPE
see BILL EVANS - EVERYBODY DIGS BILL EVANS

THAD JONES (TRUMPET, BIG BAND)

THE FABULOUS THAD JONES, Fantasy: OJC-625 (Debut 127), CD/LP/AC, 1954-55.
with Charles Mingus, Max Roach & Kenny Clarke.

* DETROIT-NEW YORK JUNCTION, Blue Note: 1513, 1956.
with Billy Mitchell, Kenny Burrell, Tommy Flanagan, Oscar Pettiford, and Shadow Wilson; three of the tunes were written by Jones (Tarriff, Scratch, and Zec), the others by Richard Rodgers (Blue Room, Little Girl Blue).

* THE MAGNIFICENT THAD JONES, Blue Note: 46814 (1527), 1956.
with Billy Mitchell, Barry Harris, Percy Heath, and Max Roach; two of the tunes were written by Jones (Billie Doo and Thedia).

see COUNT BASIE - CHAIRMAN OF THE BOARD
see CHARLES MINGUS - JAZZICAL MOODS

THAD JONES - MEL LEWIS BIG BAND

* PRESENTING THAD JONES-MEL LEWIS AND THE JAZZ ORCHESTRA, Solid State: 18003 (17003), 1966.
with Bob Brookmeyer, Joe Farrell, Eddie Daniels, Pepper Adams, and Richard Davis: ABC Blues, Mean What You Say, Willow Weep for Me, etc.

* LIVE AT THE VILLAGE VANGUARD, Solid State: 18016, 1967.

* MONDAY NIGHT!, Solid State: 18048, 1968.

* CENTRAL PARK NORTH, Solid State: 18058, 1969.
with Jimmy Knepper, Roland Hanna, and Richard Davis; Jones wrote Tow Away Zone, Groove Merchant, Big Dipper, etc.

THAD JONES/MEL LEWIS, LRC: 9004, CD, 1969-70.
includes 1969 Solid State sessions.

Note: Mosaic Records has announced a forthcoming set of the Thad Jones/Mel Lewis Solid State recordings (1966-1970) (mail order - see page 78).

* NEW LIFE, A&M/Horizon: 0810-2 (SP-707), 1975.
Greetings and Salutations, Little Rascal on the Rock, Forever Lasting, Love to One Is One to Love, and Cherry Juice; all tunes composed and arranged by Jones.

WYNTON KELLY (PIANO)

see CANNONBALL ADDERLEY - CANNONBALL & COLTRANE
see MILES DAVIS - KIND OF BLUE, SOMEDAY MY PRINCE WILL COME, FRIDAY NIGHT, SATURDAY NIGHT, and AT CARNEGIE HALL
see J.J. JOHNSON - THE EMINENT
see WES MONTGOMERY - SMOKIN' AT THE HALF NOTE

STAN KENTON (BIG BAND)

Note: See page 78 for mail-order information on Creative World. All original issue numbers in parentheses in the Kenton section are Capitol.

* MILESTONES, Creative World: 1047 (Capitol T 190), 1943-47.
Artistry in Rhythm, Eager Beaver, Concerto to End All Concertos, and Opus in Pastels.

NEW CONCEPTS OF ARTISTRY IN RHYTHM, Capitol: 92865 (T 383), CD, 1952.
arrangements by Gerry Mulligan, Bill Russo, Bill Holman; solos by Conte Candoli, Lee Konitz, Maynard Ferguson, and Frank Rosolino: 23 N-82 W, My Lady, and Portrait of a Count.

ADVENTURES IN JAZZ, Creative World: 1010 (T 1796), LP, 1961.
with mellophoniums; Kenton felt this to be one of his best recordings; includes Bill Holman's arrangement of Malaguena and Dee Barton's Turtle Talk and Waltz of the Prophets.

RETROSPECTIVE, Capitol: 97350, 4CD set, 1943-1968.

The following list of Kenton recordings is organized by arranger:

DEE BARTON
STAN KENTON CONDUCTS THE JAZZ COMPOSITIONS OF DEE BARTON, Creative World: 1022 (Capitol ST 2922), LP, 1967.
Man, Lonely Boy, Three Thoughts, etc.

BOB CURNOW
NATIONAL ANTHEMS OF THE WORLD, Creative World: 1060, 2LP set, 1972.

STAN KENTON PLAYS CHICAGO, Creative World: 1072, CD, 1974.
Alone, Inner Crisis, The Rise and Fall of a Short Fugue, etc.

RUSS GARCIA
STAN KENTON CONDUCTS THE LOS ANGELES NEOPHONIC ORCHESTRA, Creative World: 1013 (Capitol SMAS 2424), LP, 1965.
Adventure in Emotions Parts I-V.

ROBERT GRAETTINGER
* THE CITY OF GLASS & THIS MODERN WORLD, Creative World: 1006 (T 736), 1951.

BILL HOLMAN
STAN KENTON: THE COMPLETE CAPITOL RECORDINGS OF THE HOLMAN AND RUSSO CHARTS, Mosaic: MD4-136/4CD set, MR6-136/6LP set, 1950-63.
(mail order - see page 78)

KENTON SHOWCASE, Creative World: 1026 (W 524), LP, 1952-54.
Bags, The Opener, Solo for Buddy, etc.

* CONTEMPORARY CONCEPTS, Creative World: 1003 (T 666), 1955.
What's New, Stella by Starlight, Yesterdays, etc.

STAN KENTON
COLLECTOR'S CHOICE, Creative World: 1027, LP, 1951.
Southern Scandal, September Song, Artistry in Tango, etc.

JAZZ COMPOSITIONS OF STAN KENTON, Creative World: 1078, LP, 1946-56.
Eager Beaver, Opus in Pastels, Concerto to End All Concertos, etc.

KENTON/WAGNER, Creative World: 1024 (Capitol 2217), LP, 1964.
Ride of the Valkyries, Siegfried's Funeral March, etc.

BILL MATHIEU
* STANDARDS IN SILHOUETTE, Creative World: 1049 (1394), 1959.
Willow Weep for Me, Django, When Sunny Gets Blue, etc.

LENNIE NIEHAUS
THE STAGE DOOR SWINGS, Creative World: 1044 (1166), LP, 1958.
Hey There, Lullaby of Broadway, On the Street Where You Live, etc.

THE SOPHISTICATED APPROACH, Creative World: 1018 (1674), LP, 1961.
But Beautiful, You Stepped Out of a Dream, Like Someone in Love, etc.

* ADVENTURES IN STANDARDS, Creative World: 1025, 1961.
Some Enchanted Evening, Just In Time, Come Rain or Come Shine, etc.

JOHNNY RICHARDS
CUBAN FIRE, Capitol: 96260 (T 731), CD, 1956.
Fuego Cubano, El Congo Valiente, Recuerdos, etc.

* BACK TO BALBOA, Creative World: 1031 (Capitol T 995), 1958.
Rendezvous at Sunset, Out of this World, I Concentrate on You, etc.

* ADVENTURES IN TIME, Creative World: 1011 (Capitol 1844), 1962.
Commencement, March to Polaris, Artemis, etc.

GENE ROLAND
* VIVA KENTON, Creative World: 1063 (Capitol 1305), 1959.
Adios, Opus in Chartreuse Cha Cha Cha, Chocolate Caliente, etc.

ADVENTURES IN BLUES, Creative World: 1012 (1985), LP, 1961.
Reuben's Blues, Fitz, Exit Stage Left, etc.

PETE RUGOLO
STAN KENTON ENCORES, Creative World: 1034 (T 155), LP, 1946-47.
Peg O' My Heart, He's Funny That Way, Abstraction, etc.

* A CONCERT IN PROGRESSIVE JAZZ, Creative World: 1037 (T 172), 1947.
Cuban Carnival, Elegy for Alto, Impressionism, etc.

THE KENTON TOUCH, Creative World: 1033 (1276), LP, 1958.
Opus in Chartreuse, Theme for Sunday, Minor Riff, etc.

BILL RUSSO
* PORTRAITS OF STANDARDS, Creative World: 1042 (T 462), 1951-54.
Street of Dreams, Under a Blanket of Blue, Crazy Rhythm, etc.

KENTON SHOWCASE, Creative World: 1026 (W 524), LP, 1954.
A Theme for Four Values, Blues Before and After, Egdon Heath, etc.

see under KENTON ARRANGERS: BILL HOLMAN

see ANTHOLOGIES - BIG BAND JAZZ and MIRAGE

EARL KLUGH (GUITAR)

LIVING INSIDE YOUR LOVE, Capitol: 48385 (Liberty 667), CD/AC, 1976.

LEE KONITZ (ALTO SAX)

SUBCONSCIOUS LEE, Fantasy: OJC-186 (Prestige 7004), CD/LP/AC, 1949-50.
with Lennie Tristano, Warne Marsh, and Shelly Manne.

KONITZ MEETS MULLIGAN, Pacific Jazz: 46847 (PJ 20142), CD, 1953.

IDEAL SCENE, Soul Note: 121119-2, CD, 1986.
Konitz on tenor.

see MILES DAVIS - THE BIRTH OF THE COOL
see GERRY MULLIGAN - COMPLETE PACIFIC JAZZ AND CAPITOL RECORDINGS
see CLAUDE THORNHILL
see LENNIE TRISTANO - CROSSCURRENTS
see ANTHOLOGIES - THE BEBOP ERA and SMITHSONIAN COLLECTION OF CLASSIC JAZZ

GENE KRUPA (DRUMS/BIG BAND)

* GENE KRUPA, Columbia Special Products: 753, 1940-47.
  with Roy Eldrige: After You've Gone and Let Me Off Uptown.

see BENNY GOODMAN
see ROY ELDRIDGE WITH THE GENE KRUPA ORCHESTRA

JOHN LEWIS (PIANO)

see MILES DAVIS - THE BIRTH OF THE COOL
see DIZZY GILLESPIE - SHAW NUFF and DIZZIEST
see MODERN JAZZ QUARTET
see CHARLIE PARKER - SAVOY recordings
see ANTHOLOGIES - JAZZ COMPOSITIONS, JAZZ PIANO, and SMITHSONIAN COLLECTION OF CLASSIC JAZZ

MEADE LUX LEWIS (PIANO)

see SIDNEY BECHET - COMPLETE BLUE NOTE RECORDINGS
see ANTHOLOGIES - CUTTIN' THE BOOGIE, JAZZ PIANO, and SMITHSONIAN COLLECTION OF CLASSIC JAZZ

JEFF LORBER (KEYBOARDS)

* SOFT SPACE, Inner City: 1056, 1978.

JIMMIE LUNCEFORD (BIG BAND)

* WILLIE BRYANT & JIMMIE LUNCEFORD & THEIR ORCHESTRAS, RCA: AXM2-5502.
  1934 Lunceford big band recordings: White Heat, Jazznocracy, Sy Oliver's Swingin' Uptown, etc. The majority of the selections in this set is 1935-36 Willie Bryant big band material.

STOMP IT OFF, Decca Jazz/GRP: GRD-608 (MCA 1302/Decca 9237), CD, 1934-35.
Rhythm Is Our Business, Runnin' Wild, etc.

* HARLEM SHOUT, MCA: 1305 (Decca 9238), 1935-36.
  Organ Grinder's Swing, Harlem Shout, etc.

* FOR DANCERS ONLY, MCA: 1307 (Decca 9239), 1936-37.
  For Dancers Only, Annie Laurie, etc.

* BLUES IN THE NIGHT, MCA: 1314 (Decca 9240), 1938, 1941.
  Yard Dog Mazurka, Strictly Instrumental, etc.

see ANTHOLOGIES - ANTHOLOGY OF BIG BAND SWING, BIG BAND JAZZ, EARLY BLACK SWING, and SMITHSONIAN COLLECTION OF CLASSIC JAZZ

SHELLY MANNE (DRUMS)

THE THREE AND THE TWO, Fantasy: OJC-172 (Contemporary 3584), CD/LP, 1954.
each side is a different group; side one: Shorty Rogers, Jimmy Giuffre, and Manne; side two: Russ Freeman and Manne; Abstract #1 is a "free" improvisation with no preset melody or chord progressions; also includes Autumn in New York, Russ Freeman's The Sound Effects Man, A Slight Minority, Speak Easy, etc.

see SHORTY ROGERS - SHORTSTOPS and COLLABORATION: WEST

JOHN MCLAUGHLIN (GUITAR)

MY GOAL'S BEYOND, Rykodisc: RCD-10051 (Douglas 9), CD, 1970.

MAHAVISHNU ORCHESTRA: INNER MOUNTING FLAME, Columbia: 31067, CD/AC, 1971.

MAHAVISHNU ORCHESTRA: BIRDS OF FIRE, Columbia: 31996, CD/AC, 1972.

see LARRY CORYELL - SPACES
see MILES DAVIS - IN A SILENT WAY, BITCHES BREW, JACK JOHNSON, and LIVE-EVIL
see TONY WILLIAMS - EMERGENCY!

JAY MCSHANN (PIANO/BIG BAND)

BLUES FROM KANSAS CITY, Decca Jazz/GRP: GRD-614 (MCA 1338), CD, 1941-43.
includes Charlie Parker solos on Hootie Blues, Swingmatism, The Jumpin' Blues, and Sepian Stomp.

see ANTHOLOGIES - ANTHOLOGY OF BIG BAND SWING
see CHARLIE PARKER - EARLY BIRD

PAT METHENY (GUITAR)

PAT METHENY GROUP, ECM: 825593 (1114), CD/AC, 1978.

OFFRAMP, ECM: 817138 (1216), CD/AC, 1981.
above two with Lyle Mays.

PAT METHENY/ORNETTE COLEMAN: SONG X, Geffen: 24096, CD/AC, 1985.

see GARY BURTON - RING and DREAMS SO REAL

GLENN MILLER (big band)

CHATTANOOGA CHOO CHOO: THE #1 HITS, RCA Bluebird: 3102, CD/AC, 1939-42.

THE POPULAR RECORDINGS, RCA Bluebird: 9785, 3CD/3AC set, 1938-42.

see ANTHOLOGIES - BIG BAND JAZZ

CHARLES MINGUS (BASS/BANDLEADER)

JAZZICAL MOODS, Fresh Sound: FSRCD-62 (Period), CD, 1954.
* CHARLIE MINGUS, Everest: FS 235 (Period), 1954.
with Thad Jones, Teo Macero, John LaPorta, Jackson Wiley, and Clem DeRosa: Minor Intrusions, Spur of the Moment, Four Hands, and Thrice Upon a Theme.

PITHECANTHROPUS ERECTUS, Atlantic: 8809-2 (1237), CD, 1956.
with Jackie McLean, J.R. Monterose, and Mal Waldron.

NEW TIJUANA MOODS, RCA Bluebird: 5644-2-RB/CD, 5635-4-RB/AC (LSP-2533), 1957.
combo recordings that Mingus has stated to be among his best; with Clarence Shaw, Jimmy Knepper, and Shafi Hadi: Flamingo, Tia Juana Gift Shop, Dizzy Moods, etc.

MINGUS AH UM, Columbia: 40648 (CL 1370), CD/AC, 1959.
with Shafi Hadi, John Handy, Booker Ervin, Jimmy Knepper, Horace Parlan, Roland Hanna, and Dannie Richmond: Better Git It in Your Soul, Bird Calls, Fables of Faubus, Pussy Cat Dues, Jelly Roll, Goodbye Pork Pie Hat, etc.

THE COMPLETE 1959 CBS CHARLES MINGUS SESSIONS, Mosaic: MQ4-143, 4LP set, 1959. (mail order - see page 78)
includes MINGUS AH UM and MINGUS DYNASTY plus unreleased unedited takes.

CHARLES MINGUS PRESENTS CHARLES MINGUS, Candid: 79005, CD, 1960.
THE COMPLETE CANDID RECORDINGS, Mosaic: MD3-111/3CD, MR4-111/4LP set, 1960-1961. (mail order - see page 78)
with Eric Dolphy, Ted Curson, and Dannie Richmond: What Love, Original Faubus Fables, All the Things You Could Be by Now If Sigmund Freud's Wife Was Your Mother, and Folk Forms, No. 1.

MINGUS REVISITED (PRE-BIRD), Emarcy: 826496-2 (MG-20627), CD, 1960.
with 5 trumpets, 4 trombones, tuba, cello, piano, oboe, flute, voice, etc.: Prayer for Passive Resistance, Eclipse, Half-Mast Inhibition, etc. All compositions by Mingus except Billy Strayhorn's Take the 'A' Train and Ellington's Do Nothing Til You Hear From Me.

MINGUS PLAYS PIANO, Mobile Fidelity: MFCD-783 (Impulse 60), CD, 1963.

MINGUS MOVES, Rhino/Atlantic: 71454 (SD 1653), CD, 1973.
with George Adams and Don Pullen.

see LIONEL HAMPTON - MIDNIGHT SUN
see J.J. JOHNSON - EMINENT
see ANTHOLOGIES - JAZZ COMPOSITIONS, JAZZ IN REVOLUTION, MIRAGE, NICA'S DREAM, and SMITHSONIAN COLLECTION OF CLASSIC JAZZ

THE MODERN JAZZ QUARTET

MJQ40: THE BOXED SET, Atlantic: 82330-2, 4CD set, 1952-1988.
includes Prestige & Atlantic material.

DJANGO, Fantasy: OJC-057 (Prestige 7057), CD/LP/AC, 1953-54.
with Milt Jackson, John Lewis, Percy Heath, and Kenny Clarke: Milano, Django, La Ronde, The Queen's Fancy, etc.

CONCORDE, Fantasy: OJC-002 (P-7005), CD/LP/AC, 1955.
with Jackson, Lewis, Heath, and Connie Kay.

EUROPEAN CONCERT, Atlantic: CS2-603-4, 2AC set, 1960.
concert by Jackson, Lewis, Heath, and Kay: Django, Bluesology, etc.

see ANTHOLOGIES - NICA'S DREAM

MIFF MOLE (TROMBONE)

see ANTHOLOGIES - THESAURUS OF CLASSIC JAZZ

THELONIOUS MONK (PIANO)

GENIUS OF MODERN MUSIC, VOLS. 1 & 2, Blue Note: 81510/81511, CDs, 1947-52.
* THE COMPLETE BLUE NOTE RECORDINGS OF THELONIOUS MONK, Mosaic: MR4-101, 4LP set, 1947-52.
with Milt Jackson, Art Blakey, Idris Sulieman, etc.: Humph, In Walked Bud, Epistrophy, Misterioso, Well You Needn't, Off Minor, Straight No Chaser, Evidence, Criss Cross, etc.

BEST OF THELONIOUS MONK: THE BLUE NOTE YEARS, Blue Note: 95636, CD/AC, 1947-52.
includes many of the above selections.

THELONIOUS MONK: THE COMPLETE RIVERSIDE RECORDINGS, Riverside: RCD-022-2/15CD set, R-022/22LP set, 1955-1961.

THELONIOUS HIMSELF, Fantasy: OJC-254 (Riverside R-235), CD/LP/AC, 1957.
solo piano: Functional, I Should Care, and 'Round Midnight.

* MONK'S TIME, Columbia: CS 8984 (CL 2184), 1964.
with Charlie Rouse, Butch Warren, and Ben Riley: Brake's Sake, Lulu's Back in Town, and Nice Work If You Can Get It.

STANDARDS, Columbia: 45148, CD/AC, 1963-67.
compilation from various sessions: Tea for Two (1963).

see CHARLIE CHRISTIAN (HOT LIPS PAGE - TRUMPET AT MINTON'S)
see MILES DAVIS - MILES DAVIS & THE MODERN JAZZ GIANTS and BAG'S GROOVE
see MILT JACKSON QUINTET
see CHARLIE PARKER - THE VERVE YEARS and BIRD AND DIZ
see ANTHOLOGIES - BEBOP, JAZZ PIANO, and SMITHSONIAN COLLECTION OF CLASSIC JAZZ

WES MONTGOMERY (GUITAR)

INCREDIBLE JAZZ GUITAR, Fantasy: OJC-036 (Riverside 9320), CD/LP/AC, 1960.
with Tommy Flanagan, Percy Heath, and Al Heath: West Coast Blues, Mister Walker, etc.

SMOKIN' AT THE HALF NOTE, Verve: 314 521434-2 (V6-8633), CD, 1965.
with Wynton Kelly, Paul Chambers, and Jimmy Cobb.

AIRTO MOREIRA (PERCUSSION)

see CHICK COREA - RETURN TO FOREVER and LIGHT AS A FEATHER
see MILES DAVIS - BLACK BEAUTY
see WEATHER REPORT - WEATHER REPORT

LEE MORGAN (TRUMPET)

see ART BLAKEY - COMPLETE 1960, NIGHT IN TUNISIA, and INDESTRUCTIBLE
see JOHN COLTRANE - BLUE TRAIN
see WAYNE SHORTER - NIGHT DREAMER

JELLY ROLL MORTON (PIANO)

THE PIANIST AND COMPOSER, Smithsonian: RD-043, CD, 1923-26.

JELLY ROLL MORTON, Milestone: MCD-47018-2 (Gennett), CD, 1923-26.

CHICAGO: THE RED HOT PEPPERS, Smithsonian: RD-044, CD, 1926-28.
THE PEARLS, RCA Bluebird: 6588 (LPM-1649), CD/LP/AC, 1926-38.
with Kid Ory, George Mitchell, Johnny St. Cyr, etc.: Black Bottom Stomp, The Chant, etc.

THE JELLY ROLL MORTON CENTENNIAL: HIS COMPLETE VICTOR RECORDINGS, RCA Bluebird: 2361, 5CD/5AC set, 1926-30, 1939.

see ANTHOLOGIES - ENCYCLOPEDIA OF JAZZ ON RECORD VOL.1, JAZZ PIANO, PIANO IN STYLE, RIVERSIDE COLLECTION OF CLASSIC JAZZ, and SMITHSONIAN COLLECTION OF CLASSIC JAZZ

GERRY MULLIGAN (BARITONE SAX)

THE BEST OF THE GERRY MULLIGAN QUARTET WITH CHET BAKER, Pacific Jazz: 95481, CD/AC, 1952-53.
Walkin' Shoes, Soft Shoe, and Freeway.

* THE COMPLETE PACIFIC JAZZ AND CAPITOL RECORDINGS OF THE ORIGINAL GERRY MULLIGAN QUARTET AND TENTETTE WITH CHET BAKER, Mosaic: MD3-102/MR5-102, 1952-53.
1952 with Chet Baker, Bob Whitlock, and Chico Hamilton: Walkin' Shoes, Soft Shoe, and Freeway; live 1953 session with Lee Konitz, Baker, Carson Smith or Joe Mondragon, and Larry Bunker: I Can't Believe That You're in Love With Me, Broadway, All the Things You Are, Almost Like Being in Love, and Lover Man (a transcription of the Konitz solo on this tune is available in John Mehegan, *Jazz Improvisation, Vol. 2*); the 1953 Mulligan Tentette with Baker, Pete Candoli, Bob Enevoldsen, John Graas, Ray Siegel, Bud Shank, Don Davidson, Mondragon, Hamilton, and Bunker; includes Walkin' Shoes, Rocker, Flash, etc.; Mulligan considers this session to represent some of his best work.

* WHAT IS THERE TO SAY?, Columbia Special Products: JCS 8116, 1959.
with Art Farmer, Bill Crow, and Dave Bailey: What Is There to Say?, Just in Time, As Catch Can, etc. Mulligan feels this recording to be some of his best work.

* THE CONCERT JAZZ BAND, Verve: V-8388, 1960.
  big band featuring Mulligan and Bob Brookmeyer: Sweet and Slow, Out of This World, Duke Ellington's I'm Gonna Go Fishin, and Mulligan's Bweebida, Bobbida, etc.

GERRY MULLIGAN CONCERT JAZZ BAND, Verve: 838933 (MGV 8396), CD/AC, 1960.
* GERRY MULLIGAN & THE CONCERT JAZZ BAND AT THE VILLAGE VANGUARD, Mobile Fidelity: 179, 1960.
  the above band in concert, featuring Clark Terry and Bob Brookmeyer: Black Nightgown, Body and Soul, Come Rain or Come Shine, etc; the CD also includes big band material from a 1960 European tour.

see MILES DAVIS - THE BIRTH OF THE COOL
see PAUL DESMOND - TWO OF A MIND
see DUKE ELLINGTON - NEWPORT 1958
see LEE KONITZ MEETS GERRY MULLIGAN
see ANTHOLOGIES - THE BIRTH OF THE COOL, VOL. 2

FATS NAVARRO (TRUMPET)

NOSTALGIA, Savoy/Denon: SV-0123 (12133), CD, 1946-47.
  with Tadd Dameron, Dexter Gordon, Art Blakey, etc.

FATS NAVARRO MEMORIAL, Savoy/Denon: SV-0181 (12011), CD, 1946-47.
  with Bud Powell, Kenny Dorham, Sonny Stitt, Tadd Dameron, Kenny Clarke, etc.

* THE FABULOUS FATS NAVARRO, VOLS. 1 & 2, Blue Note: 81531/81532, 1947-49.
  1948 with Howard McGhee: Double Talk and Boperation; 1948 with Tadd Dameron: Our Delight and Dameronia; and 1948 with Wardell Gray and Allen Eager: Lady Bird. Vol. 1 (CD only) includes Dameron's 1949 sessions for Capitol with Navarro or Miles Davis.

see COLEMAN HAWKINS - BODY AND SOUL
see BUD POWELL - AMAZING
see ANTHOLOGIES - BEBOP, THE BEBOP REVOLUTION, JAZZ IN REVOLUTION, and SMITHSONIAN COLLECTION OF CLASSIC JAZZ

OLIVER NELSON (SAXOPHONE)

BLUES AND THE ABSTRACT TRUTH, MCA/Impulse: MCAD-5659 (A-5), CD, 1961.
  with Freddie Hubbard, Eric Dolphy, Bill Evans, and Roy Haynes.

NEW ORLEANS RHYTHM KINGS

NEW ORLEANS RHYTHM KINGS, Milestone: MCD-47020-2, CD, 1922-23.

see ANTHOLOGIES - STEPPIN' ON THE GAS

RED NICHOLS (TRUMPET)

see ANTHOLOGIES - THESAURUS OF CLASSIC JAZZ

JIMMIE NOONE (CLARINET)

THE JIMMIE NOONE COLLECTION, VOL. 1, Gazell/Collectors Classics: COCD-6 (MCA 1313), CD, 1928. (import - see page 78)
  with Earl Hines, Joe Poston, Bud Scott, Lawson Buford, and Johnny Wells: Apex Blues, My Monday Date, King Joe, I Know That You Know, and two versions of Every Evening and Sweet Lorraine.

see ANTHOLOGIES - ENCYCLOPEDIA OF JAZZ ON RECORDS VOL. 1 and SMITHSONIAN COLLECTION OF CLASSIC JAZZ (REVISED)

KING OLIVER (CORNET)

* KING OLIVER'S JAZZ BAND, Smithsonian: 2001, 1923.
  with Louis Armstrong, Johnny Dodds, Honore Dutrey, Lil Hardin, etc.: Snake Rag, Sweet Lovin' Man, High Society Rag, Dippermouth Blues, West End Blues, etc.

LOUIS ARMSTRONG & KING OLIVER, Milestone: MCD-47017-2, CD, 1923-1924.
Dippermouth Blues (1923) with Oliver, Armstrong, Johnny Dodds, Honore Dutrey, Baby Dodds, etc.; Cakewalking Babies from Home (1924) with Armstrong, Sidney Bechet, Lil Hardin, and Charlie Irvis; Tom Cat Blues (1924), duet between King Oliver and Jelly Roll Morton.

see ANTHOLOGIES - THE SMITHSONIAN COLLECTION OF CLASSIC JAZZ

ORIGINAL DIXIELAND JAZZ BAND

THE 75TH ANNIVERSARY, RCA Bluebird: 61098 (LPV-547), CD/AC, 1917-1921.
usually considered the first recording of jazz; 1917 sessions feature Nick LaRocca, Larry Shields, Eddie Edwards, Henry Ragas, and Tony Sbarbaro: Livery Stable Blues (1917), Tiger Rag (1918), Clarinet Marmalade (1918), etc.

see ANTHOLOGIES - AN EXPERIMENT IN MODERN MUSIC and RAGTIME

CHARLIE PARKER (ALTO SAX)

COMPLETE BIRTH OF THE BEBOP, Stash: ST-CD-535, CD, 1940-46.
includes Parker's first known recording: Honey & Body (1940) and a 1942 session with Parker on alto plus a guitar; also a 1943 jam session with Dizzy Gillespie, Oscar Pettiford, and Parker on tenor sax, made in the hotel room of Billy Eckstine's valet, Robert Redcross: Sweet Georgia Brown, Three Guesses, Boogie Woogie. These performances are among the most valuable on record for documenting formative Parker, and, because they are on tenor, clarifying his Lester Young and Coleman Hawkins roots.

EARLY BIRD, Stash: ST-CD-542 (Onyx 221/Spotlite 120), CD, 1940-44.
1940 Wichita transcriptions with Bernard Anderson, Orville Minor, Bud Gould, Jay McShann, Gene Ramey, and Gus Johnson: I Found A New Baby, Body and Soul, Moten Swing, Coquette, Lady Be Good, Wichita Blues, and Honeysuckle Rose; Cherokee (1942) by Parker with an unidentified rhythm section; 1942 broadcast from the Savoy Ballroom with Jay McShann.

* BIRD/THE SAVOY RECORDINGS (MASTER TAKES), Savoy: 8801 (2201), 1944-48.
1944 with Tiny Grimes, Clyde Hart, etc.: Tiny's Tempo and Red Cross; 1945 with Miles Davis, Dizzy Gillespie, Argonne Thornton, Curly Russell, and Max Roach: Billie's Bounce, Now's the Time, Ko Ko; 1947 with Davis, Bud Powell, Tommy Potter, and Roach: Donna Lee and Cheryl; 1947 with Davis, John Lewis, Nelson Boyd, and Roach: Half Nelson and Sippin' at Bells; 1947 with Davis, Duke Jordan, Potter, and Roach: Blue Bird; 1948 with Davis, Lewis, Russell, and Roach: Barbados, Parker's Mood, etc.

* COMPLETE SAVOY STUDIO SESSIONS, Savoy: 5500, 3CD set, 1944-48.

THE IMMORTAL CHARLIE PARKER, Savoy/Denon: SV-0102 (12001), CD, 1944, 1947-48.

THE CHARLIE PARKER STORY, Savoy/Denon: SV-0105 (12079), CD, 1945.

THE GENIUS OF CHARLIE PARKER, Savoy/Denon: SV-0104 (12014), CD, 1945-48.

CHARLIE PARKER MEMORIAL. VOL. 1, Savoy/Denon: SV-0101 (12000), CD, 1947-48.

CHARLIE PARKER MEMORIAL. VOL. 2, Savoy/Deno: SV-0103 (12009), CD, 1945-48.
Note: The above Savoy/Denon reissues, which are replicas of the original Savoy LPs, are poorly organized (frequently mixing different sessions and master takes with incomplete takes), but they are the only Parker Savoy's currently in print.

THE COMPLETE DIAL SESSIONS, Stash: ST-CD-567-70 (Spotlite 101-106), 4CD set, 1946-47.
1946 with Dizzy Gillespie, Lucky Thompson, etc.: Diggin' Diz; 1946 with Miles Davis, Lucky Thompson, Dodo Marmarosa, etc.: Moose The Mooch, Yardbird Suite, Ornithology, and Night In Tunisia; 1946 with Howard McGhee, etc.: Lover Man; 1947 with Erroll Garner, etc.: This Is Always, Cool Blues, and Bird's Nest; 1947 with McGhee, Wardell Gray, Marmarosa, etc.: Relaxin' at Camarillo and Cheers; 1947 with Davis, Duke Jordan, Max Roach, etc.: Dexterity, Embraceable You, Dewey Square, Klactoveesedstene, Crazeology, etc.

THE LEGENDARY DIAL MASTERS, VOL. 1 & 2, Stash: ST-CD-23 & -25, CD, 1946-47.
master takes of Dial sessions; see above.

THE VERY BEST OF BIRD, Warner Bros: 3198, 2AC set, 1946-47.
selection of Dial recordings; see above.

BIRD/ THE COMPLETE CHARLIE PARKER ON VERVE, Verve: 837141-2, 10CD set, 1946-1954.

* THE VERVE YEARS 1948-50, Verve: 827151-4 (VE2-2501), 1948-50.
April in Paris and Just Friends with strings; Star Eyes with Hank Jones; and Bloomdido and Relaxin' with Lee with Gillespie, Monk, and Buddy Rich.

BIRD AND DIZ, Verve: 831133-2 (MGV 8006), CD, 1950.
with Dizzy Gillespie, Thelonious Monk, and Buddy Rich.

NOW'S THE TIME, Verve: 314 521437-2 (MGV 8005), CD, 1952-53.
with Al Haig and Max Roach.

JAZZ AT MASSEY HALL, Fantasy: OJC-044 (Debut 124), CD/LP/AC, 1953.
concert with Dizzy Gillespie, Bud Powell, Charles Mingus, and Max Roach.

see DIZZY GILLESPIE - SHAW NUFF
see JAY MCSHANN - BLUES FROM KANSAS CITY
see ANTHOLOGIES - BEBOP and SMITHSONIAN COLLECTION OF CLASSIC JAZZ

JACO PASTORIUS (ELECTRIC BASS GUITAR)

JACO PASTORIUS, Epic: 33949, CD/AC, 1976.

WORD OF MOUTH, Warner Bros: 3535, CD/AC, 1981.

see WEATHER REPORT - BLACK MARKET, HEAVY WEATHER, MR. GONE, 8:30, NIGHT PASSAGE, and WEATHER REPORT (1981)

ART PEPPER (ALTO SAX)

MODERN ART, Blue Note: 46848 (Intro 606), CD, 1956-57.
with Russ Freeman.

* THE COMPLETE PACIFIC JAZZ SMALL GROUP RECORDINGS OF ART PEPPER, Mosaic: MR3-105, 3LP set, 1956-57.
with Chet Baker, Russ Freeman, and Shorty Rogers.

INTENSITY, Fantasy: OJC-387 (Contemporary 7607), CD/LP/AC, 1960.

OSCAR PETERSON (PIANO)

* TENDERLY, Verve: 2046 (Clef 696), 1950.
with Ray Brown or Major Holley: Tenderly, Debut, Nameless, and All The Things You Are.

JAZZ AT THE PHILHARMONIC - THE OSCAR PETERSON TRIO SET, Verve: 825099-4, AC, 1952-3.
with Barney Kessell or Herb Ellis, and Ray Brown.

* THE MODERN JAZZ QUARTET AND THE OSCAR PETERSON TRIO AT THE OPERA HOUSE, Verve: MGV 8269, 1957.
concert; one side is the MJQ, the other is the Oscar Peterson Trio with Herb Ellis and Ray Brown: Indiana, Joy Spring, etc. This recording is included for Peterson's fastest solo, Indiana.

THE WILL TO SWING: OSCAR PETERSON AT HIS VERY BEST, Verve: 847203, 2CD set/AC, 1947-73.

see ANTHOLOGIES - JAZZ PIANO

OSCAR PETTIFORD (BASS)

see LUCKY THOMPSON - TRICOTISM
see ANTHOLOGIES - CLASSIC TENORS

BUD POWELL (PIANO)

THE BUD POWELL TRIO PLAYS, Roulette: 93902 (Roost 2224), CD, 1947-1953.
Nice Work If You Can Get It with Curly Russell and Max Roach.

THE AMAZING BUD POWELL, VOL. 1 & 2, Blue Note: 81503/81504, CDs, 1949-53.
* THE COMPLETE BUD POWELL BLUE NOTE RECORDINGS, Mosaic: MR5-116, 5LP set, 1949-58.
with Max Roach, Sonny Rollins, Fats Navarro, Tommy Potter, and Roy Haynes: Un Poco Loco, Bouncing with Bud, and Dance of the Infidels.

JAZZ GIANT, Verve: 829937-2 (MGV 8153), CD, 1949-50.
with Ray Brown, Curly Russell, Max Roach: Get Happy.

THE GENIUS OF BUD POWELL, Verve: 827901-2 (V 8115), CD, 1950-51.
Hallucinations, Tea for Two, etc.

see DEXTER GORDON - DEXTER RIDES AGAIN
see FATS NAVARRO - MEMORIAL
see CHARLIE PARKER - SAVOY recordings and JAZZ AT MASSEY HALL
see SONNY STITT - STITT/POWELL/JOHNSON
see ANTHOLOGIES - BEBOP, THE BEBOP REVOLUTION, JAZZ PIANO, and SMITHSONIAN COLLECTION OF CLASSIC JAZZ

JIMMY RANEY (GUITAR)

see STAN GETZ - Mosaic set and AT STORYVILLE

DJANGO REINHARDT (GUITAR)

DJANGOLOGIE U.S.A., VOL. 1, DRG/Swing: 8421/23, 2CD set, 1936-37.
DJANGOLOGIE U.S.A., VOL. 2, DRG/Swing: 8424/26, 2CD set, 1937-40.
Swing Guitars, Swinging with Django, Minor Swing, Honeysuckle Rose, Crazy Rhythm, etc.

* PARISIAN SWING, GNP Crescendo: 9002, 1935-39.
Djangology, Nocturne, Louise, and Improvisation.

see COLEMAN HAWKINS & BENNY CARTER
see ANTHOLOGIES - SMITHSONIAN COLLECTION OF CLASSIC JAZZ (REVISED)

MAX ROACH (DRUMS)

see CLIFFORD BROWN - BROWN & ROACH and BASIN STREET
see MILES DAVIS - BIRTH OF THE COOL
see DEXTER GORDON - DEXTER RIDES AGAIN
see THAD JONES - THE MAGNIFICENT THAD JONES
see CHARLIE PARKER - SAVOY and DIAL recordings and NOW'S THE TIME
see BUD POWELL - THE AMAZING BUD POWELL and JAZZ GIANT
see SONNY ROLLINS - SAXOPHONE COLOSSUS and PLUS FOUR
see SONNY STITT - STITT/POWELL/JOHNSON
see ANTHOLOGIES - BEBOP and SMITHSONIAN COLLECTION OF CLASSIC JAZZ

SHORTY ROGERS (TRUMPET/COMPOSER)

SHORTSTOPS, RCA Bluebird: 5917, CD/AC, 1953-54.
with Milt Bernhart, John Graas, Gene England, Art Pepper, Jimmy Giuffre, Hampton Hawes, Joe Mondragon, and Shelly Manne: Morpo, Diablo's Dance, Pirouette, etc.

TEDDY CHARLES/SHORTY ROGERS COLLABORATION: WEST, Fantasy: OJC-122 (Prestige 7028), CD/LP, 1953.
with Jimmy Giuffre, Teddy Charles, Shorty Rogers, Curtis Counce, and Shelly Manne; Etudiez Le Cahier employs mode-based improvisation; Variations on a Motive by Bud uses a tone center based improvisation instead of conventional chord progression based improvisation.

see WOODY HERMAN - KEEPER OF THE FLAME
see SHELLY MANNE - THE THREE AND THE TWO
see ANTHOLOGIES - ATLANTIC JAZZ: WEST COAST and BIRTH OF THE COOL, VOL. 2

SONNY ROLLINS (TENOR SAX)

SONNY ROLLINS: THE COMPLETE PRESTIGE RECORDINGS, Prestige: 7PCD-4407-2, 7CD set, 1949-56.

SONNY ROLLINS PLUS FOUR, Fantasy: OJC-243 (Prestige 7038), CD/LP/AC, 1956.
with Clifford Brown, Richie Powell, George Morrow, and Max Roach: Pent Up House, Kiss and Run, and Valse Hot; Rollins has said that this is some of his best playing on record.

SAXOPHONE COLOSSUS, Fantasy: OJC-291 (Prestige 7079), CD/LP/AC, 1956.
with Tommy Flanagan and Max Roach: Blue Seven, St. Thomas, etc.

WAY OUT WEST, Fantasy: OJC-337 (Contemporary 7530), CD/LP/AC, 1957.
with Ray Brown and Shelly Manne.

NIGHT AT THE VILLAGE VANGUARD, VOL. 1 & 2, Blue Note: 46517/46518, CD, 1957.
with Wilbur Ware and Elvin Jones: A Night in Tunisia, I'll Remember April, etc. The 2 CDs include all the material on Blue Note 1581 and MORE FROM THE VANGUARD (Blue Note 475).

QUARTETS FEATURING JIM HALL (THE BRIDGE), RCA Bluebird: 5643-2-RB/CD, 5634-4-RB/2AC, (LSP-2527), 1962.

ON THE OUTSIDE (OUR MAN IN JAZZ), RCA Bluebird: 2496 (LSP-2612), CD/AC, 1962.
live with Don Cherry, Henry Grimes, and Ed Blackwell.

see CLIFFORD BROWN - AT BASIN STREET
see MILES DAVIS - DIG, COLLECTOR'S ITEMS, and BAG'S GROOVE
see DIZZY GILLESPIE - DUETS and SONNY SIDE UP
see BUD POWELL - AMAZING
see ANTHOLOGIES - NICA'S DREAM and THE SMITHSONIAN COLLECTION OF CLASSIC JAZZ

FRANK ROSOLINO (TROMBONE)

see STAN KENTON - NEW CONCEPTS OF ARTISTRY IN RHYTHM

GEORGE RUSSELL (PIANO/COMPOSER)

see DIZZY GILLESPIE - DIZZIEST
see LENNIE TRISTANO - CROSSCURRENTS
see ANTHOLOGIES - JAZZ COMPOSITIONS and MIRAGE

LUIS RUSSELL (BIG BAND)

THE LUIS RUSSELL COLLECTION, VOL. 1, Gazell/Collectors Classics: COCD-7 (Columbia 32338), CD, 1926-34. (import - see page 78)
big band recordings featuring Henry Red Allen, J.C. Higginbotham, etc: Plantation Joys, Jersey Lightning, Higginbotham Blues, etc.

PEE WEE RUSSELL (CLARINET)

see ANTHOLOGIES - THESAURUS OF CLASSIC JAZZ

ARTIE SHAW (CLARINET/BIG BAND)

BEGIN THE BEGUINE, RCA Bluebird: 6274, CD/AC, 1938-41.
1938 big band: Begin the Beguine; 1940 big band: Star Dust, etc.

COMPLETE GRAMERCY FIVE, RCA Bluebird: 7637 (LPV-582), CD/LP/AC, 1940-45.
combo with Roy Eldridge, Barney Kessel, Dodo Marmarosa, Morris Rayman, and Lou Fromm: Scuttlebutt, Mysterioso, Grabtown Grapple, etc.

see ANTHOLOGIES - BIG BAND JAZZ

GEORGE SHEARING (PIANO)

LULLABY OF BIRDLAND, Verve: 827977-4 (MGM), AC, 1949-54.
with Marjorie Hyams, Don Elliott, Chuck Wayne, John Levy, Denzil Best, etc: September in the Rain, Conception, Pick Yourself Up, Lullaby of Birdland, etc.

THE BEST OF GEORGE SHEARING: ORIGINAL CAPITOL RECORDINGS, Curb/CEMA: 77631 (Capitol 2104), CD/AC, 1955-68.
not necessarily his best, but a good survey, including a remake of Lullaby of Birdland.

WAYNE SHORTER (SOPRANO & TENOR SAX)

NIGHT DREAMER, Blue Note: 84173, CD, 1964.
with Lee Morgan, McCoy Tyner, Reggie Workman, and Elvin Jones; all tunes composed by Shorter: Night Dreamer, Oriental Folk Song, Virgo, Black Nile, Charcoal Blues, Armageddon, and House of Jade.

SPEAK NO EVIL, Blue Note: 46509 (84194), CD, 1964.
with Freddie Hubbard, Herbie Hancock, Ron Carter, and Elvin Jones; all tunes composed by Shorter: Witch Hunt, Fee Fi Fo Fum, Dance Cadaverous, Speak No Evil, Infant Eyes, and Wild Flower.

SUPER NOVA, Blue Note: 84332, CD, 1969.
with John McLaughlin, Chick Corea, Jack DeJohnette, etc.

see ART BLAKEY - MOSAIC, THREE BLIND MICE, CARAVAN, UGETSU, and INDESTRUCTIBLE
see MILES DAVIS - HEARD ROUND THE WORLD, E.S.P., PLUGGED NICKEL, MILES SMILES, SORCERER, NEFERTITI, MILES IN THE SKY, FILLES DE KILIMANJARO, IN A SILENT WAY, and BITCHES BREW
see WEATHER REPORT
see JOE ZAWINUL - ZAWINUL

HORACE SILVER (PIANO)

HORACE SILVER AND THE JAZZ MESSENGERS, Blue Note: 46140 (81518), CD, 1954.
with Kenny Dorham, Hank Mobley, and Art Blakey: Doodlin', The Preacher.

* SIX PIECES OF SILVER, Blue Note: 81539, 1956.
Senor Blues.

FINGER POPPIN', Blue Note: 84008, CD, 1959.
with Blue Mitchell, Junior Cook, Gene Taylor, and Louis Hayes: Finger Poppin', Cookin' at the Continental, Mellow D, etc.

BLOWIN' THE BLUES AWAY, Blue Note: 46526 (84017), CD, 1959.
with Mitchell and Cook: Sister Sadie, Peace, etc.

HORACE-SCOPE, Blue Note: 84042, CD, 1960.
with Blue Mitchell and Junior Cook.

SONG FOR MY FATHER, Blue Note: 84185, CD/AC, 1964.
with Carmell Jones, Joe Henderson: Song For My Father, The Kicker.

CAPE VERDEAN BLUES, Blue Note: 84220, CD, 1965.
with Joe Henderson, Woody Shaw and J.J. Johnson.

* IN PURSUIT OF THE 27TH MAN, Blue Note: 054, 1972.
with Randy Brecker, Michael Brecker, David Friedman, Bob Cranshaw, and Mickey Roker: Liberated Brothers, Kathy, Gregory Is Here, Summer in Central Park, Nothin' Can Stop Me Now, In Pursuit of the 27th Man, and Strange Vibes; included because it contains the best recorded solos of the Brecker Brothers to date; it also hangs together very well, displays delightful Silver writing, and, on some tunes, an unusual format for Silver: vibes, piano, bass and drums.

see ART BLAKEY - A NIGHT AT BIRDLAND and JAZZ MESSENGER
see MILES DAVIS - WALKIN' and BAG'S GROOVE
see ANTHOLOGIES - BEBOP, JAZZ PIANO, NICA'S DREAM, and SMITHSONIAN COLLECTION OF CLASSIC JAZZ (REVISED)

ZOOT SIMS (TENOR SAX)

ONE TO BLOW ON, Biograph: 12062 (Dawn 1102), LP/AC, 1956.
with Bob Brookmeyer.

SLY AND THE FAMILY STONE (FUNK-ROCK BAND)

GREATEST HITS, Epic: 30325, CD/AC, 1968-70.

FRESH, Epic: 32134, CD, 1973.
includes In Time, drum part for which appears on page 431 of text.

BESSIE SMITH (BLUES SINGER)

THE COLLECTION, Columbia: 44441, CD/AC, 1923-33.
includes selections with accompaniment by Louis Armstrong.

JABBO SMITH (TRUMPET)

JABBO SMITH'S RHYTHM ACES. Classics: 669 (MCA 1347), CD, 1929-38.
(import - see page 78)
Sweet and Low Blues and Till Times Get Better.

see ANTHOLOGIES - SWEET AND LOW

JIMMY SMITH (ORGAN)

MIDNIGHT SPECIAL, Blue Note: 84078, CD/AC, 1960.
with Kenny Burrell.

PINETOP SMITH (PIANO)

see ANTHOLOGIES - CUTTIN' THE BOOGIE, ENCYCLOPEDIA OF JAZZ ON RECORDS VOL. 1, and PIANO IN STYLE

SPYRO GYRA (FUSION BAND)

SPYRO GYRA, MCA: 1651 (Amherst 1014), CD/AC, 1977.
MORNING DANCE, MCA: MCAD-37148/CD, MCAC-1650/AC (Infinity 9004), 1979.

SONNY STITT (ALTO & TENOR SAX)

SONNY STITT/BUD POWELL/J.J. JOHNSON (BUD'S BLUES), Fantasy: OJC-009 (Prestige 7024), CD/LP/AC, 1949-50.
with Bud Powell, Curly Russell, and Max Roach: All God's Chillun Got Rhythm, Bud's Blues, Sonny Side, Sunset, Strike Up the Band, I Want to Be Happy, Taking a Chance on Love, and Fine and Dandy; with J.J. Johnson, John Lewis, Nelson Boyd, and Max Roach: Blue Mode, Teapot, Afternoon in Paris, and Elora.

CONSTELLATION, Muse: 5323 (Cobblestone 9021), CD/LP/AC, 1972.
with Barry Harris, Sam Jones, and Roy Brooks.

see GENE AMMONS - BOSS TENORS
see DIZZY GILLESPIE - DUETS and SONNY SIDE UP
see ANTHOLOGIES - THE BEBOP REVOLUTION

SUN RA (KEYBOARDS/BIG BAND)

SUN SONG, Delmark: 411 (Transition J 10), CD/LP/AC, 1956.
portions of this recording and SUPER-SONIC JAZZ (see below) resemble updated Ellington big band styles.

SUPER-SONIC JAZZ (SOUNDS), Evidence: ECD 22015-2 (Saturn 216/Impulse 9271), CD, 1956.

ANGELS & DEMONS AT PLAY (Saturn 9956/Impulse 9245) / NUBIANS OF PLUTONIA (Saturn 406/Impulse 9242), Evidence: ECD 22069-2, CD, 1955-57, 1958.
the selections on side two of NUBIANS OF PLUTONIA resemble mode-based work of later John Coltrane and Pharoah Sanders pieces.

ATLANTIS, Evidence: ECD 22067-2 (Saturn 507/Impulse 9239), CD, 1960.
much of side two of this recording and HELIOCENTRIC WORLDS OF SUN RA resembles the work of Edgard Varese.

THE FUTURISTIC SOUNDS OF SUN RA, Savoy/Denon: SV-0213 (12169), CD, 1960-61.
with John Gilmore, Marshall Allen, Pat Patrick, Bernard McKinney, Ronnie Boykins, and Willie Jones: Bassism, Of Sounds and Something Else, What's That?, Where Is Tomorrow?, The Beginning, China Gates, New Day, Tapestry from an Asteroid, Jet Flight, Looking Outward, and Space Jazz Reverie. Gilmore's solo on Jet Flight influenced John Coltrane's work on his own albums IMPRESSIONS and CHASIN' THE TRANE.

WE TRAVEL THE SPACEWAYS (Saturn 5445) / BAD AND BEAUTIFUL (Saturn 532/Impulse 9276), Evidence: ECD 22038-2, CD, 1958-59, 1961.
BAD AND BEAUTIFUL includes Just in Time.

MAGIC CITY, Evidence: ECD 22069-2 (Saturn 711/Impulse 9243), 1960?, 1965?.

HELIOCENTRIC WORLDS OF SUN RA, VOL. 1, ESP-DISK: 1014, CD, 1965.

HELIOCENTRIC WORLDS OF SUN RA, VOL. 2, ESP-DISK: 1017, CD, 1965.

* ASTRO BLACK, Impulse: 9255, 1972.
portions of this recording, side two of HELIOCENTRIC WORLDS, VOL. 2, and MAGIC CITY sound collectively improvised, free of preset chord progressions and tempos.

ART TATUM (PIANO)

PIANO STARTS HERE, Columbia: PCT 9655, AC, 1933, 1949.
Tea for Two, Humoresque, Tiger Rag, St. Louis Blues, Willow Weep for Me, The Man I Love, Yesterdays, etc.

I GOT RHYTHM, VOL. 3, Decca Jazz/GRP: GRD-630 (MCA 4019), CD, 1935-44.
with Tiny Grimes and Slam Stewart; includes amazing 1944 versions of I Got Rhythm and Tea for Two, plus Deep Purple, Cocktails for Two, etc.

* PIECES OF EIGHT, Smithsonian: 2029, 1939-55.

ART TATUM: SOLOS (1940), Decca Jazz/MCA: 42327, CD/AC, 1940.

COMPLETE CAPITOL RECORDINGS, VOL. 1 & 2, Capitol: 92866/92867, CDs, 1949-52.
VOL. 1 includes Willow Weep For Me and Aunt Hagar's Blues.

TATUM GROUP MASTERPIECES, VOL. 8, Pablo: 2405-431-2 (2310 737), CD, 1956.
ballads by Ben Webster, Tatum, Red Callender, and Bill Douglass: All the Things You Are, Where Or When, My One and Only Love, etc.

see ANTHOLOGIES - JAZZ PIANO and SMITHSONIAN COLLECTION OF CLASSIC JAZZ

CECIL TAYLOR (PIANO)

JAZZ ADVANCE, Blue Note: 84462 (Transition), CD, 1955.
with Steve Lacy, Buell Neidlinger, and Dennis Charles: Bemsha Swing, Charge 'Em Blues, Azure, Song, You'd Be So Nice to Come Home To, Rick Kick Shaw, and Sweet and Lovely.

* IN TRANSITION, Blue Note: LA458-H2 (Transition/UA), 1955 & 1959.
above recording plus 1959 session with Ted Curson, Bill Barron, Chris White, and Rudy Collins: Get Out of Town, Carol/Three Points, Love For Sale, Little Lees, and I Love Paris.

LOOKING AHEAD!, Fantasy: OJC-452 (Contemporary 7562), CD/LP/AC, 1958.
quartet session.

THE WORLD OF CECIL TAYLOR, Candid: 79006, CD, 1960.
THE COMPLETE CECIL TAYLOR/BUELL NEIDLINGER CANDID SESSIONS, Mosaic: MD4-127/4CD set, MR6-127/6LP set, 1960-61.
(mail order - see page 78)
with Archie Shepp, Buell Neidlinger, and Dennis Charles: Air, This Nearly Was Mine, Port of Call, Eb, and Lazy Afternoon.

* CAFE MONTMARTRE, Fantasý: 86014; or * NEFERTITI, Arista: 1905, 1962.
with Jimmy Lyons and Sunny Murray.

UNIT STRUCTURES, Blue Note: 84237, CD, 1966.
with Eddie Gale Stevens, Jr., Jimmy Lyons, Ken McIntyre, Henry Grimes, Alan Silva, and Andrew Cyrille.

* CONQUISTADOR, Blue Note: 46535 (84260), 1966.
with Bill Dixon, Jimmy Lyons, and Andrew Cyrille.

SILENT TONGUES, Freedom: FCD-41005 (Arista 1005), CD, 1974.
unaccompanied piano improvisations recorded live at the Montreux Jazz Festival: Abyss, Petals and Filaments, and Jitney.

* FLY, FLY, FLY, Pausa: 7108 (MPS), 1980; solo piano.

see ANTHOLOGIES - MASTERS OF THE MODERN PIANO and SMITHSONIAN COLLECTION OF CLASSIC JAZZ

JACK TEAGARDEN (TROMBONE)

* KING OF THE BLUES TROMBONE, Columbia Special Products: JSN 6044, 1928-40.
with Benny Goodman, Frankie Trumbauer, Bud Freeman and His Famous Chicagoans, etc.: Texas Tea Party (1933), I Got a Right to Sing the Blues (1939), and 47th and State (1940).

see BENNY GOODMAN - B.G. & BIG TEA IN NYC
see ANTHOLOGIES - JAZZ HOLIDAY and SMITHSONIAN COLLECTION OF CLASSIC JAZZ (REVISED)

TEN WHEEL DRIVE

* CONSTRUCTION NO. 1, Polydor: 24-4008, 1969.
* BRIEF REPLIES, Polydor: 24-4024, 1970.

LUCKY THOMPSON (TENOR & SOPRANO SAX)

TRICOTISM, Impulse/GRP: GRD-135 (ABC 111), CD, 1956.
with Jimmy Cleveland, Hank Jones, Oscar Pettiford, & Osie Johnson: Tom Kattin', Old Reliable, Deep Passion, & Translation; with Pettiford & Skeeter Best: Tricrotism, Bo-Bi My Boy, A Lady's Vanity, & OP Meets LT.

CLAUDE THORNHILL (BIG BAND)

* THE MEMORABLE CLAUDE THORNHILL, Columbia: 32906, 1941-47.
  featuring Lee Konitz: Snowfall, Hungarian Dance #5, Traumerai, Portrait of a Guinea Farm, Where or When, Night and Day, Grieg's Piano Concerto, I Don't Know Why, Moonlight Bay, Buster's Last Stand, Moments Like This, A Sunday Kind of Love, Warsaw Concerto, Robbin's Nest, Lover Man, For Heaven's Sake, and the following Gil Evans arrangements: There's a Small Hotel, Anthropology, Yardbird Suite, and Donna Lee.

BEST OF THE BIG BANDS: CLAUDE THORNHILL, Columbia: 46152, CD/AC, 1941-47.

see ANTHOLOGIES - THE BEBOP ERA, BIG BAND JAZZ, and JAZZ IN REVOLUTION

LENNIE TRISTANO (PIANO)

* CROSSCURRENTS, Capitol: M 11060, 1949.
  one side with Tristano, Lee Konitz, Warne Marsh, Billy Bauer, etc.: Wow, Crosscurrent, Yesterdays, Marionette, Sax of a Kind, Intuition, and Digression; other side is Buddy DeFranco in combo and big band settings.

* DESCENT INTO THE MAELSTROM, Inner City: 6002 (East Wind 8040), 1953-66.
  Descent into the Maelstrom (1953).

* REQUIEM, Atlantic: SD2-7003, 1955, 1961.
  combines LENNIE TRISTANO (1224) and THE NEW TRISTANO (1357): Line Up and Turkish Mambo.

Note: Mosaic Records has announced a forthcoming set to reissue all of Tristano's studio recordings (Capitol, East Wind, Atlantic, etc.) including all recordings cited here. (mail order - see page 78).

see LEE KONITZ - SUBCONSCIOUS LEE
see ANTHOLOGIES - THE BEBOP ERA, JAZZ PIANO, MIRAGE, and SMITHSONIAN COLLECTION OF CLASSIC JAZZ

MCCOY TYNER (PIANO)

see JOHN COLTRANE - most Atlantic and Impulse LPs
see ART FARMER - MEET THE JAZZTET
see WAYNE SHORTER - NIGHT DREAMER
see ANTHOLOGIES - JAZZ PIANO

MIROSLAV VITOUS (BASS)

* INFINITE SEARCH, Embryo: 524 (MOUNTAIN IN THE CLOUDS, Atlantic 1622), 1969.
  with Joe Henderson, Herbie Hancock, John McLaughlin, and Jack DeJohnette.

see CHICK COREA - NOW HE SINGS, NOW HE SOBS and TRIO MUSIC
see WEATHER REPORT - WEATHER REPORT (1971), I SING THE BODY ELECTRIC, and SWEETNIGHTER

FATS WALLER (PIANO)

THE FATS WALLER PIANO SOLOS: TURN ON THE HEAT, RCA Bluebird: 2482 (AXM2-5518), 2CD/2AC set, 1927-41.
Numb Fumblin and Valentine Stomp (1929).

see ANTHOLOGIES - JAZZ PIANO and SMITHSONIAN COLLECTION OF CLASSIC JAZZ

GROVER WASHINGTON (SAXOPHONE)

MR. MAGIC, Motown: 5175 (Kudu 20), CD/AC, 1974.

WEATHER REPORT (FUSION GROUP)

WEATHER REPORT, Columbia: 48824 (30661), CD/AC, 1971.

I SING THE BODY ELECTRIC, Columbia: 46107 (31352), CD/AC, 1971-72.
includes edited live performance by Joe Zawinul, Wayne Shorter, Miroslav Vitous, Eric Gravatt, and Dom Um Romao: Vertical Invader, T.H., Dr. Honoris Causa, Surucucu, and Directions; also includes studio date with added singers, English horn (Andrew White), flute, trumpet & 12-string guitar: Unknown Soldier, The Moors, Crystal, & Second Sunday in August.

* SWEETNIGHTER, Columbia: 32210, 1973.

MYSTERIOUS TRAVELLER, Columbia: 32494, CD/AC, 1974.

* TALE SPINNIN', Columbia: 33417, 1975.

BLACK MARKET, Columbia: 34099, CD/AC, 1976.

HEAVY WEATHER, Columbia: 47481 (34418), CD/AC, 1977.

MR. GONE, Columbia: 46869 (35358), CD/AC, 1978.

* 8:30, Columbia: PC2-36030, 1979.

NIGHT PASSAGE, Columbia: 36793, CD/AC, 1980.

WEATHER REPORT, Columbia: 37616, CD/AC, 1981.

BEN WEBSTER (TENOR SAX)

see DUKE ELLINGTON - THE BLANTON-WEBSTER BAND and ELLINGTON 1940
see ART TATUM - GROUP MASTERPIECES, VOL. 8
see ANTHOLOGIES - SMITHSONIAN COLLECTION OF CLASSIC JAZZ (REVISED) and THREE GREAT SWING SAXOPHONISTS

TONY WILLIAMS (DRUMS)

EMERGENCY!, Polydor: 849068-2 (25-3001), CD, 1969.
* ONCE IN A LIFETIME, Verve: 833563 (VE2-2541), 1969-70.
with John McLaughlin and Larry Young.

see MILES DAVIS - SEVEN STEPS TO HEAVEN, IN EUROPE, COMPLETE CONCERT 1964, HEARD ROUND THE WORLD, E.S.P., PLUGGED NICKEL, MILES SMILES, SORCERER, NEFERTITI, MILES IN THE SKY, FILLES DE KILIMANJARO, and IN A SILENT WAY
see ERIC DOLLPHY - OUT TO LUNCH
see HERBIE HANCOCK - EMPYREAN ISLES and MAIDEN VOYAGE

GERALD WILSON (BIG BAND)

* YOU BETTER BELIEVE IT, Pacific Jazz: 10097 (PJ 34), 1961.

MOMENT OF TRUTH, Pacific Jazz: 92928 (PJ 61), CD, 1962.
seven of the nine selections were composed and arranged by Wilson; Viva Tirado features solos by Teddy Edwards, Joe Pass, and Carmell Jones; Latino features solos by Joe Pass and Harold Land; Nancy Jo has solos by Harold Land, Carmell Jones, and Joe Pass; rhythm section includes Jack Wilson, Jimmy Bond, and Mel Lewis.

* ON STAGE, Pacific Jazz: 10100 (PJ 88), 1965.

* FEELIN' KINDA BLUE, Pacific Jazz: 10101 (PJ 10099), 1965.

TEDDY WILSON (PIANO)

* STATEMENTS AND IMPROVISATIONS, Smithsonian: 2005, 1934-42.

see ROY ELDRIDGE - LITTLE JAZZ
see BENNY GOODMAN - AFTER YOU'VE GONE, AVALON, and CARNEGIE HALL JAZZ CONCERT
see BILLIE HOLIDAY
see ANTHOLOGIES - JAZZ PIANO and SMITHSONIAN COLLECTION OF CLASSIC JAZZ

WORLD SAXOPHONE QUARTET

STEPPIN', Black Saint: 120027-2 (BSR 0027), CD, 1978.
with Julius Hemphill, Oliver Lake, David Murray, and Hamiet Bluiett.

W.S.Q., Black Saint: 120046-2 (BSR 0046), CD, 1980.

REVUE, Black Saint: 120056-2 (BSR 0056), CD, 1980.

LESTER YOUNG (TENOR SAX)

* THE LESTER YOUNG STORY, VOLUME 1, Columbia: 33502;
* VOLUME 2, Columbia: 34837; * VOLUME 3, Columbia: 34840;
* VOLUME 4, Columbia: 34843; * VOLUME 5, Columbia: 34849, 1936-40.
Count Basie combo and big band with Buck Clayton, Dicky Wells, Freddie Green, Walter Page, and Jo Jones: Shoe Shine Boy, Lady Be Good, Lester Leaps In, Dickie's Dream, Moten Swing, Taxi War Dance, Pound Cake, Easy Does It, Ham 'n' Eggs, etc.

LESTER YOUNG & FRIENDS, Commodore/Pair: 7002, CD/LP/AC, 1938, 1944.
selections feature Young (on clarinet and tenor saxophone), Buck Clayton, Eddie Durham, Freddie Green, Walter Page, and Jo Jones: Way Down Yonder in New Orleans, I Want a Little Girl, Countless Blues, and Pagin' the Devil (1938).

* ALADDIN SESSIONS, Blue Note: 456 (Aladdin 801), 1945-48.
D.B. Blues.

see COUNT BASIE - COMPLETE DECCA RECORDINGS, ONE O'CLOCK JUMP, BEST OF, and ESSENTIAL
see BILLIE HOLIDAY
see ANTHOLOGIES - CLASSIC TENORS, 1930'S - SMALL COMBOS, and SMITHSONIAN COLLECTION OF CLASSIC JAZZ

JOE ZAWINUL (KEYBOARDS)

ZAWINUL, Atlantic: 1579, CD/AC, 1970.
with Wayne Shorter, Earl Turbinton, Woody Shaw, George Davis, Hubert Laws, Herbie Hancock, Miroslav Vitous, Walter Booker, Jack DeJohnette, Joe Chambers, Billy Hart, and David Lee: Doctor Honoris Causa, In A Silent Way, Double Image, etc. This recording displays some of Zawinul's best composing and arranging.

see CANNONBALL ADDERLEY - CANNONBALL IN EUROPE and MERCY, MERCY, MERCY
see MILES DAVIS - IN A SILENT WAY and BITCHES BREW
see WEATHER REPORT

ANTHOLOGIES (ALPHABETICALLY BY TITLE)

AN ANTHOLOGY OF BIG BAND SWING, Decca Jazz: GRD2-629, 2CD set, 1930-55.
includes Duke Ellington, Fletcher Henderson, Jimmie Lunceford, Count Basie, Benny Carter, Jay McShann, Roy Eldridge, etc.

ATLANTIC JAZZ: WEST COAST, Atlantic: 81703, CD/AC, 1947-66.
1958 Jimmy Giuffre, Bob Brookmeyer, Jim Hall: Topsy, originally on Giuffre's WESTERN SUITE (Atlantic 1330); 1955 Shorty Rogers, Giuffre, Pete Jolly, Curtis Counce, Shelly Manne: Not Really the Blues; 1955 Jack Montrose, Bob Gordon, Paul Moer, Red Mitchell, Shelly Manne: Paradox; 1955 Conte Candoli, Bill Holman, Lou Levey, Leroy Vinnegar, Lawrence Marable: Cheremoya; and others.

* BEBOP, New World: NW 271, 1945-56.
Parker's Mood, Relaxin' at Camarillo, Ko-Ko, and Embraceable You by Charlie Parker; Things to Come by Dizzy Gillespie's big band; Un Poco Loco by Bud Powell; Jahbero by Tadd Dameron and Fats Navarro; Misterioso by Thelonious Monk; What is This Thing Called Love by Clifford Brown and Max Roach; Stop Time by Horace Silver, etc.

THE BEBOP ERA, Columbia: 40972, CD/AC, 1942-51.
Gil Evans' arrangements for Claude Thornhill of Yardbird Suite and Donna Lee; and No Figs by the Metronome All Stars with Stan Getz and Lennie Tristano.

THE BEBOP REVOLUTION, RCA Bluebird: 2177, CD/AC, 1946-49.
Dizzy Gillespie combo (1946) and big band (1947-49); and Kenny Clarke & His 52nd Street Boys with Fats Navarro, Sonny Stitt, and Bud Powell (1946).

BIG BAND JAZZ: FROM THE BEGINNINGS TO THE FIFTIES, Smithsonian: 2202/4CD set, 2201/3AC set, 1924-56. (mail order - see page 78)
FLETCHER HENDERSON - Copenhagen, Henderson Stomp, Hop Off, New King Porter Stomp, and Down South Camp Meetin'.
JIMMIE LUNCEFORD - Mood Indigo, Stratosphere, Stomp It Off, Organ Grinder's Swing, and Uptown Blues.
BENNY GOODMAN - Sometimes I'm Happy; King Porter Stomp; Sing, Sing, Sing; Ridin' High; and Mission To Moscow.
TOMMY DORSEY - Song Of India, Well Git It, On The Sunny Side Of The Street, and Opus Number One.
COUNT BASIE - One O'Clock Jump, Sent For You Yesterday, Jumpin' At The Woodside, Volcano, 9:20 Special, and Shiny Stockings.
ARTIE SHAW - Begin The Beguine, Rose Room, and Star Dust.
BENNY CARTER - Shufflebug Shuffle.
DUKE ELLINGTON - A Gypsy Without A Song, Take The 'A' Train, Just A-Settin' And A-Rockin', Perdido, C-Jam Blues, Main Stem, and Happy-Go-Lucky Local.
LIONEL HAMPTON - Till Tom Special and Flying Home.
WOODY HERMAN - Down Under, Apple Honey, and Four Brothers.
BILLY ECKSTINE - Cool Breeze.
DIZZY GILLESPIE - Our Delight and Things To Come.
CLAUDE THORNHILL - Robbins Nest and Donna Lee.

THE BIRTH OF THE COOL, VOL. 2, Capitol: 98935, CD, 1951-53.
Gerry Mulligan Tentette (1953): Walking Shoes, Rocker, Flash, etc.; Mulligan considers this session to represent some of his best work; Shorty Rogers & His Giants (1951); and the Metronome All Stars (1951) with Miles Davis, Lee Konitz, Stan Getz, etc.

* BLACK CALIFORNIA, Savoy: 2215, 1945-52.
with Sonny Criss, Wardell Gray, Roy Porter, Harold Land, and Hampton Hawes.

* THE CHANGING FACE OF HARLEM, Savoy: 2208, 1944-45.
included for Earl Bostic solos which show possible origins of certain Coltrane devices.

* THE CHICAGOANS: THE AUSTIN HIGH GANG, MCA: 1350 (Decca 9231), 1928-30.
Chicago-style combo recordings featuring Frank Teschemacher: Prince of Wails (1929) by Elmer Schoebel and His Friar's Society Orchestra, with Dick Feige, Jack Read, Floyd Towne, Elmer Schoebel, Charlie Berger, John Kuhn, and George Wettling.

CLASSIC TENORS, Signature/CBS: 38446, CD/AC, 1943.
Coleman Hawkins with Eddie Heywood, Oscar Pettiford, and Shelly Manne: The Man I Love, Sweet Lorraine, etc.; Lester Young with Bill Coleman and Dicky Wells: I Got Rhythm, etc.

* CUTTIN' THE BOOGIE, New World: NW 259, 1926-41.
Pinetop's Boogie Woogie by Pinetop Smith and Honky Tonk Train Blues by Meade Lux Lewis.

EARLY BLACK SWING: THE BIRTH OF BIG BAND JAZZ, RCA Bluebird: 9583, CD/AC, 1927-34.
Fletcher Henderson: Sugar Foot Stomp; Bennie Moten: Moten Swing; Jimmie Lunceford: White Heat and Swingin' Uptown; Duke Ellington, Louis Armstrong, Earl Hines, McKinney's Cotton Pickers, Charlie Johnson, and the Missourians.

* THE ENCYCLOPEDIA OF JAZZ ON RECORDS, VOL. 1, MCA: 2-4061 (Decca), 1926-38.
Boogie Woogie by Pinetop Smith; You've Got To Be Modernistic by James P. Johnson; selections by Jelly Roll Morton, Johnny Dodds, Duke Ellington, etc.

* AN EXPERIMENT IN MODERN MUSIC: PAUL WHITEMAN AT AEOLIAN HALL, Smithsonian: 2028, 1919-24.
Livery Stable Blues by the Original Dixieland Jazz Band.

THE GREATEST JAZZ CONCERT IN THE WORLD, Pablo: 2625-704-2, 3CD set, 1967.
concert with the entire Ellington band (Chromatic Love Affair, featuring Harry Carney; Swamp Goo, featuring Russell Procope) plus the Oscar Peterson Trio (Sam Jones and Louis Hayes), singer Ella Fitzgerald, and others.

HITSVILLE USA: THE MOTOWN SINGLES COLLECTION, Motown: 6312, 4CD/4AC set, 1959-1971.
Marvin Gaye, Supremes, Four Tops, Temptations, Miracles, etc.

* JAMMIN' FOR THE JACKPOT, New World: NW 217, 1929-41.
includes 1941 Ebony Silhouette featuring Milt Hinton on bass with Cab Calloway.

* JAZZ COMPOSITIONS, Columbia: 37012 (WL 127/CL 941), 1956-57.
Revelations by Charles Mingus; All About Rosie by George Russell featuring Bill Evans; Three Little Feelings by John Lewis; and Poem for Brass by J.J. Johnson.

* JAZZ HOLIDAY, MCA: MCA2-4018 (Decca), 1928-34.
combos led by Red Nichols and Adrian Rollini; plus Venuti-Lang (1931): Farewell Blues and Beale St. Blues, with Jack Teagarden, Frank Signorelli, Joe Tarto, and Neil Marshall; Muskrat Ramble (1928) with Benny Goodman, Wingy Manone, Bud Freeman, Joe Sullivan, Herman Foster, Harry Goodman, and Bob Conselman; That's A' Plenty and Clarinetitis (1928) with Benny Goodman, Mel Stitzel, and Conselman.

* JAZZ IN REVOLUTION, New World: NW 284, 1940-49.
Mingus Fingers featuring Charles Mingus with the Lionel Hampton band; Donna Lee arranged by Gil Evans for the Claude Thornhill band; The Chase by Dexter Gordon and Wardell Gray; Royal Roost by Fats Navarro and Kenny Clarke; etc.

JAZZ PIANO: A SMITHSONIAN COLLECTION, Smithsonian: 7002 (RD-039)/4CD set, 7001/4AC set, 1924-78. (mail order - see page 78)
selections by Jelly Roll Morton(2), James P. Johnson(2), Willie "The Lion" Smith, Fats Waller(3), Earl Hines(4), Teddy Wilson(3), Jimmy Yancey, Meade Lux Lewis, Pete Johnson, Avery Parrish, Count Basie, Billy Kyle, Art Tatum(5), Duke Ellington(2), Nat King Cole(2), Erroll Garner(3), Bud Powell(4), Lennie Tristano, Dodo Marmarosa, Al Haig, Oscar Peterson, Thelonious Monk(3), Horace Silver, Herbie Nichols, Hank Jones(3), Tommy Flanagan(2), John Lewis, Bill Evans(3), McCoy Tyner, Chick Corea, Keith Jarrett, and Herbie Hancock.

* JIVE AT FIVE, New World: NW 274, 1927-46.
Every Tub and Jive at Five by Count Basie; Passion Flower by Johnny Hodges; Pitter Panther Patter by Duke Ellington and Jimmy Blanton; Body and Soul by Coleman Hawkins; etc.

LEGENDS OF THE BLUES, VOL. 1, Columbia: 46215, CD/AC, 1925-1965.
LEGENDS OF THE BLUES, VOL. 2, Columbia: 47467, CD/AC, 1929-1940.
VOL. 1: Bessie Smith, Robert Johnson, Leadbelly, Lonnie Johnson, etc.
VOL. 2: Roosevelt Sykes, Tampa Red, Charlie Spand, etc.

* MASTERS OF THE MODERN PIANO, Verve: VE2-2514, 1955-66.
Jimmy Giuffre with Paul Bley (1961), and Cecil Taylor (1957).

* MIRAGE, New World: NW 216, 1947-61.
Mirage (arranged by Pete Rugulo) and Egdon Heath (arranged by Bill Russo) performed by the Stan Kenton big band; Eclipse by Charles Mingus; Yesterdays by Lennie Tristano; Concerto for Billy the Kid by George Russell; etc.

* NICA'S DREAM, New World: NW 242, 1955-64.
Nica's Dream by Art Blakey; Blues March by the Jazztet; Original Faubus Fables by Charles Mingus; Sonny Rollins; Modern Jazz Quartet; etc.

THE 1930'S - THE SMALL COMBOS, Columbia: 40833, CD/AC, 1930-39.
Shoe Shine (1936) by Jones-Smith Inc.(Basie/Lester Young); Wabash Stomp (1937) by Roy Eldridge; Echoes of Harlem (1938) by Cootie Williams.

* PIANO IN STYLE, MCA: 1332, 1926-30.
includes Pinetop Smith, James P. Johnson, and Jelly Roll Morton.

RAGTIME: PIANOS, BANJOS, SAXOPHONES, CAKE-WALKS, BRASS BANDS, JASS..., RCA: PM 45687 (France), 2LP set, 1900-1930. (import - see page 78)
includes the Sousa Band, Jim Europe's Society Orchestra, Earl Fuller, the Original Dixieland Jazz Band, etc.

THE RIVERSIDE HISTORY OF CLASSIC JAZZ, Riverside/Fantasy: RB-005, 5LP set, ca.1900-1956.
Jelly Roll Morton's 1923 The Pearls, 1924 Steady Roll; New Orleans Rhythm Kings 1922 Livery Stable Blues; Louis Armstrong and Sidney Bechet 1924 Cake Walkin' Babies From Home; Scott Joplin's The Cascades; Street Cries of Charleston (that illustrate Afro-American pitch bending by Southern Negro street vendors); also brass bands, vocal blues, ragtime, black religious music, and numerous selections by early New Orleans and Chicago musicians.

THE ROOTS OF THE BLUES, New World: 80252-2, CD, 1959.
(mail order - see page 78)
field recordings by Alan Lomax.

THE SMITHSONIAN COLLECTION OF CLASSIC JAZZ, revised edition, Smithsonian: 2502 (RD-033)/5CD set, 2501/5AC set, 1916-1981.
(mail order - see page 78)
Critic-journalist Martin Williams has drawn from the vaults of many record companies to compile an ambitious collection for the Smithsonian Institute. It is an excellent place to find one or more good examples of a particular musician's work without purchasing the albums from which the selections were taken. It would take months, even years, to obtain the selections contained in this collection separately. However, it should not be purchased with the intention of gaining a well-balanced view of jazz history because of the lengthy list of historically

significant players and groups omitted: tenor saxophonist Albert Ayler, pianist-composer-bandleader Sun Ra, The Original Dixieland Jazz Band, Stan Kenton's big bands, Woody Herman's big bands, Stan Getz (SMITHSONIAN COLLECTION OF CLASSIC JAZZ (revised) has 8 measures of Getz on a Red Norvo recording of Body and Soul), post-1963 John Coltrane, pianist-composer-bandleaders Herbie Hancock, Chick Corea, Keith Jarrett, combos led by composer- baritone saxophonist Gerry Mulligan, the combos of Art Blakey and Horace Silver (*SCCJ-R* (revised) has one selection by a Silver quintet of 1958), and combos led by Miles Davis during the 1960's and 1970's, etc. There is nothing representing the past 30 years of jazz history, except one selection by the World Saxophone Quartet.
Of course, it is not what the collection omits that is important, but what it includes.

The following is a partial listing:

LOUIS ARMSTRONG - eight selections including the 1928 West End Blues with Earl Hines; 1928 duet with Hines called Weather Bird; 1927 Hotter Than That with Johnny Dodds, Kid Ory, Lil Hardin Armstrong, Lonnie Johnson, and Johnny St. Cyr.

BIX BEIDERBECKE - 1927 Singin' the Blues with Frankie Trumbauer.

DON BYAS - 1945 I Got Rhythm: duet with Slam Stewart.

ORNETTE COLEMAN - includes Congeniality and Lonely Woman with Don Cherry, and an excerpt from his FREE JAZZ.

MILES DAVIS - includes Boplicity (BIRTH OF THE COOL), and So What (KIND OF BLUE) with Cannonball Adderley, John Coltrane, Bill Evans, Paul Chambers, and Jimmy Cobb.

DUKE ELLINGTON - eight big band selections including Concerto for Cootie, Harlem Air Shaft, and Ko-Ko, all from 1940 (SCCJ-R has Cottontail but not Harlem Airshaft).

ROY ELDRIDGE - 1941 big band version of Rockin' Chair.

DIZZY GILLESPIE - 1945 I Can't Get Started and 1945 Shaw 'Nuff with Charlie Parker, Al Haig, Curly Russell, and Sid Catlett.

BENNY GOODMAN - 1935 Body and Soul with Teddy Wilson, and 1941 I Found a New Baby and Breakfast Feud with Charlie Christian.

COLEMAN HAWKINS - the famous 1939 Body and Soul.

FLETCHER HENDERSON - 1926 Stampede and 1934 Wrappin' It Up.

JAMES P. JOHNSON - 1921 Carolina Shout.

LEE KONITZ - 1949 Crosscurrent with Konitz, Warne Marsh, Billy Bauer, and Lennie Tristano (SCCJ-R substitutes Subsconsious Lee with all but Marsh).

MEADE LUX LEWIS - the famous 1937 Honky Tonk Train Blues.

JIMMIE LUNCEFORD - 1939 Lunceford Special (SCCJ-R substitutes 1936 Organ Grinder's Swing).

CHARLES MINGUS - 1963 Hora Decubitus (SCCJ-R substitutes 1957 Haitian Fight Song).

THELONIOUS MONK - six selections including Criss Cross and Misterioso (SCCJ-R contains five Monk selections).

JELLY ROLL MORTON - 1926 Black Bottom Stomp, Dead Man Blues, and Grandpa's Spells.

KING OLIVER - 1923 Dippermouth Blues with Johnny Dodds and Louis Armstrong.

CHARLIE PARKER - seven selections including two 1947 versions of Embraceable You, one version of Parker's Mood, and one of his fastest performances: a 1945 version of Ko-Ko. (SCCJ-R has eight Parker selections.)

BUD POWELL - 1947 Somebody Loves Me with Curly Russell and Max Roach. (SCCJ-R substitues a 1951 A Night In Tunisia).

SONNY ROLLINS - 1956 Blue Seven with Tommy Flanagan, Doug Watkins, and Max Roach.

ART TATUM - 1949 Willow Weep for Me and 1956 Too Marvelous for Words.

CECIL TAYLOR - a selection from his UNIT STRUCTURES.

FATS WALLER - 1927 I Ain't Got Nobody (solo piano).

WORLD SAXOPHONE QUARTET - 1981 Steppin' (only in REVISED).

LESTER YOUNG - 1939 Lester Leaps In and Taxi War Dance, both with Count Basie.

* STEPPIN' ON THE GAS, New World: NW 269, 1913-1927.
She's Cryin' for Me Now (1925) by the New Orleans Rhythm Kings; Ory's Creole Trombone and Society Blues (1922) by Kid Ory; as well as several nonjazz pieces that cast light on where jazz originated (1914 band ragtime by James Reese Europe, etc.).

THE STORY OF THE BLUES, Columbia: CGT 30008, AC, 1928-1968.
compiled by Paul Oliver.

* SWEET AND LOW, New World: NW 256, 1926-33.
Sweet and Low Blues and Til Times Get Better by Jabbo Smith.

* THESAURUS OF CLASSIC JAZZ, Columbia: C4L 18.
boxed set: twelve 1927-30 recordings by Miff Mole and His Molers (At the Darktown Strutters Ball with Red Nichols and Jimmy Dorsey, That's a Plenty with Jimmy Dorsey and Eddie Lang, etc.); eleven 1927 recordings with Red Nichols and the Charleston Chasers (Farewell Blues with Jimmy Dorsey and Miff Mole, Five Pennies with Pee Wee Russell, etc.); and other groups.

THREE GREAT SWING SAXOPHONISTS, RCA Bluebird: 9683, CD/AC, 1929-1946.
with Coleman Hawkins, Benny Carter, and Ben Webster: Body and Soul (1939) by Hawkins; Cotton Tail and All Too Soon (1940) by Webster with Duke Ellington.

* TRUMPETER'S HOLIDAY, Epic: LN 3252.
included for Frankie Newton's solos and Henry Red Allen's 1935 Body and Soul; also has Roy Eldridge's 1937 After You've Gone.

WHAT IS JAZZ? / Leonard Bernstein, Sony Music Special Products: 11459 (CL919), AC, 1956. (mail order - see page 78)
This presentation remains the single most effective tool for explaining the principles and concepts underlying jazz, as well as for comparing different styles of jazz. With his typical clarity, humor, and eclecticism, Bernstein provides definitions and musical examples for mutes, vibraphone, cymbals, cow bell, maracas, bongo drums, jazz shading of tone, syncopation, blue notes, vibrato, improvisation, instrumental break, collective improvisation, jazz swing feeling, 12-bar blues form, 32-bar AABA form, theme and variations, etc. He is assisted by an all-star set of jazz musicians including Louis Armstrong, Bessie Smith, Miles Davis, Buck Clayton, Buster Bailey, John Coltrane, Teo Macero, Turk Murphy, Coleman Hawkins, etc. He also compares jazz styles by offering different renditions of Sweet Sue.